FLORIDA STATE
UNIVERSITY LIBRARIES

JAN

TALLAHASSEE, FLORIDA

MULTICULTURALISM IN PRACTICE

Multiculturalism in Practice
Irish, Jewish, Italian and Pakistani migration to Scotland

SUZANNE AUDREY

Ashgate
Aldershot • Burlington USA • Singapore • Sydney

© Suzanne Audrey 2000

All rights reserved. No part of this publication may be reproduced, stored in a retrieval system, or transmitted in any form or by any means, electronic, mechanical, photocopying, recording or otherwise without the prior permission of the publisher.

Published by
Ashgate Publishing Ltd
Gower House
Croft Road
Aldershot
Hants GU11 3HR
England

Ashgate Publishing Company
131 Main Street
Burlington, VT 05401-5600
USA

Ashgate website: http://www.ashgate.com

British Library Cataloguing in Publication Data
Audrey, Suzanne
  Multiculturalism in practice : Irish, Jewish, Italian and Pakistani migration to Scotland. - (Interdisciplinary research series in ethnic, gender and class relations)
  1.Multiculturalism - Scotland - Glasgow 2.Pluralism (Social sciences) - Scotland- Glasgow 3.Multiculturalism - Scotland - Glasgow - History 4.Govan Hill (Glasgow, Scotland) - Race relations 5.Scotland - Race relations
  I.Title
306'.094144

Library of Congress Control Number: 00-134482

ISBN 0 7546 1511 1

Printed and bound by Athenaeum Press, Ltd.,
Gateshead, Tyne & Wear.

Contents

List of Tables vi
Acknowledgements xi
Terminology xii
Series Editor's Preface xiv

Introduction 1

1 The Irish in Glasgow 13

2 Italians in Glasgow 33

3 Glasgow Jewry 46

4 Pakistanis in Glasgow 61

5 A History of Govanhill 85

6 Past and Present 104

7 School-age Education: a Pragmatic Approach 118

8 Youth Services: the Socialisation Model 154

9 Elderly Care: a Case of Benevolent Trial and Error 191

10 Conclusion: the Process of Multiculturalism 225

Bibliography 239
Index 251

List of Tables

Table 1.1	Irish Emigration 1841-1861	16
Table 1.2	Irish-born Population in Scotland 1911-1991	32
Table 2.1	Italian-born Population in Scotland 1861-1931	35
Table 2.2	Distribution of Italians in Britain 1927	35
Table 2.3	Italian-born Population in Scotland 1951-1991	37
Table 2.4	Italian-born Population in Scotland 1991	43
Table 3.1	Jewish Population in UK and Glasgow 1955-1985	48
Table 3.2	Jewish Participation in Trade 1945	49
Table 4.1	Population of Glasgow 1951-1971	65
Table 4.2	Lessons Outside of School	66
Table 4.3	Census 1991: Population by Ethnic Group	68
Table 4.4	Census 1991: Ethnic Group of Non-White Population	69
Table 4.5	Census 1991: Country of Birth of Pakistani Population	69
Table 4.6	Census 1991: Pakistani Population by Age and Gender	70
Table 4.7	Census 1991: Pakistani Household Composition	71
Table 4.8	Census 1991: Household Conditions	72
Table 4.9	Census 1991: Housing Tenure	73
Table 4.10	Census 1991: Economic Position by Ethnic Group (Males)	74
Table 4.11	Census 1991: Economic Position by Ethnic Group (Females)	75

Table 4.12	Census 1991 Scotland (10% Sample): Occupational Classification of Pakistani Population	76
Table 4.13	Census 1991 Scotland (10% Sample): Employers and Managers	77
Table 4.14	Census 1991 Scotland (10% Sample): Hours Worked	78
Table 4.15	Census 1991 Glasgow City (10% Sample): Ethnic Group and Qualified Manpower	79
Table 4.16	Census 1991 Scotland (10% Sample): Social Class Based on Occupation	79
Table 4.17	Reported 'Racial Incidents' in Scotland	83
Table 5.1	Housing Tenure 1971-1991	91
Table 5.2	Govanhill: Residents by Country of Birth	94
Table 5.3	Govanhill: Residents by Ethnic Group	95
Table 5.4	Govanhill: Distribution of Ethnic Groups by Sector	95
Table 5.5	Govanhill: Migrants	96
Table 5.6	Govanhill: Ethnic Group of Migrants	97
Table 5.7	Govanhill: Age and Ethnic Group of Residents	97
Table 5.8	Unemployment by Ethnic Group	98
Table 5.9	Govanhill: Economic Position by Sex and Ethnic Group	98
Table 5.10	Govanhill: Households with Dependent Children	99
Table 5.11	Single Adult Households	100
Table 5.12	Govanhill: Housing Tenure and Household Amenities	101
Table 5.13	Govanhill: Housing Tenure by Ethnic Group	101
Table 5.14	Govanhill: Occupancy Rates by Ethnic Group	102

Table 5.15	Govanhill: Distribution of Population by Sector	103
Table 7.1	Govanhill Sample: Which of the Following Points are 'Very Important' for a 'Good' Education?	132
Table 7.2	Govanhill Sample: How Important is it to Teach Islamic Studies in School?	135
Table 7.3	Govanhill Sample: Which are the Two Most Important School Subjects?	135
Table 7.4	Govanhill Sample: How Important is it to Teach Urdu (and English) at School?	136
Table 7.5	Govanhill Sample: How Important is it for Girls to Wear *Shalwar Kamiz* to School?	139
Table 7.6	Govanhill Sample: Qualifications of 14-24 Age-band	143
Table 7.7	Govanhill Sample: Qualifications of 25-50 Age-band	144
Table 7.8	Govanhill Sample: Qualifications of Children of 25-50 Age-band	144
Table 7.9	Govanhill Sample: Qualifications of 50+ Age-band	145
Table 7.10	Govanhill Sample: Qualifications of Children of 50+ Age-band	146
Table 8.1	Govanhill Youth Survey: Use of Youth Facilities in Last 5 Years	157
Table 8.2	Govanhill Youth Survey: Youth Facilities Used	157
Table 8.3	Govanhill Youth Survey: Youth Facility Preferences	158
Table 8.4	Govanhill Youth Survey: Reason for Facilities (Order of Preference)	158
Table 8.5	Youth Project: Involvement of Minority Ethnic Groups	162
Table 8.6a	Govanhill Sample: Which of the Following Problems Affect Young People?	165

Table 8.6b	Govanhill Sample: Which are the Two Worst Problems Affecting Young People?	165
Table 8.7	Govanhill Sample: Participation in Youth Groups	171
Table 8.8	Govanhill Sample: Separate Muslim Provision (Youth)	174
Table 8.9	Govanhill Sample: Religiously Specific Provision (Youth)	175
Table 8.10	Govanhill Sample: Culturally Specific Provision (Youth)	176
Table 8.11	Govanhill Sample: Gender Separation (Youth)	177
Table 8.12a	Govanhill Sample: Equal Opportunities (Youth)	179
Table 8.12b	Govanhill Sample: Equal Opportunities Discussion (Youth)	179
Table 8.13a	Govanhill Sample: Sexual Health Problems (Youth)	181
Table 8.13b	Govanhill Sample: Sexual Health Discussion (Youth)	181
Table 8.14	Govanhill Sample: Recreational Activities (Youth)	183
Table 8.15	Govanhill Sample: Sports (Youth)	185
Table 9.1a	Govanhill Sample: Which of the Following Problems Affect the Elderly?	201
Table 9.1b	Govanhill Sample: Which are the Two Worst Problems Affecting the Elderly?	201
Table 9.2a	Govanhill Sample: Who Should Care for the Elderly?	208
Table 9.2b	Govanhill Sample: Who Should Have the Most Responsibility for Care of the Elderly?	208
Table 9.3a	Govanhill Sample: Which Services are Important for the Elderly?	215
Table 9.3b	Govanhill Sample: Which are the Two Most Important Services for the Elderly?	215

Table 9.4	Govanhill Sample: Which of the Following Points are Important for Organisations Working with the Elderly?	217
Table 10.1	Govanhill Sample: Country of Birth	226
Table 10.2a	Govanhill Sample: How Would You Describe Your Identity?	227
Table 10.2b	Govanhill Sample: Which Single Identity Would You Choose?	227

Acknowledgements

I would like to thank the many individuals, families, and community groups who offered me support while I was working and researching in Govanhill. In particular, the fieldwork would have been impossible without the help of Sumbla Bashir Qur'eshi, and the respondents who gave their time for no other reason than to promote understanding. I am very grateful to them all.

I would also like to thank Bob Miles for his encouragement and supervision over many years; Derek Lang for his assistance with the preparation of the manuscript; and the 'Thursday night' crowd, especially Margaret Black, for their friendship.

My parents, Audrey Betty Honeywell and S Norman J Hawken, have been constant in encouraging me to pursue the opportunities that they were denied. This book is dedicated to them and to my son, James Thomas. During the course of the research, James married Toni and I was delighted to gain the status of 'granny' when Grace was born. May she grow up, with her soon-to-be-born brother Max, to cherish the diversity and the symmetry of humankind.

Suzanne Audrey
Glasgow, July 2000

Terminology

This book does not focus on semantics but it is recognised that a number of the terms used are problematic and require some clarification. Additional references to terminology occur throughout the text, particularly in the introduction and chapter ten.

Immigrant

Unfortunately, racist discourse often portrays immigration as a problem and the term 'immigrant' has developed negative connotations. The word is used here simply to refer to someone who changes his or her place of abode from one country to another. Thus it is possible to distinguish those who moved from Pakistan to Scotland, from their descendants who were born in Scotland. This is important because it will be argued that a sense of location is an important aspect of identity.

'White' and 'Wider Population'

These terms refer to the majority of the population in Scotland who would not classify themselves, using the categories available in the Census 1991 Report for Scotland, as 'Pakistani', 'Indian', 'Bangladeshi', 'Chinese', 'Other Asian', 'Black African', 'Black Caribbean' or 'Black Other'. Although 'White' and 'wider population' are unsatisfactory terms, they are used in preference to 'indigenous', 'host' or 'Scottish' which, it will be shown, are entirely inappropriate.

Minority Ethnic Group

This is used in preference to 'ethnic minority group' as it expresses more clearly that we all have ethnicity, but some 'ethnic groups' constitute a minority in Scotland. However, on occasions the language used is that of the particular agency under discussion e.g. some reports refer to 'ethnic minorities' or 'black and ethnic minority groups'.

Pakistani

Most of fieldwork respondents were not born in Pakistan and would not choose this as a single preferred identity. However, respondents who were born in India, Pakistan, Scotland and England accepted 'Pakistani' as an aspect of a multiple identity. It was also an ethnic category in the Census 1991 Report for Scotland. As such, it represents a common factor of identification for the individuals who are the subjects of this thesis.

Multiculturalism and Integration

Throughout this book 'integration' and 'multiculturalism' are linked and refer to a continuous process through which newcomers arrive and settle and, in negotiating aspects of their identity, shape local conditions into which subsequent newcomers settle. Thus, 'multiculturalism' refers to the process through which aspects of different cultures are asserted and acknowledged within a wider social context; and 'integration' refers to the interaction between relative newcomers and an existing population through which aspects of culture are adapted and shared.

It is not suggested that this process involves actors with equal access to power, or that the process is linear. However, it is argued that policies that promote multiculturalism and integration can undermine exclusionary practices that act as barriers to minority ethnic group participation in the labour market, education system and welfare services.

Series Editor's Preface

This is a very important book because the author was able to execute her preference for a focus on anti-racism and how to encourage multiculturalism in practice without ignoring crucial theoretical issues that are essential for understanding the practical problems. Dr Suzanne Audrey started by examining the growing scepticism in research towards grand theory and rightly concluded that attempts to theorise multiculturalism and anti-racism should be grounded on research rather than encouraging theoretical factionalism that tends to become an obstacle to research. Another quality that recommends this book to a wide range of readership is the close attention to history that the author systematically presents.

This is not just a book about one immigrant community but a fascinating account of the history of Glasgow as a religious and trading city at the height of the transatlantic slave trade and the British Raj in India. With that broad historical background, the reader is quickly introduced, one chapter at a time, to the dramatic histories of Irish, Italian, Jewish and Pakistani immigration to the city of Glasgow. Each of these groups came with a rich cultural heritage of different religious faiths, labour traditions and entrepreneurial skills. Each of them faced crude racism of the biological sort and yet each strove to assert their cultural identity, resulting in a rich multicultural heritage in modern day Glasgow.

However, the book warns that emphasis on multiculturalism the way it is practised in the USA could blind researchers and policy makers to the prevalence of racism and the need to develop anti-racist strategies suitable to conditions on the ground.

Dr Biko Agozino
Associate Professor
Indiana University of Pennsylvania

Introduction

This book is concerned with multiculturalism as a practical process through which different cultures are accommodated within a wider social context. Through historical comparison and empirical investigation it will be shown that there is nothing new about this process but that there is value in reasserting the important part it plays in undermining exclusionary practices and informing anti-racist strategies. Before describing the study in more detail, a number of key concepts require discussion.

Some Problems of 'Grand Theory'

In recent years a number sociologists have criticised modern attempts to seek all-embracing explanations for social behaviour. It has been argued that this approach can engender a cycle of exaggeration and counter exaggeration which impedes rather than progresses our understanding of the complexity of social relations [Turner 1985, Mason 1996]. In this context research workers 'seem more often to select the sorts of questions which provide the best opportunities for advancing their general theoretical or political views, than come to favour a theory because it offers the best way to account for the data' [Banton 1996: 34]. Furthermore, where the meanings ascribed by actors contradict a preferred theory they may be undervalued as deriving from their status as victims of social forces beyond their control.

Such tendencies exist in the study of racism and 'race relations' where there is evidence of 'fragmentation into entrenched theoretical paradigms' [Solomos & Back 1996: 2] and where it has been asserted that empirical case studies are a superficial form of inquiry involving the simple documentation of 'phenomenal relations' [Miles 1982: 62-64].

While it is important to understand the structural factors that constrain social relations, I would argue that a key purpose of research in this field is to challenge racism and contribute to effective anti-racist strategies. If this is the case then the study of racism is an area in which theory and practice should inform each other. Arguing in favour of empirical research, Modood has persistently asserted that a strategy of anti-racism that is not informed by appropriate ethnic histories is seriously inadequate [1988a, 1988b, 1992, 1996: 96]. It will be shown later that the fieldwork undertaken as part of this study supports this argument. Furthermore, since ethnic histories are continually developing, documenting the way in which identity is asserted and negotiated at local level is essential to an understanding of the way in which people make (ethnic) history.[1]

'Race', Racism, Culture and New Racism

During the nineteenth and early twentieth centuries, claims that humankind could be divided into categories on the basis of phenotypical characteristics such as skin colour and hair texture ('races') were linked to personal, social and cultural competencies and used to legitimise differential treatment (racism) [Stepan 1982, Banton 1987, Miles 1989]. In this way the idea of 'race' and racism were closely connected. Systems of racial typology are now widely discredited [Banton 1977, Miles 1982, Barkan 1992] but a notion of 'race' remains and opinions vary about whether the term should be abandoned entirely, acknowledged as an aspect of political and popular discourse, or retained as a concept for social scientific purposes [Gilroy 1987, Anthias 1992, Miles 1993, Mason 1996]. This debate continues but the somewhat indiscriminate use of the word 'race' during the 1960s, reinforced by events in the USA which were conceptualised as a 'race struggle', had a significant impact on the vocabulary used in British legislation. In 1965 the first Race Relations Act came into force where 'race' was stated to include 'race, colour, nationality and ethnic or national origins'.[2] Subsequent legislation and policy guidelines continue to use this terminology and, although a positive aspect of the British legislation is the assertion that unequal treatment on such grounds is unlawful, one effect has been to 'freeze and legitimate ... the idea of "race relations" as social relations between races' [Miles 1993: 45].

During the 1980s anti-racist discourse in Britain included the identification of 'new racism' [Barker 1981] which attested the natural preference of human beings for their 'own culture' and the potential for social conflict when incompatible cultures were forced to mix. This new racism is said to have emerged in the second half of the twentieth century after the racism based on biological theories of inferior and superior races was no longer viable as a public discourse [Modood 1997c: 154]. Its most

---

[1] 'Men make their own history, but they do not make it just as they please; they do not make it under circumstances chosen by themselves, but under circumstances directly encountered, given and transmitted from the past' [Marx & Engels quoted in McLellan 1972: 61].

[2] Thus 'race' is used tautologically with no clear definition.

blatant articulation in Britain is often traced back to Enoch Powell's 'rivers of blood' speech in April 1968 [reproduced in *New Statesman* 17 April 1998], through Ray Honeyford's attack on multicultural education [*Salisbury Review* January 1984] and the anti-Muslim fervour evident throughout the *Satanic Verses* affair [Lewis 1994: 4, Runnymede Trust 1997]. However, it has also been argued that this form of racist discourse is not new and that nineteenth century race science is an exception in a history of European cultural racism which has included centuries of anti-Semitism and 'Islamophobia'[3] [Modood 1997b: 155]. One aspect of the historical research in this study is to consider whether cultural and phenotypical differences, actual or putative, were linked in the racist discourse surrounding migrations to Scotland during the nineteenth and early twentieth centuries, before 'new racism' was conceptualised.

An important consequence of the identification of cultural racism was the impact on anti-racist strategies. During the 1970s and 1980s emphasis on opposing White racism through a collective Black identity discouraged discussion of cultural differences within the Black population. Highlighting such differences was thought to blame the victims of racism, and to give insufficient recognition to economic and social processes that influence the position of racialised minorities in society [Lawrence 1982, Solomos & Back 1996: 130]. But it has been increasingly argued that the imposition of an all inclusive Black identity underestimated the significance of cultural and religious identity to individuals who prioritised ethnic ties over other patterns of group formation, and the extent to which cultural differences were being exploited as justification for exclusion and harassment [Rex 1991: 11, Jenkins 1996: 72, Modood 1992, 1994].

The fieldwork in this study focused on the Pakistani population of Govanhill on the south side of Glasgow.[4] The majority of this population have settled in Scotland on a permanent basis so that it is important to regard them as local and not as 'the other, the exotic' [Ahmed & Hastings 1994: 5]. At the same time it will be shown that differences of language, religion, diet, dress and social mores do exist and are reproduced. Modood has argued that cultural racism is likely to be particularly aggressive against those who 'far from denying their difference ... want to assert this difference in public' [1997c: 165], but it would be wrong to assume that asserting

---

[3] This term, described as 'a useful shorthand way of referring to dread or hatred of Islam', appears to have developed during the 1980s and its first known use in print was in February 1991 [Runnymede Trust 1997: 1]

[4] This is the terminology used in the 1991 Census. It will be shown later that although respondents would not choose 'Pakistani' as their primary term of identity, the majority were happy to include it as one aspect of their identity.

difference in public invariably triggers hostility. While cultural racism is directed at the Pakistani population, it will be shown through the local case studies that their interaction with service providers also includes notions of fair and equal treatment.

Essentialism and Identity

The systematising trends of modern thought included the tendency to portray culture as discreet, bounded and continuous (essentialism) but such ideas are now widely criticised [Gilroy 1987, van de Veer 1997, Wicker 1997, Caglar 1997]. The notion of discreet culture, like 'race', can form the basis on which difference is exaggerated and incorporated into racist discourse to reinforce exclusion and disadvantage. Moreover, those who unquestioningly assert the rights of minorities to maintain 'their culture' may, in effect, collude with authoritarian leaders who claim to represent the true essence of their collectivity's culture and religion [Yuval-Davis 1997: 201]. In order to avoid essentialism, the concept of a coherent, territorially based culture has been replaced by notions of cultural complexity changing with space and time [Wicker 1997: 39, Hannerz 1992, Barth 1993: 339]. Some go further and argue that it is necessary to 'write against culture' and develop a 'multi-culturalism of the market, in which consumers are left to define for themselves who they are, away from top-down constructions by the state or by fictive "communities"' [Caglar 1997: 180-182].

Yet, while the analytical concern to avoid essentialism remains, for the purposes of policy development and implementation it is important to acknowledge that not all ethnic and cultural representations essentialise in the same way [Werbner 1997: 229, Spivak 1987]. Local authority and voluntary organisations may identify themselves as serving 'Chinese elderly', 'Asian youth', and so on, and such terms inevitably essentialise. But the motive, both intended and perceived, may be to signal sensitivity to specific cultural requirements and, as such, is quite different from the motives of those who assert that 'Pakis stink' [Cohen 1988: 83]. Furthermore, those who wish to access services may not regard themselves as individual consumers in the market but may deliberately assert an essentialised group identity. They may, at different times and in different ways, perceive themselves, and project themselves to others, as belonging to real collectivities with shared language, customs, religion and so on: 'not just modes of oppression but modes of being' [Modood 1996: 95]. Such collectivities should not be dismissed as fictive, or as constructions imposed by the state or authoritarian leaders, without assessing their significance to the actors involved.

While it may be possible to identify aspects of shared culture at a given moment, it is important to remember that the movements of people ensure that 'all cultures are the results of a mishmash, borrowings, mixtures that have occurred, though at different rates, ever since the beginning of time' [Levi-Strauss 1994: 424]. Thus the identity of an individual, or a collectivity, is dependent upon relationships with others and a sense of location [Bhabha 1994: 185]. Bhabha suggests that migration may stimulate the emergence of 'hybrid identities' made up of elements of different cultures. Once again it can be argued that conceptualising such hyphenated identities contributes to essentialism by implying the combination of discreet cultures, as well as feeding notions of dual loyalties and potential conflict [Caglar 1997: 175-177]. This points to an inherent, and apparently insoluble, problem in conceptualising cultural identity in that 'the model starts off arguing that ethnicity is dynamic and situational, but ends up allowing a relatively static conceptualisation of the social system or subsystem' [Solomos & Back 1996: 6]. While this is an interesting theoretical conundrum, for the practical purpose of service provision it may be best to be alert to the danger and move on. In relation to this study, the potential exists for the evolution of hyphenated identities which include 'Pakistani', 'Muslim', 'Asian', 'Scottish', 'British', 'Black' and so on. The development of such identities and their significance to the actors involved are not explored here as theoretical issues but through examining the assertion and negotiation of identity in practice.

Modood has persistently argued that the Black/White terminology, emphasised in anti-racist discourse throughout the 1970s and 1980s, deprived 'Asians' of a language in which to debate cultural difference [1992, 1996, 1997a]. Ironically, a similar criticism might be levelled at his use of the term 'Asian' which also conflates a variety of cultural and religious identities [Solomos & Back 1996: 135]. The fieldwork respondents in this study were interviewed primarily as local residents and service users rather than as Pakistanis, Muslims etc. They were not asked about their preferred identity until the end of the interviews in order to reduce the tendency to which they answered questions with a specific identity in mind. Their preferred identities are discussed later but it is significant to note that during the 1991 Census less than 9% of the non-White population in the whole of Scotland described themselves as 'Black' (i.e. 2,773 African, 934 Caribbean, and 2,646 Other). Over 50% of the total 'ethnic minority' population chose identities associated with the Indian sub-continent (34% Pakistani, 16% Indian and 2% Bangladeshi), with 17% Chinese and 7% Other Asian [Scottish Office *Factsheet 15*]. It might therefore be assumed that the Black/White terminology is even less relevant in the Scottish context than it is in Britain as a whole.

The Significance of Religion

In asserting that it is not only Black people who are the objects of racism, Miles has made reference to the experience of Irish and Jewish populations [Miles 1989]. His concern was primarily with economic and political explanations and the significance of religious identity was largely neglected. But historical investigation indicates that religious identity was highly significant to both Irish and Jewish migrants and to the wider population, and that it played an important part in shaping racist discourse and local conditions.

There was no opportunity in the 1991 Census for individuals to identify themselves by religious affiliation and so it is not possible to use the data to gauge the importance, if any, individuals placed upon their religious identity. Current anti-racist and equal opportunities policies in Britain also tend to avoid religious terminology, although there are some glaring anomalies that have implications for fieldwork respondents in this study. Muslims (defined as members of a religious group) are not entitled to protection under the Race Relations Act 1976, but Sikhs and Jews (considered to be members of 'ethnic groups') are entitled to such protection. Meanwhile in Northern Ireland discrimination against Protestants or Roman Catholics is unlawful under the Fair Employment (Northern Ireland) Acts 1976 and 1989. Thus, in different parts of Britain, Jews, Sikhs, and Christians have recourse to anti-discrimination law, while other faiths do not. Other legal inequalities were brought sharply into focus with the publication of Salman Rushdie's novel *The Satanic Verses* when it was made clear that British blasphemy law offered no protection to non-Christian faiths. Muslims and non-Muslims continue to raise these issues and argue for change [Runnymede Trust 1997].

Despite the persistence of religion as a component of identity, the degree of adherence to faith is likely to vary and cannot be ascertained through consideration of religious texts, the proclamations of religious leaders, or theoretical reflection. An important aspect of this study is, therefore, to consider the importance of religious identity to individuals through examining the ways in which it is expressed in daily life. It has been asserted that Islam is impervious to secularisation [Gellner 1994: xiii, Gerholm 1994: 191]. If so, this would constitute a significant difference from the experience of Jewish and Catholic migrants to Scotland where secularisation was, and continues to be, acknowledged as an issue [Collins 1987, 1993; Gallagher 1991]. Consideration is, therefore, also given to the potential for a secular Muslim identity to develop in Scotland.

'New Multiculturalism'

The prominence of recent debates about the place of Islam in a western liberal democracy apparently supports the assertion that religious migrants are in the vanguard of a 'new European multiculturalism' [van de Veer 1997]. In a similar vein it has been asserted that this 'new multiculturalism' does not relegate cultural diversity to the private sphere [Modood 1997b]. But historical consideration of Catholics and Jews in Scotland indicates that they might also be described as 'religious migrants' and that they did not relegate their cultural diversity to the private sphere. Thus in practice 'new multiculturalism' is not new. Rather 'each society is multicultural and over centuries has arrived at its own original synthesis' [Levi-Strauss 1994: 424]. While it may be possible to describe a particular synthesis at a given moment, the process is continuous as the cultural mores of migrants are reconstituted according to local conditions and, in turn, contribute to the conditions encountered by subsequent generations and newcomers [Ahmed & Hastings 1994: 3, Miles 1993: 117].

The process is not defined solely by events at one end of a migratory chain. Visits to, and visitors from, the 'homeland' contribute to the maintenance, reproduction or redefinition of identity. Events abroad (in the West Bank, Northern Ireland, Kashmir and so on), together with local and international responses to them, have the potential to reinforce or reshape the identity of individuals whether or not they have ever been to the places concerned. In this study the historical material and fieldwork interviews confirm that the significance of diasporic ties to immigrants and their descendants is likely to vary with time and place, and the significance presumed by others also varies according to particular historical circumstances.

Theoretical concerns about culture and essentialism have prompted the assertion that multiculturalism is an important rhetoric and an impossible practice: as rhetoric it proposes that marginal cultures should be accorded respect, yet this is impossible in practice because of the 'intrinsically sited, negotiated, hybrid nature of culture' [Werbner 1997: 22-3]. But empirical investigation suggests that the converse may apply. Academic analysis requires precision in the definition of terms, and theoretical propositions are subject to detailed scrutiny and rigorous debate. But the 'exercise in avoiding specifics' [Saggar 1996: 177] which is the reality of local anti-racist and multicultural policies, whilst often the source of frustration and inactivity, also allows room for flexibility and innovation. Similarly, the argument that multiculturalism involves an 'institutionalisation of cultures in the public sphere' in which only recognised groups will be given rights [Caglar 1997: 179] overestimates the precision with which the local state implements policy. In practice, the imprecise use of terms such as 'ethnic minority' allows for multiple and changing definitions of group membership. Furthermore, the suggestion that collective identities must inevitably become sources of constraints imposed on individuals by religious or community leaders [Appiah 1994: 163, Caglar 1997: 179], underestimates the ability of the actors involved to negotiate multiple identities and allegiances. It is in practical attempts to implement multiculturalism that the potential for flexibility becomes apparent and where academic incompatibilities are translated into practical compromises.

Integration

Questions of multiculturalism are linked to ideas of the nation state and the right of each 'naturally distinct' nation to self-determination within defined spatial boundaries [Miles 1993: 61]. If the nation state is constructed as 'home' for 'our people' then questions arise about how 'our people' are defined and whether, and under what conditions, outsiders are permitted to enter. The history of Britain's immigration laws is well documented [Jones 1977, Bevan 1986, Dummett & Nicol 1990] but the primary concern of this study is the extent to which those who are allowed to enter are expected to 'fit in'. Following the Second World War, when there were concerns about labour shortages, the Royal Commission on Population asserted that immigration on a large scale could only be welcomed 'if the immigrants were of good human stock and were not prevented by their religion or race from intermarrying with the host population and becoming merged in it' [1949: 124].

Some twenty years later, Enoch Powell made his infamous 'rivers of blood' speech in which he implied that immigrants from the New Commonwealth and Pakistan posed a threat because they did not wish to become 'for all practical purposes indistinguishable from' the (imagined, homogeneous) British population. But official discourse had already begun to move away from such vigorous notions of assimilation and Roy Jenkins' definition of integration, in a speech as Home Secretary in 1966, was widely articulated as the elusive goal for many years. He defined integration 'not as a flattening process of assimilation but as equal opportunity, accompanied by cultural diversity, in an atmosphere of mutual tolerance' [Jones 1977: 148]. The apparent generosity of this definition was undermined because it was asserted within a broader discourse that continued to portray the arrival of immigrants from the New Commonwealth and Pakistan as a problem [Dummett & Dummett 1982]. It has since been further tainted by his more recent suggestion, as Lord Jenkins, that 'in retrospect we might have been more cautious about allowing the creation in the 1950s of substantial Muslim communities here' [*The Independent* 4/3/89].

Yet, in response to the recent phase of Islamophobia, discussion about the importance of religious tolerance and equality under the law also emerged [St Catherine's Conference 1991, Runnymede Trust 1997]. Such a response is not new and historical comparison will show that hostility and exclusionary practices towards the Irish, Italian and Jewish immigrants of the nineteenth and early twentieth centuries co-existed with notions of fair and equal treatment. Thus, while a charge of British ethnocentricity is valid, it might also be described as an uneven ethnocentricity which permits multiple, and changing, definitions of what it is to be British, Scottish, Christian, Conservative and so on. Such pragmatism is not necessarily renounced, and may be actively supported, by members of minority ethnic groups.

In practice integration and multiculturalism are aspects of an evolutionary process, linked to the evolution of society as a whole, through which newcomers arrive and settle, and, in negotiating aspects of their identity, shape local conditions into which subsequent newcomers settle. Thus integration is an interactive process in which 'both parties are an active ingredient and so something new is created' [Modood 1997c: 24]. It can, of course, be argued that the process involves the unequal distribution of power between dominant and minority groups [Solomos & Back 1996: 126]. But the notion of an interactive process avoids conceptualising immigrants and their descendants solely as victims. It may also reduce the tendency for researchers to be 'trapped in an orthodoxy which always requires them to see the world as an awful place getting worse' [Fenton 1996: 160]. For the anti-racist strategist and the social policy practitioner it is important to identify and build on examples of good practice.

The Scottish Context

It has been argued that there are dangers in using information from the USA to explain or predict the course of 'race relations' in Britain, particularly where this has focused on an African American history that has little relevance for those who migrated to Britain from the Indian sub-continent [Banton 1983, Miles 1993, Modood 1996]. Although there are likely to be similarities between the Scottish experience and other parts of Britain, the extent and significance of any differences are difficult to assess if boundaries are blurred or even ignored. For this reason the sources used here are those which refer to Scotland in general and, wherever possible, to Glasgow and Govanhill in particular. The resulting narrative is inevitably patchy but, since the aim is to present a Scottish study, gaps have not been filled using 'British' data which, in reality, refers solely to England and Wales. Historical comparison is focused *within* Scotland and there is no cross border comparison, but the presentation of specifically Scottish data allows distinctions to emerge which may enable others to make comparisons with similar studies in England and Wales.

When Norman Tebbit expressed concern that some British citizens did not support the English cricket team it is unlikely that he was thinking of the Scots. He was probably unaware that, in Glasgow, T-shirts were produced emblazoned with the Scottish flag and the words 'I failed the English cricket test'. Many Scots are proud of 'not being English' and one aspect of this has been the popular conception that Scottish tolerance has contributed to the absence of the serious 'race relations' problems evident south of the border [Armstrong 1989, Miles & Dunlop 1987]. In reality, research has repeatedly shown that racism does exist: cases of 'racial discrimination and harassment' are regularly handled by Racial Equality Councils, and police annual statistics show a steady increase in reported 'racial incidents'[5] [Walsh 1987, TCRC 1987, Fife Regional Council 1991, Cant et al 1995, West Of Scotland CRC 1997].

To explain this incongruity it has been argued that while racism does exist, politics have not been racialised in Scotland. The clash between Roman Catholic and Protestant identity, and a political nationalism that has tended to focus on the perceived economic and political disadvantages of the Union, have been offered as factors contributing to the lack of racialisation of the political process [Miles & Dunlop 1986, Miles 1993: 78]. But such explanations conceptualise South Asian immigrants and their descendants as victims, or potential victims, whose status is dependent on changes in political circumstances to which they are peripheral. In contrast, this study places immigrants and their descendants at the heart of a multicultural process and examines some of the ways in which they assert and negotiate their priorities in the wider social context.

The Study

Govanhill was established as a working class neighbourhood in the nineteenth century. The history of the area has been inextricably linked with

---

[5] An increase in the reporting of incidents may indicate greater confidence that issues will be addressed and is not necessarily evidence of an increase in the number of actual incidents.

the development and subsequent decline of Glasgow as an industrial city, and with nineteenth and twentieth century migrations to the West of Scotland. Irish Catholic, Italian and Jewish immigrants have all played a part in the history of Govanhill and in the first three chapters consideration is given to the factors influencing these migrations, the response of the local population to the migration and settlement of these (relative) newcomers, and the priorities and strategies of the immigrants and their descendants as they established themselves in their new surroundings.

In chapter four attention is focused on the history of migration to Scotland from the Indian sub-continent and the response of the local population to the arrival and settlement of South Asian immigrants. This is followed by analysis of the 1991 Census data for those who identified themselves as Pakistani.

To contextualise the fieldwork, chapter five describes the neighbourhood of Govanhill from its early history, through its development as Glasgow became a major industrial centre, and subsequent decline to the status of a 'deprived' area. Govanhill was not subjected to major slum clearance and redevelopment, and the tenements, school buildings, shops and places of worship continue to reflect much of this history. The second part of the chapter concentrates on Govanhill in the 1990s, including a description of the physical environment and an analysis of 1991 Census data with particular reference to the local Pakistani population.

Having established both the historical and contemporary context, the study proceeds to a more detailed examination of the way in which multiculturalism is negotiated. The problem of managing 'race relations' has been effectively devolved from central to local government through Section 71 of the Race Relations Act 1976 which requires local authorities to 'eliminate unlawful racial discrimination' and 'promote equality of opportunity and good relations between persons of different racial groups'. In practice, responsibility has been further devolved to Racial Equality Councils ('Community Relations Council' in the West of Scotland) and a range of voluntary sector initiatives. Thus it is at local level that the implementation of these policies can best be examined.

Three policy areas (school-age education, youth work and care of the elderly) are examined. In each case, national and local government policy guidelines are outlined before consideration is given to the attempts of local projects and organisations to meet needs and implement policy. In addition, a series of interviews were conducted and collated by age and gender to ascertain the priorities of actual or potential clients from the Pakistani population. Some methodological issues are discussed in chapter six, followed by analysis of the case studies and fieldwork interviews in chapters seven (school-age education), eight (youth work) and nine (care of the elderly).

Finally, the theoretical issues outlined in this introduction are re-examined in chapter ten. In particular, consideration is given to the assertion and negotiation of identity by Pakistani immigrants and their descendants in Scotland, the historical continuity of 'new racism' and multiculturalism, and the importance of multiculturalism as an integrative process in a Scottish context.

1 The Irish in Glasgow

Three major migrations to Glasgow took place during the nineteenth and early twentieth centuries: those of Irish Catholics, Italians and Jews. Despite diversity of history and origin, it will be shown that there were similarities in the assertion and acknowledgement of ethnic and religious identity that have relevance for the more detailed study of the Pakistani population in Glasgow today. But first it is necessary to understand something of the place to which they migrated.

A Brief Early History of Glasgow

It has been said that Glasgow owes its origins to 'the impulse of religion' [Massie 1989]. The city is thought to have been founded by Saint Mungo in the sixth century, and later incorporated Govan parish on the other side of the River Clyde where Saint Constantine had reputedly built a church in the seventh century. A cathedral was built on the site of St Mungo's original wooden church during the twelfth century [Edward 1993: 12] and a Papal Bull was obtained from Pope Alexander VI some three hundred years later elevating Glasgow to the status of an Archbishopric. Catholic bishops dominated the mediaeval city but during the sixteenth century Scotland embraced the Reformation. In 1560, as the Lords of the Congregation in Edinburgh gave instructions to 'purge the Kirk of all kynd of monuments of adolatrye', Glasgow's Archbishop went into exile [Massie 1989: 11].

A second impulse that shaped the history of the city was that of trade. In 1651 one of Cromwell's commissioners wrote that 'with the exception of the colleges, all the inhabitants are traders' [Ibid: 28] and this propensity increased rapidly as a result of the Act of Union in 1707. The Act created a free market within the British Isles and enabled Scotland to trade with English colonies in the West Indies, America and India. Hostility to union with England had been intense in Glasgow but the city's merchants took full advantage of the new opportunities. The wealth that was generated was evident in their conspicuous consumption, their mansions, and the streets to which they gave their names, but was also invested in manufacturing industry [Miles & Muirhead 1986: 112]. Glasgow was eventually known as 'Second City of the Empire' and the prosperity generated did much to convince Scots that there were advantages to the Union. However, resentment of English political domination survived and helped to shape a Scottish identity that is, to this day, determinedly 'not English'.

As trade developed, educational establishments played their part in advancing Scotland's industrial revolution. The University of Glasgow, founded in 1451, was moved 'from the mediaeval to the modern world' during the eighteenth century by Frances Hutcheson, who held the Chair of Moral Philosophy from 1729 until 1746, and began lecturing in the English language as an aid to understanding [Massie 1989: 33]. Also during the eighteenth century, in keeping with the emphasis on promoting knowledge with a practical application, John Anderson set up an Institution, later to become the University of Strathclyde, which offered 'a complete scientific course on physics and chemistry with their application to the arts and manufactures' [Ibid: 36].

Industrialisation and increased prosperity were accompanied by rapid growth in the population. The first official census in 1801 showed that the population of Glasgow was 77,000 and within a hundred years this figure had increased tenfold to over three-quarters of a million [Edward 1993: 13]. This growth was partly due to the incorporation of surrounding districts, but of greater significance was the arrival of people from further afield, many attempting to escape poverty or persecution, who were seeking opportunities to improve their situation. The new arrivals entered a vibrant and expanding city: founded through the Roman Catholic faith, yet wholeheartedly embracing the Reformation; initially hostile to the Union, yet prospering as a result of industrialisation and increased trade; generating extremes of wealth and poverty to create magnificent buildings and some of the worst slums in Europe. The remainder of this chapter examines the Irish migration that played a part in the subsequent history of Glasgow.

Irish Migration

Only twelve miles of sea separate Ireland and Scotland at the shortest crossing and so it is not surprising that links between Ireland and Scotland developed well before the nineteenth century. The name Scotland derives from the Gaelic Scots of Ulster who crossed to Argyll in the fifth and sixth centuries, bringing with them their language and Scotland's first experience of the Christian religion [Kay 1982]. Migration was in the opposite direction at the beginning of the seventeenth century when attempts were made to extend British influence by attracting settlers, including Calvinist Lowlanders, to six of the nine counties of Ulster [Curtis 1990: 226-32]. The settlers were given favourable terms in exchange for swearing allegiance to the Crown (and agreeing not to inter-marry or learn the language of the native Irish).

Strong links between Ulster and the West of Scotland were maintained through education, as the sons of tenant farmers and Presbyterian ministers favoured Scottish universities because of their Presbyterian ethos [Bishop 1987]. These students often returned to live in Ulster, although the career of Frances Hutcheson illustrates the reciprocal connections between the two destinations. He was born in Ulster, educated at Glasgow University, became a minister in Ulster, and then returned to Glasgow to become the first Irish-born Professor at the University (where he famously began lecturing in English). Other reciprocal links were maintained through the linen industry. Weavers and bleachers from Ulster first gave instruction to the Scottish labour force and later, when the Irish linen industry began to decline in the 1770s, moved to Scotland to seek employment [Durie 1979].

At the beginning of the nineteenth century, seasonal migration from the West of Ireland to Scotland was an integral part of the lives of many people, and enabled small farmers and cottiers to supplement their income in increasingly difficult circumstances [Collins 1991]. Thousands of them looked for work during the Scottish corn harvest and their journey was made easier by the regular steam boat passenger services which began to operate between Derry and Glasgow in the 1820s. Conditions on board were far from luxurious. On 11 May 1836, the *Scots Times* was moved to report that the boats were 'crowded on deck with hundreds of poor creatures, who are huddled together and mixed up with horned cattle, pigs, sheep and lambs'. Nevertheless the experience was generally regarded as a worthwhile method of subsidising life in Ireland. In 1845 the *Glasgow Examiner* reported:

> Immense numbers of Irish reapers have passed through Glasgow on their return from different parts of Scotland ... on questioning a small party that looked exceedingly pleased we learned that each had saved £3 of money which they were carrying home with ineffable delight. [Edward 1993: 46]

These established patterns of migration, together with the improved transport systems, made Scotland an obvious destination for the poor when blight caused the failure of successive Irish potato crops between 1845 and 1849, and the Great Famine struck. Estimates suggest that about a million people left Ireland at this time with a further million dying of starvation and fever [Edward 1993: 50]. Throughout this period Ireland was producing large quantities of food for export so that this was a famine in which the poor 'did not starve for want of food but for want of the means to pay for it from the lack of employment' [Davis 1991: 14, Handley 1947].

Table 1.1 Irish Emigration 1841-1861

Total Irish emigration	1841-1851	1,194,866
	1851-1861	1,163,418
Irish emigrants to Scotland	1841-1851	approx.115,000
Total Irish-born in Scotland	1841-1851	207,367
Total population of Glasgow	1851	358,951
'Irish' population of Glasgow	1851	64,185

[Source: Handley 1947: 20-21]

After the Great Famine opportunities for agricultural labourers and cottiers in Ireland declined even further, while the position of larger farmers strengthened.[6] Large-scale emigration continued as people searched for opportunities abroad and the population fell from 6.5 million in 1851 to 3.2 million in 1911 [Collins 1991: 10]. America was the favoured destination but not everyone could afford the fare. Many felt the West of Scotland, and Glasgow in particular, offered at least the chance of a better life. Statistics relating to this migration are by no means irrefutable, but there is no doubt that a considerable number of desperately poor people left Ireland for Scotland, with as many as 8,000 per week arriving in Glasgow at the height of the famine [Edward 1993: 52]. Handley's statistics indicate that at the time of the 1851 Census over 30% of the Irish-born in Scotland were based in Glasgow, and they constituted 18% of the city's total population.

Attitudes Towards Irish Immigrants

The majority of these immigrants were caught up in the rapid industrial expansion of the period, and the misery and exploitation of whole families working long hours in appalling conditions is well documented [Handley 1947: 130-136]. Men, women and children provided cheap labour in the textile industry, chemical works, potteries and tobacco factories. Many men were employed as unskilled labourers in mines, iron and steel works, docks, locomotive works and the construction industry. The terms 'navvy' and

---

[6] Between 1845 and 1910 the number of labourers and cottiers fell by 65%, small farming decreased by 50%, but the number of farmers with over fifteen acres increased by 10% [Lee 1973: 2-3].

'Paddy' became synonymous in the public mind despite one estimate that only 10% of 'navvies' were actually Irish by birth [Treble 1973: 228-9].

Regular employment was not ensured and poverty, illness and destitution led to applications for Poor Relief. Hundreds of desperate cases were investigated by Inspectors and documented in an *Irish Series* of the volumes of Poor Law Applications of Glasgow City Parish, but public sympathy was limited and it became commonplace to accuse the Irish of migrating to Scotland specifically to be kept by charity. The *Poor Law Magazine* began publication in 1858 and one Inspector contributed a poem entitled 'The Irish Pauper in Ireland to his Neighbours' [Edwards 1993: 54]. A few lines from the poem illustrate the derisive attitude that was evident amongst some Poor Law officials:

> Then come where there's praties and whisky galore
> They'll feed us and clothe us, with all of the rest
> And make us their own though we come from the West.
> In the poorhouse of Scotland we'll live at our aise

Negative stereotypes are often contradictory and this was the case with the Irish who were charged with laziness and living off charity, and with undermining attempts to strengthen employment rights by their willingness to work hard for low wages. The *Report on the State of the Irish Poor in Great Britain* [1936] included evidence from witnesses largely supporting the allegation that wages were lowered by Irish workers. Irish labourers were commonly accused of undercutting wage rates, and the practice of separating groups of workers to 'prevent trouble' may indeed have been used as a way of imposing lower pay on the Irish [Treble 1973]. Whatever the accuracy or inaccuracy of these assertions, the belief was widespread and contributed to hostility amongst Scottish trade unionists towards them [Gallagher 1987: 31]. Even Engels, who one might assume to have had a deeper understanding of the exploitation of labour power, was not above contributing to negative stereotypes:

> For when in almost every great city, a fifth or a quarter of workers are Irish or children of Irish parents who have grown up among Irish filth, no one can wonder if the life, habits, intelligence, moral status - in short the whole character of the working class - assimilates a great part of the Irish characteristics. [Engels 1958: 125]

This quotation refers not only to people born in Ireland but to their children, and this became an increasing concern for those who were attempting to measure the size of the 'problem'. In the 1851 *Report on the Census of the City of Glasgow and Suburbs*, it was asserted that:

> Within the last ten years the children born here of Irish parents have been very numerous; but these, of course, are all put under the heading of Scotch. While, therefore, there appears to be an increase of 2.07 percent in the present enumeration, above that which the Irish bore to the population of 1841, the real number of inhabitants who are imbued with Irish characteristics, habits, feelings and religious sentiments is infinitely greater. [Handley 1947: 46]

Thus concern was growing that the immigrants were bringing up their Scottish-born children with an Irish identity, which included 'characteristics, habits, feelings and religious sentiments' that were incompatible with being 'Scotch'. The worrying religious sentiments were those of the Roman Catholic faith and such was the *anti-Catholic* fervour that Protestant Irish immigrants were rendered almost invisible in *anti-Irish* discourse. Reports, books, articles and press coverage frequently used the terms 'Irish' and 'Catholic' interchangeably but before focusing on the Catholic population in more detail, consideration will be given to the Irish Protestant population in Scotland.

Irish Protestant Immigrants

Census data did not distinguish immigrants by religion, so that estimates of the number of Irish Protestants have been calculated by subtracting the known number of Catholics from the total number of Irish. Such estimates are crude but the proportion of Irish Protestants is generally accepted to be about 25% [Walker 1991: 48-9]. It has already been shown that connections between lowland Scots and Ulster can be traced back at least as far as the Ulster Plantation in the reign of King James VI (James I of England), and that these were maintained through education and the linen industry. From the middle of the nineteenth century the shipbuilding industry established additional links between Belfast and Glasgow, reinforcing the potential for Glasgow to be perceived as a suitable destination for the Irish Protestant migrant. The long-held assumption of a broad compatibility between Ulster Protestantism and the religious values of lowland Scotland might lead to the conclusion that these immigrants were soon barely discernible from the majority population, but there were some distinguishing factors.

The most conspicuous manifestation of identity was evident in the activities of the Orange Order which had been established in Armagh in

1795 to 'maintain the laws and peace of the country and the Protestant Constitution, and to defend the King and his heirs as long as they shall maintain the Protestant ascendancy' [Curtis 1990: 336-7]. On 12 July 1823 the first full dress procession commemorating the Battle of the Boyne took place in Glasgow and the annual march to the statue of King William at Glasgow Cross became an important part of the Orangeman's calendar.[7] While not all the Irish Protestants who migrated to Scotland were members of the Orange Order, research has shown a strong correlation between the strength of the Orangeism and the number of Protestant Irish in a given area [McFarland 1986, Walker 1991].

Membership of the Orange Order was a means by which Protestants could distinguish themselves from the Catholic Irish, but this may not have been the primary motive. Membership also gave access to practical support for the newly arrived immigrant. This included the Glasgow Orange Union Funeral Society, the Glasgow Ulster Association, and the Glasgow Antrim and Down Benevolent Association [McFarland 1986: 50, 176]. Apprenticeships were commonly allocated by Unions in conjunction with foremen who were often Orangemen [Walker 1991: 58, McLean 1983]. And some firms, such as Bairds of Coatbridge, adopted a paternalistic style of management, allocating houses for workers and company schools for children, whilst encouraging an identity between the firm and Orange values [Campbell 1979, McFarland 1986].

As far as religious practice was concerned, the compatibility between Scottish and Irish Protestant traditions could not be taken for granted. For many years the Church of Scotland had regarded itself as speaking for the *Scottish* nation and there was a reluctance to be drawn into *Irish* causes (such as the dispute over Irish Home Rule which will be discussed later). Many of the immigrants were Episcopalian, but the Scottish Episcopal Church was largely upper class and was unprepared for the arrival of thousands of migrant workers from Ulster [McFarland 1986: 44]. Working class Irish migrants were not welcomed with open arms and one estimate suggests that in the late 1830s there were already 7,000 Episcopalians in Glasgow and the suburbs 'consisting chiefly of Irish emigrants without a place of worship' [Walker 1991: 64, Note 43]. Meanwhile, the Orange Order was a largely Episcopalian organisation and the local Lodge may have provided a more supportive and congenial environment than the local church.

---

[7] In the history of Ireland, the Battle of the Boyne in 1690 has been described as 'one of the half-dozen events that completely changed her history ... The Protestant and Anglican ascendancy, social, religious and political, became securely established for another century and a half.' [Curtis 1990 271].

Religious affiliation shaped political allegiance and the influence of the Ulster Protestant immigrant population on Conservatives in Scotland was evident from the 1880s until well into the twentieth century [Pugh 1985, McFarland 1986]. The priorities of the Scottish politician and the Irish immigrant did vary, since at this stage they were often those of the respective country of origin, but there is compelling evidence of an Orange-Conservative alliance operating between 1912 and 1914 [Walker 1991 cites Scott 1912-14]. Debates about Irish Home Rule provided the Conservative and Unionist Party with an opportunity to strengthen their support amongst the newly enfranchised, predominantly Protestant, working class population and they were not slow to recognise this. The *Belfast Weekly News* of 23 January 1913 reported a meeting of the Glasgow Ulster Association at which the President stated that the Association was not attached to any political party but could not disregard the fact that the Conservatives were opposing Home Rule.

When Sir Edward Carson, leader of the Irish Unionist Party, visited Glasgow in October 1913 he addressed a rally in St Andrew's Hall and referred to 'the Ulstermen of Glasgow', some 8,700 of whom had signed the Ulster Covenant pledging resistance to Home Rule. With Sir Edward Carson on the platform were: Parker Smith, Conservative MP for Partick; John Gilmour, Conservative MP and Orangeman; and John Ure-Primrose, Chairman of Rangers Football Club which was increasingly portrayed as the Protestant rival to Catholic Celtic [Walker 1991: 62]. Thus, the bodies represented on the platform at this rally give a clear indication of the political, religious and sporting preoccupations of a large section of the Irish Protestant population in Glasgow at the time.

Overall, the relative compatibility between the religious identity of many Irish Protestant immigrants and that of the existing majority population in Scotland did ease the process of migration and settlement. The 'Irishness' of their descendants is hardly visible today, although one aspect of their history remains evident through those active members of the Orange Order who continue to march through the streets of Glasgow on and around the 12th of July.

Nineteenth and early twentieth century concern about the 'Irish' was predominantly a concern about 'Catholics'. This religious preoccupation was interspersed with nationalist and racist sentiments, as was evident in a report to the General Assembly of the Church of Scotland entitled *The Menace of the Irish Race to our Scottish Nationality* which stated:

> Nor is there any complaint of an Orange population in Scotland. They are the same race as ourselves and of the same faith, and are readily assimilated to the Scottish population ... The problem is of

the Irish Roman Catholic population in Scotland. They cannot be assimilated and absorbed into the Scottish race. They are a people by themselves, segregated by reason of their race, their customs, their traditions, and above all, by their loyalty to their church. [Edinburgh, 1923]

Irish Catholic Immigrants

Reactions to the arrival of a sizeable Catholic population should be considered in the light of Scottish history. The Scottish Presbyterian tradition had been achieved after considerable struggle and sacrifice, and such was the strength of feeling at the end of the eighteenth century that in Glasgow 'there were only thirty-nine Catholics, but forty-three anti-Catholic societies' [Murray 1984: 93]. These sentiments were exacerbated in 1850 when Pope Pius IX decreed that 'the hierarchy of bishops ordinary, taking their titles from their sees, should, according to the usual rules of the church, again flourish in the Kingdom of England' [Handley 1947: 93]. This was considered to be an act of provocation and meetings were held in almost every town in Scotland, including Glasgow where nineteen speakers talked on the subject of 'Papal Aggression'. The following year the Lord Rector of Glasgow University chose 'the intolerance of the Catholic church through the ages' as the topic for his inaugural address [Handley 1947: 111]. Two new anti-Catholic periodicals were set up: the *Bulwark* (or *Reformation Journal*) and the *Scottish Protestant*. Meanwhile, the slogan of the *Scottish Guardian* (1832-1861) was 'No Compromise with Popery'. This was the atmosphere in the West of Scotland at the peak of Irish Catholic immigration.

The earlier references to families, working and living in appalling conditions as they were caught up in the industrial expansion of the period, applied to the vast majority of the Irish Catholic immigrants of the mid-nineteenth century. They were often the least skilled, undertook the least desirable jobs and lived in the worst housing. Negative stereotypes were in abundance: they were a filthy, inferior 'race', arriving in large numbers, multiplying at an alarming rate and turning whole areas into slums; they were immoral yet obsessed with their religion; they were lazy and living off charity, yet taking the jobs of others. Variations on these themes were articulated by their non-Catholic neighbours, the Poor Law Inspectors, non-Catholic clergy, politicians and academics. Antagonism erupted into violence that ranged from relatively minor attacks to major riots [Handley 1943, Campbell 1979, Miles 1982]. There were others who were more sympathetic, although hardly more flattering, about the poor Irish immigrant. The *Glasgow Herald* of 11 June 1947 reported:

> The streets of Glasgow are at present literally swarming with vagrants from the sister kingdom, and the misery which many of these poor creatures endure can scarcely be less than what they have fled or been driven from at home. Many of them are absolutely without means of procuring a lodging of even the meanest description, and are obliged consequently to make their bed frequently with a stone for a pillow. [Kinealy 1992: 11]

Gallagher argues that many of these immigrants 'yearned for the kind of certainty that unquestioning religious commitment could provide', while the Catholic clergy, fearing apostasy, saw an urgent priority in counteracting external influences by establishing organisations to absorb the energies of parishioners [1991: 21]. But the situation was more complicated than that.

Prior to the 1840s there was evidence of inter-marriage and the loss of Irish forms of surnames, suggesting that some Irish immigrants in Scotland drifted away from the Catholic faith [Handley 1947: 242, Gallagher 1991: 20]. This may have been due to the lack of priests since in 1836 there was only one Catholic clergyman for every 9,000 to 11,000 Catholics in Glasgow [Sloan 1991: 69]. However, it seems that some of those who drifted from the faith did so intentionally because if they had asked a priest to administer essential sacraments their requests would probably have been met. Parliamentary Papers of the 1830s described 'the great numbers, scattered situations, and distance of the Roman Catholic population' but pointed out that 'the rites of religion are always administered to persons ill at whatever distance they live' [PP 1837-38: 275]. Thus it seems likely that the faith of some migrants did lapse.

However, many others began to recreate space in which they felt comfortable with their religious identity. In the home, religious pictures and ornaments were used to ensure that 'a Catholic interior' was easily recognised [*Glasgow Free Press*, 6 June 1861]. Some reinforced this by asking the priest to bless their accommodation, or even to consecrate an entire tenement block [*Scottish Guardian*, 5 September 1856]. Soon whole streets were recognised as Catholic territory and 'a sense of Catholicism prevailed' [Sloan 1991: 78].

As numbers grew, and more priests were available to minister to them, neighbourhoods became organised around the parish with its church, school and branch of the Society of St Vincent de Paul offering assistance to the needy. These institutions were partly funded by voluntary contributions from the parishioners and, bearing in mind their impoverished status, represented considerable commitment and sacrifice on their part. On a wider scale the sense of a Catholic community was promoted by newspapers such as *The Glasgow Observer* which provided religious, political, sporting and cultural news for the Irish Catholic population. Thus, while parishioners engaged in sacramental activities to varying degrees, their sense of belonging to a Catholic community was tenacious and continued to incite hostility:

> ... the non-practising majority of Catholics, in their financial support of the Catholic church, in their respect for and deference towards the Catholic clergy, in their unwillingness to forego the Catholic rites of passage, and in their disdain of Protestant proselytism, demonstrated an allegiance and loyalty to Catholicism which could only be interpreted by the Protestant majority as an expression of religious identity and virility. [Ibid: 85]

In many ways Catholic and Irish loyalties were inextricably intermingled but this was not always the case. In 1888 a Marist brother, Brother Walfrid, founded Celtic football team as a focus for the recreational energies of Catholic young men [Murray 1984, Campbell & Woods 1987]. Four years later the Gaelic Football Association imposed a ban on soccer and other 'foreign sports' being played by its Irish membership, but the expatriate Irish Catholics in Glasgow had built up such enthusiasm for the game that they refused to comply with the ruling [Gallagher 1991]. Celtic Football Club became a powerful symbol of Irish Catholic sporting success in Scotland and was an early example of a Scottish influence predominating, but in other ways the opinions of the Catholic population were strongly influenced by events in Ireland.

Home Rule

The widening of the franchise in 1884 and 1885, with full extension to men and the majority of women in 1918, and universal suffrage in 1928, meant that the voting intentions of the poor became more significant as the nineteenth century ended and the twentieth century progressed. The 'Irish vote' was usually highly disciplined, following instructions from the head of the Irish Parliamentary Party to vote for whichever British party was most likely to promote 'Irish interests'. Support was usually given to the Liberal Party which attempted twice under Gladstone to introduce Home Rule, and when James Keir Hardie stood as the Labour candidate at the Mid-Lanark bi-election the Catholic *Glasgow Observer* commented:

> We cannot afford, much as we would like to serve the interests of workmen - if Mr Hardie's return would be a gain to them, which we question - to throw in our lot with any new causes or new programmes. We want to settle Home Rule first. [28 April 1888]

Such comments prompted suggestions that the presence of Irish Catholic immigrants undermined radical labour movements. But again the situation was more complicated. The *Glasgow Observer* questioned whether the gains to the working man from Keir Hardie's election would be sufficient to outweigh the benefits of achieving Irish independence 'first'. On balance their conclusion was 'no', but the Scottish miners themselves appeared to have little confidence in radical working class movements at this stage. By 1897, when about 31,000 men were employed in the Lanarkshire coal-fields, the Miners Federation had only 3,000 members [Howell 1983: 35]. Furthermore, Irish Catholics would have experienced difficulty in becoming involved with the skilled unions and trades councils, some of whom determined entry around criteria such as membership of the freemasons, while others accused them of undermining the struggle for improved wages and working conditions [Gallagher 1987: 27].

Home Rule remained the significant political issue of the day for many Irish immigrants, and Catholic opinion in Glasgow was concerted and visible. When Gladstone's Home Rule Bill was rejected by the House of Lords in 1893, the United Irish League, with both Liberal and Labour support, organised 'a procession through principle streets of Glasgow to the Green where from six platforms speakers addressed a vast audience on the short comings of the hereditary house' [Handley 1947: 284]. At the turn of the century, when Sinn Fein began to look for support in Scotland, a number of prominent activists addressed meetings in Glasgow and the city became the headquarters in Scotland for the collecting and dispatching of rifles, revolvers, cartridges and detonators [Ibid: 298]. It was not until the setting up of the Free State in 1922, as the *Glasgow Observer* quotation hinted, that the majority of Irish Catholics did 'throw in their lot' with the new Labour party that claimed to represent the interests of the working class.

The Catholic clergy in Scotland had not been committed to preserving an *Irish* identity amongst the immigrants, and had made strenuous efforts to promote a respectable *Catholic* reputation [Hickman 1995]. But many of their parishioners continued to be as Irish as they were Catholic and concerns that they might be drawn towards the Fenian movement, which combined a commitment to Home Rule with an anti-clerical stance, caused the church to review its approach:

Priests consciously used Irish symbols to draw migrants into church activities. Through the naming of associations and parish churches after Irish saints and the elaborate parish celebrations of St Patrick's Day, they united the appeal of religion with that of nationalism. [Lees 1979: 195, Aspinwall 1982]

Education and Domestic Politics

Home Rule represented an *Irish* priority, but there was also a *Catholic* priority to be addressed. The Catholic Schools Society had been formed in Glasgow in 1817 and provided some rudimentary education but by 1835 Bishop Andrew Scott of Glasgow made reference to funding difficulties in his representations to the Poor Law Commission:

> There are many Charitable schools in Glasgow, but the teachers all being Protestants always mix up with the elements of education the principles of the Protestant religion. This necessarily excludes Roman Catholic children from attending these schools ... An attempt has been made to get schools for the education of these poor people, but that attempt, for want of funds, and the daily increasing poverty of the lower orders, will render it impossible for them to keep up schools for themselves. To improve the feelings, the conduct, the morals, and the loyalty of the Irish Roman Catholic poor in this country, it would be necessary that the Government should, at least, extend the same assistance for education as is granted them in Ireland. [Jones 1977: 62]

This quotation highlights a number of points. Firstly, schools at this time could not be regarded as 'non-denominational' and if separate Catholic education was not provided then children would effectively be attending Protestant schools. Secondly, even before large-scale immigration, the Catholic population in Glasgow was struggling to fund its schools. Thirdly, the Church authorities at the time regarded the schools as a means of 'improving' the Irish Roman Catholic poor. And finally it was suggested that assistance with school funding would encourage their 'loyalty' to the British government. Hickman [1995] argues that this latter point is proof of compatibility between the agendas of the British state and the Catholic church who both aimed to 'denationalise' the children of Irish immigrants. But while this may have been evident in the discourse relating to Catholic education, it has been shown that at local level the clergy adopted a pragmatic approach and even promoted Irish identity to attract the loyalty of their congregations.

Funding problems continued in the schools and were not eased by the 1847 Education Act. This Act made grants available for school buildings except where the building was also used for church purposes, but such dual-purpose buildings were common in poorer Catholic areas.[8] In 1872 The Education (Scotland) Act introduced compulsory education for children aged five to thirteen years and enabled voluntary schools to transfer into the local authority system. The Catholic authorities chose to remain outside of the system, fearing that if it schools were handed over they would lose their denominational character. The issue became one of control of the schools in return for public finance [Hickman 1995: 197].

For almost half a century the schools struggled to keep up with improvements in the national system as the Catholic school population increased, new buildings were required, the curriculum expanded, and there was a shortage of staff who not only had the necessary religious commitment but were educated and trained to the required standard. By the turn of the century Catholic schools provided mainly primary education in poorly equipped, overcrowded, understaffed buildings [FitzPatrick 1986b: 39]. It was clear that the system was working to the disadvantage of the Catholic population and in 1906 Father Eric Hansen, in his speech to the Catholic Truth Society, made reference to the situation in Glasgow:

> How many Catholic employers of labour have we? Where are the master engineers or shipbuilders who are Catholics? ... It is a University city. Among the 2,500 students at Gilmorehill could we find a dozen Catholics? Is there one reading for a degree in Arts? ... Is there a single schoolmaster in the whole Archdiocese, elementary or secondary, who possesses a University degree? ... With marvellous unanimity they are as a class the least ambitious of all, the humblest in their ideas and inspirations, the least independent and enterprising, the most willing to take back seats and to be pushed aside by others. [Ibid: 20]

Yet the majority of the Catholic population tenaciously held to the belief that their children should be educated in Catholic schools. In 1918 Sir John Struthers, the Head of the Scottish Education Department, advised the Secretary of State for Scotland that the Department should be sympathetic to the Catholic case, and recommended that Catholic parents should have the same advantages as others in the state sector [Kenneth 1968: 104]. But in return for equality of financial provision the Catholic Church had to agree to their schools coming under public control. A solution was eventually reached with the 1918 Education (Scotland) Act as a result of which

---

[8] Including Govanhill, see later.

Catholic voluntary schools were managed and funded through the local authority, whilst the church retained control over appointments and religious instruction. The Act enabled the Catholic education system in Scotland to expand, broaden the curriculum and raise academic standards. Part of this process involved a sustained campaign to increase the number of suitable teachers so that, as well as the general improvement in educational standards, teaching became 'the first generation move into the professions' for some older pupils [FitzPatrick 1986b: 71].

The 1918 Education (Scotland) Act gave rise to the expression 'Rome on the Rates' [Smout 1986: 274] and the Labour Party has been accused of compromising its principles over denominational schools in order to win the Catholic vote. However, Labour was not strong enough at this stage to take blame or credit for the legislation and Catholics presented their case in terms of fairness and equal citizenship to as wide an audience as possible. In Glasgow this included the support of the Chairman of the Local Education Authority, Sir Charles Cleland, who was a former Unionist leader [McCaffrey 1991: 130]. Nevertheless, once the two major political concerns of the Irish Catholic community had been settled (Home Rule for Ireland and Catholic education within Scotland), the party political loyalties of this population turned towards the party that claimed to represent their interests as a predominantly working class population.

Meanwhile the clergy, having been initially hostile to socialism, also recognised that Irish Catholic interests appeared to be increasingly allied to the interests of Labour. This transition is well illustrated through the life of John Wheatley (1869-1930) who came from a mining background and 'took the path of self-improvement' to become a leading political figure [Gallagher 1991: 28, Hannan 1988, Wood 1990]. Wheatley earned a reputation for his organising ability in the Home Rule movement, but was increasingly committed to a broader struggle for social justice. Following Labour's successes in the general election of 1906, he formed the Catholic Socialist Society with his brother Patrick and undertook speaking tours to persuade workers that Socialism and the Catholic faith were compatible. Wheatley attended mass regularly and was regarded as a pillar of his local community so that the Catholic hierarchy were unwilling to issue an outright condemnation of his views. His perspective was that of 'radical Christianity', stressing that the inequalities of capitalism were damaging to faith.

While Wheatley was a committed Roman Catholic, it has been argued that Catholic support for the Labour Party took place at a period of general political realignment in Scotland during which the strongest determining factor was class rather than religion [Butler & Stokes 1969: 303, McCaffrey 1991]. As such, this can be seen as another example of the Irish

Catholic population, especially the Scottish-born descendants of the original immigrants, identifying themselves in terms of their contemporary Scottish experience. As for Wheatley, he was elected a Labour Member of Parliament in 1922 and became Minister of Health a year later, which suggests that his Irish Catholic origins were eventually regarded, by the wider population and the political establishment, as less significant than his commitment to social justice.

Assertion of Identity at Local Level: the Parish of Holy Cross

The legacy of the Irish Catholic population remains visible in Govanhill today and in considering the development of the Parish of Holy Cross it is possible to trace the continuity of both Irish and Catholic identity at local level [CHC 1936 & 1961, FitzPatrick 1986a]. The history of Govanhill is considered in more detail later but here it is sufficient to say that the area was well established as a working class community with a population of about 10,000 when the Parish of Holy Cross was established and a small 'chapel of ease' was instituted in 1882. At this time the Catholic population of Govanhill was so small that the ecclesiastical authorities had decided not to erect an independent parish church, and by 1886 the 'neat little building' was being used as a chapel and a school with one teacher, three pupil-teachers and 179 children. Three years later the congregation had grown to over 1,000 and Father O'Brien was appointed as the first of a number of Irish clergy involved with the developing parish [CHC 1936: 11]. From this point the congregation grew rapidly and it was clear that the building was inadequate. Work began on a new chapel school which was completed in 1900, with a ground floor built to accommodate 500 children and an upper floor to be used as a church.

By 1904 Father O'Brien felt that the Parish of Holy Cross merited a new church and presbytery, and proposed that this be erected on a prominent site. An objection was lodged by a Dr Lachlan on the grounds that the feu charter had stipulated the site be used for tenements and dwelling houses, and that a church occupying the site would 'injuriously affect his interests as medical practitioner and neighbouring proprietor' [CHC 1961: 15]. The objection was successful but was later overruled by Lords Kinnear and Parsons who, it was asserted, 'brought joy to the hearts of the people' and 'an appreciation of the justice of Scots Law' [Ibid].

The new church opened in 1912 when the Catholic parishioners numbered 3,560. By 1961, when the building was consecrated by the Archbishop of Glasgow, the Catholic population was clearly confident about public displays of its religious heritage and the clergy and relics processed through the streets of Govanhill. This confidence was also evident in a very practical sense when, in the 1960s, the new parish of Our Lady of Consolation was created to serve the north of Govanhill. A redundant cinema was acquired as a temporary Mass centre, and, when it was demolished to allow work to begin on the new parish church, a lease was obtained on another redundant cinema. The parishioners rallied to the cause:

> The men became painters, joiners, plumbers, electricians, heating engineers, scaffolders ... The women scrubbed, swept and shampooed at all hours of the day. It was a herculean task for the building had lain empty for years. Holy Mass was offered in the new centre at midnight on Christmas. A most memorable sight was seeing the people, after the last Mass was celebrated in Inglefield Street, carrying the chairs they used and placing them in the new centre at Calder Street. [FitzPatrick 1986a: 37]

As the Catholic congregation expanded, so too did the school population. The chapel school, which had been completed in 1900 to accommodate 500 children, was too small by 1925 and two classes were accommodated in a nearby non-Catholic school to relieve congestion. The HM Inspection Report of 1929 described the majority of pupils as coming from 'good working class homes' [FitzPatrick 1986a: 42] suggesting that the local population was no longer suffering the conditions experienced by the impoverished immigrants of the mid-nineteenth century. The school population continued to expand and it was not until two Catholic primary schools were established that there were sufficient places for the Catholic children in the area.

The need to educate older children and young adults had been evident from the turn of the century when Father Eric Hansen, in his speech to the Catholic Truth Society in 1906, had decried the lack of academic and professional achievement of the Catholic population. By 1922 there were five Catholic secondary schools in Glasgow (three for girls and two for boys) and all five were managed by religious orders. It was not until 1936 that a Senior Secondary School opened in Govanhill with a lay Head Teacher and lay staff. This was the first Catholic school providing full secondary courses to have opened in Glasgow for fifty years, and the first to offer mixed secondary education to boys and girls [FitzPatrick 1986b: 61]. The school roll expanded rapidly, to be maintained in recent years at around 2,000 pupils. Recent data concerning the destinations of school leavers indicates that the school is fulfilling the hope of Father Hansen in ensuring that an above average proportion of pupils enter higher and further education.

Maintaining Identity

The key institutions in a Catholic parish remain the church and the school. It would appear that the predominantly working class population continue to attend mass irregularly. Although religious festivals and rites of passage are observed, the Archdiocese of Glasgow estimated that less than 30% of parishioners attended mass on the day chosen for its own recent census.[9]

Today, Catholic schools employ both Catholic and non-Catholic staff and adhere to the National Curriculum, and so it is reasonable to ask what distinguishes the Catholic from the non-denominational school. This varies from one institution to another, but the 'Catholic interior' is still recognisable: perhaps a statue of the Madonna and child, or a display relating to a particular sacrament, in the entrance hall. The school handbook is likely to include a special school prayer and a statement concerning the Christian ethos of the school. Mass is celebrated, if not daily then at least on certain Holy Days, and religious instruction includes preparation for specific Roman Catholic sacraments. And, while not all staff are practising Catholics, those involved with religious education adhere to the view that the importance of religious education is 'the truth encompassed within it' [FitzPatrick 1986b: 151].

Meanwhile both church and school stress the importance of a third institution - the family. A crucial aspect of Catholic family life is the practice of religious endogamy and such has been the significance placed upon this over the years that a 'mixed marriage' in Glasgow is still most likely to refer to the union of Catholic and Protestant. Despite the emphasis placed upon endogamy, a reference to Holy Cross church in the 1930s indicated that 'mixed marriages' were already common enough amongst the parishioners to justify a church notice:

> Those were the years when we knew about mixed marriages simply because there was confetti on the pavement outside the chapel house. Mixed marriage couples were not allowed to exit through the main door of the church, where Bishop Graham used to have a prominent notice - the throwing of confetti or rice or other pagan customs is not permitted in this church. [FitzPatrick 1986a: 33]

One way to encourage young people to meet a suitable marriage partner is to influence their social interactions. Until the 1950s Catholic provision for young people focused on sport, recreational clubs and dances as a way of giving young people 'a parallel Catholic social framework to move about

---

[9] Personal correspondence 26/6/98.

in'.[10] But by the 1960s young people were increasingly attracted to commercial clubs and social activities where Catholics and non-Catholics mixed freely. In 1997 the Archdiocese conducted a survey in Glasgow and found that the clergy were concerned about youth indifference to church activities [Docherty 1997]. Comments included:

> Only 110-120 attend weekly mass - of that number about 4-10 are between the 12-22 age group, but not all that number are regular or from the parish.

> One of the main difficulties is getting them interested in coming to Church, or in Church activities. The bulk of our parish is made up of older people.

When asked about the main issues affecting young parishioners, the clergy identified preoccupations that Catholic teenagers shared with their non-Catholic peers: relationships, fashion, education, work, drugs, alcohol, unemployment. In many ways young Catholics are inconspicuous in Glasgow, but this is not simply an indication of their assimilation into the predominantly Scottish Protestant culture to which their ancestors migrated. Rather, it is a sign of the 'normality' of attending a Catholic school or supporting Celtic Football Club. The Catholic population played a part in shaping the history of the city, and signs of the Catholic identity of a significant proportion of Glasgow's population are now largely taken for granted.

A discussion of Catholic identity gives no indication of whether an *Irish* heritage is visible today. Certainly, the names of some clergy and school staff denote Irish origin, but it is in leisure activities that a clear Irish identity is manifest. This is particularly noticeable in Govanhill. School handbooks indicate extra-curricular participation in activities such as Irish dancing and Gaelic Football, and the yearbook of *Tir Connaill Harps*, a local Gaelic Football Club, makes repeated references to connections with Ireland including visits to Antrim and Donegal, and playing host to Gaelic Football and Hurling teams from Derry, Donegal, Belfast, Dublin and Galway. This yearbook is full of advertisements alluding to a strong Irish heritage: a Camogie team and a School of Irish Dance based at Govanhill Neighbourhood Centre; coach tours to Ireland; live Irish folk music at several local bars; Irish language classes through the Gaelic League; the (Italian owned) Unique Restaurant in the heart of Govanhill, described as 'Second Home to the Irish Community'; and more general advertisements

---

[10] Archdiocese of Glasgow Youth Office, personal correspondence 23/6/98.

placed by Aer Lingus, the Allied Irish Bank and the *Irish Post* newspaper. These associations persist despite the increasing age and declining size of the Irish-born population.

Table 1.2 Irish-born Population in Scotland 1911-1991

Irish-born population in Scotland	1911	174,715
	1921	159,020
	1931	124,000
Irish-born population in Scotland	1991	49,184
Irish-born population of Glasgow	1991	10,384
Irish-born population of Govanhill*	1991	505

* Of the 1991 Govanhill figure 45% were of pensionable age and over

[Source: Handley 1947: 316, and Table 6 Census 1991 Report for Scotland]

During the process of migration and settlement, a number of factors shaped the identity of Irish immigrants and their descendants. But their presence also contributed to the local environment in which other immigrants settled, including those of Italian origin who are considered next.

2 Italians in Glasgow

Italian Migration to Scotland

During the eighteenth and early nineteenth centuries Italians in Scotland were largely respected as educated, skilled and artistic people. The skilled craftsmen who set up their businesses included Antoni and Gallati, the carvers and gilders who established their firm in Glasgow in 1805, and Gerletti, who manufactured looking-glasses, barometers and thermometers in Glasgow during the 1820s [Colpi 1991:30]. Meanwhile it was asserted that 'every girl in Edinburgh who plays the pianoforte learns Italian, and Italian masters are to be found on every street' [Rodgers 1982a: 13].

It was not until the second half of the nineteenth century that Italian immigrants arrived in significant numbers, and their circumstances contrasted sharply with those of their predecessors. These newcomers were predominantly unskilled peasants who were no longer able to support themselves and their families using traditional agricultural methods. Part of their story can be told through the experience of the Barghigiani who settled in Glasgow and the south west of Scotland [Sereni 1974].

During the mid-nineteenth century the population of Barga experienced increasing poverty as a result of the sharecropping system through which land was divided into ever decreasing plots as it passed from generation to generation. Many farms were no longer viable and it became common practice for sons to temporarily join up with roving statuette pedlars. Some of these pedlars travelled to England and made their way up to Glasgow where they found other Italians, from the Ciociari district, who were already laying the foundations of what was to become a flourishing ice-cream industry:

> In summer they would push their ice-cream carts to the gates of the main public parks and do business there. In under 50 years, from 1870 to 1920, with great courage and initiative, they graduated from rudimentary shops in the slum quarters to more luxurious establishments in Sauchiehall Street and the city centre, with lots of mirrors on the walls, wooden partitions and leather-covered seats.
> [Sereni 1974: 3]

The Barghigiani followed this example and began to abandon the sale of plaster figurines in favour of establishing fish and chip shops. The early shops were purchased from Scots who were moving out of the poorest parts of the city, but gradually larger shops were acquired where clients could sit at tables to eat their 'fish supper'. By the turn of the century families from Barga were running some of the most prestigious restaurants in Glasgow and a pattern of chain migration was established. This was illustrated by the career of Leopoldo Giuliani who originally left Barga for the United States where he sold statuettes. He returned to Italy but then decided to join his brother who had graduated from selling statuettes to ice-cream in Glasgow. By 1890 Giuliani owned three successful cafes in Glasgow and played an important role in finding jobs for young, newly-arrived immigrants from Barga. Giuliani, along with other Barghigiani, expanded his business through a system of partnerships and by the turn of the century he had more than sixty of these establishments in operation.

> The owners would supply the premises with all the necessary furniture and equipment plus the usual stocks of cigarettes, chocolates, soft drinks, milk and sugar which were all purchased in bulk at discounted prices. The working partner would provide the labour and accept full responsibility for the efficient running of the business, the profits being shared equally between them. [Ibid: 24].

The system of chain migration spared the later immigrants some of the difficulties of finding employment and making social contacts in their new surroundings. In return, the newcomers were dependent on a *padrone* who was able to control and exploit their labour. Thus, while Irish immigrants had formed a pool of labour for the expanding industrial economy, chain migration constituted a source of labour for expanding 'Italian' businesses. In time it would be hard to find a main street in Scotland that did not have an Italian-run cafe, ice-cream parlour or fish and chip shop.

The idea of a swift return to Italy was disappearing for many of these male immigrants and in the 1890s they began to establish family life in Scotland by sending for their wives and female relatives. As children were born and families grew in size young women were also recruited by *padrone* to become domestic servants and nannies. British Census statistics show a significant increase in the Italian-born population in Scotland from the 1880s to the 1920s. The Italian Consulate figures for 1927 suggest that some 6,000 Italians were living in Scotland and that they represented about 20% of the total Italian population in Britain.

During the 1930s, the majority of Italians in Scotland lived in Glasgow and most located their homes and businesses along the busier roads [Colpi

1991:75]. Ice-cream parlours also appeared in almost every seaside resort, with a trip to Nardini's of Largs being a favourite destination for holiday-makers from Glasgow. And Italian businesses included the manufacturing of equipment for making ice-cream.

Table 2.1 Italian-born Population in Scotland 1861-1931

1861	119
1871	268
1881	328
1891	1,025
1901	4,051
1911	4,594
1921	5,654
1931	5,216

[Source: British Census 1861 to 1931]

Not all Italians were involved with catering and a survey into the *Diet of the Labouring Classes in the City* conducted in 1911-12 contained evidence of Italian miners and railway workers [Edward 1993: 92]. But this does appear to have been a small minority. Outside of catering it was more common to find Italians engaged in specialist crafts, and there were several mosaic and *terrazzo* firms in Glasgow. One of Leopoldo Giuliani's nephews gained a degree from Glasgow University in 1900 [Sereni 1974: 30], but it was not until later that the descendants of immigrants began looking to a university education and entry into the professions in significant numbers.

Table 2.2 Distribution of Italians in Britain 1927

Consular areas	Number	% of Total
London	14,800	50
Glasgow *[Scotland]*	6,092	20
Liverpool	6,000	20
Cardiff	2,238	7
Ireland	750	3
Total	29,880	100

[Source: Colpi 1991: 74]

During the 1920s and 1930s two main factors contributed to a decline in Italian migration to Scotland. The first was the passing of the Aliens Order in 1920 which, at a time of rising unemployment, required immigrants to have a work permit and gave discretionary powers to the Ministry of Labour over the granting of such permits. The second was the rise of Fascism in Italy when large-scale emigration was no longer acceptable to an Italian government who wanted to employ the working population in large-scale public works programmes.

After the Second World War, the implications of which are discussed later, there was a change in the pattern of migration from Italy to Britain. Conditions in parts of Italy, particularly the south, had become desperate. Poverty and unemployment had reached a level where emigration was considered not so much a means of economic improvement but of physical survival. Thousands applied to their local employment offices for work anywhere in the world. Between 1948 and 1968 over 148,000 Italians entered Britain in search of work. The push of home circumstances was complemented by labour shortages in Britain and 'group recruitment' brought workers from Italy to those sectors of the economy where labour was needed. In 1952 the Duke of Argyll asked the authorities in Barga to supply foresters for his estate around the village of Inveraray:

> One of the clauses in the contract which the Barghigiani found particularly appealing specified that at the end of the four-year period they could choose between renewing the contract, returning to Italy or staying on in Scotland in any employment and town of residence of their choice. This opened up a much wider 'vista' and many of them 'took to the woods' simply as an expedient and with a view to setting themselves up in business in the traditional way once the forestry stint was over. [Sereni 1974: 42]

The arrival in Scotland of the woodcutters and farmers from Barga coincided with the changes that took place in the way of life of the descendants of earlier immigrants. Many of the shops, cafes and restaurants were taken over by the new arrivals while second and third generation Italians began to enter the professions.

> Our marriage gave us four children, all of whom became university graduates in medicine, law and in the arts ... There was, after all, a world of difference in growing up in the Gorbals in the 1920s and growing up in Bearsden in the 1960s. [Pieri 1997: 144]

The vast majority of post-war immigrants settled in England and Wales and the Italian-born population of Scotland never exceeded 6,000. Statistics indicate a steady decline in population size and, since the Italian-born population is now ageing, it seems likely that this pattern will continue.

Table 2.3 Italian-born Population in Scotland 1951-1991

1951	5,268
1961	5,920
1971	5,420
1981	4,789
1991	3,947

[Source: British Census 1951-91]

Attitudes Towards Italian Migration

At its peak the Italian-born population of Scotland was less than 6,000 and the majority arrived at a time when some 200,000 Irish-born immigrants were being portrayed as a problem. In addition, the occupations chosen by the majority of Italian immigrants meant that they were not in direct competition with the wider population but were providing a popular service to local communities. These factors may help to explain why, in relative terms, they did not experience the negative reception of other immigrant groups. But this was not the whole picture and at the turn of the century, despite (or possibly because of) the increasing popularity of ice-cream parlours, there was evidence of negative stereotyping of their owners. The United Free Church condemned Italians for keeping their shops open on Sundays and violating the Sabbath. Evidence given to the 1906 Parliamentary Committee on Sunday Opening described ice-cream parlours as 'one of the evils of Glasgow' where young people were encouraged to 'hang about and loaf'. It was suggested that 'the Italian ice-cream man as a rule tolerates conduct in his shop that no Britisher would tolerate' [Edward 1993: 93]. Police evidence to the Committee suggested that low standards of behaviour were 'acceptable only to their alien owners and to people of loose moral habits' [Rodgers 1982a: 15].

Within Catholic schools, being Italian could be the cause of torment. Outside of school, children were reminded that they were Catholic:

> In the playground many a taunt of 'dirty wee Tally' had to be answered with scuffles and fist fights, yet after school hours we would have to stand shoulder to shoulder with our tormentors in common cause against gangs of children from other schools in the

same area ... Those were the days when religion was much more polarised than it is now and you had to be ready with some sort of answer when challenged by the cry, 'Are you a Billy or a Dan or an old Tin Can?'[11] [Pieri 1997: 5]

During the 1930s Italy's invasion of Abyssinia and intervention in the Spanish Civil War created a wave of ill feeling that resulted in 'more frequent, forceful and insulting remarks' and 'dirty wee Tally' gave way to 'Tally bastard' [Pieri 1997: 8]. When Mussolini declared war on the allies on 10 June 1940 a wave of anti-Italian riots spread across Britain. That night, Italian shops became the targets of burning and looting, with some of the worst violence taking place in Glasgow. The police, who were attempting to restore order, were also instructed to arrest all Italian males between the ages of 17 and 60 as potential enemy agents [Colpi 1991: 105]. Overall, their treatment in the camps suggests that they were not really regarded as a great threat to Britain's war effort, but the way in which they were taken from their families was a shocking experience for many of them and memories of these years resonate to this day [Rossi 1991, Pieri 1997]. The sinking of the Arandora Star, bound for Canada and carrying Italian internees as well as German prisoners of war and German Jewish refugees, is still regarded as one of the most tragic events in the history of the Italian population in Britain. The ship was torpedoed by a German U-boat and over 700 men, including 446 Italians, lost their lives. Although the War Office asserted that those who died were German Nazis and Italian Fascists, there had been no adequate screening of internees, and no proper embarkation list had been compiled. The question of whether Italian men were 'Fascists' will be considered later, but today there are few who would regard the event as anything other than a tragedy [Colpi 1991: 115-124].

Meanwhile, the wives and children of internees attempted to maintain their businesses. Following the initial outburst, it appears to have been difficult for their customers and neighbours to regard them with hostility.

> The people in Scotland continued to buy ice cream and fish and chips from the Italians, many of them stopped to have a cup of tea or coffee and talked to the ladies as if nothing had happened between Italy and Great Britain; some of them sympathised with them and asked for information about their Italian friends. But for a few exceptions I must say that generally speaking the people were kind with the womenfolk who were able to hide their sorrow and heartbreak. [Rossi 1991: 63]

---

[11] i.e. 'Are you a Protestant, a Catholic or a Jew?'

Sympathetic attitudes were not only evident at local level. It had been clear from the beginning of the war that sons of Italian immigrants were fighting for the allies and this fact was discussed in the House of Lords in August 1940 when Lord Cecil expressed concerns about indiscriminate internment. He cited the case of Silvestro D'Ambrogio of Hamilton, a 68 year old man who had been living in Britain for 42 years, who was interned and drowned with the sinking of the Arandora Star despite having three sons serving in the allied armies [Pieri 1997: 73]. Even British soldiers appeared unconvinced that the majority of Italians were the enemy, and this had some beneficial effects when the war was over:

> Complete strangers, ex-soldiers who had fought in the Italian campaigns and who correctly assumed that I was Italian, would regale me with their stories of Italy. Of how they were treated as liberators, of the hospitality received from Italian families, of the help given to escaped British prisoners and of the friendliness of the population in general. For whatever reason, the war seemed to have broadened attitudes and increased people's tolerance. Paradoxically, after all that had happened, for the first time in my life I began to feel welcome and a part of the society in which I lived. [Ibid: 143]

These extremes of acceptance and rejection were related to notions of an Italian identity that the wider population linked in various ways with Catholicism, with 'foreign' ways and, due to extreme external circumstances, to 'the enemy'. But being Italian was also associated with family businesses, good food and hospitality. In the next section consideration is given to the significance placed on aspects of this identity by the immigrants themselves.

The Italian 'Community'

To talk of an Italian 'community' in Scotland at the turn of the century is to give an exaggerated notion of unity. The majority of Italians in Scotland were from just two regions - Toscana, towards the north, and Lazio, towards the south - which were more than 250 miles apart and whose inhabitants had very different backgrounds [Colpi 1991: 77]. Italians in Scotland were broadly split into two groups who spoke different dialects, could identify group membership through surnames, and some of whom even claimed to distinguish each other by appearance alone. The *Casa d'Italia*, the centre of Italian cultural activity for much of the twentieth century, acknowledged the north/south schism in its constitution until its closure in 1989 by insisting that the Board of Directors should represent both groups.

The first collective activity of Italians in Glasgow was the formation of a *Societa di Mutuo Soccorso* in 1891 which provided welfare and assistance as well as organising social activities. In reality the Italian immigrants were more likely to look to their family and friends for assistance and, being widely dispersed and working long hours, there was little time for recreation other than visiting relatives and friends on 'half days'. An element of socialising was more likely to be incorporated into the working day. Chip shop owners regarded trips to the fish market as an opportunity to meet friends and acquaintances and to congregate afterwards for coffee [Sereni 1974: 8], while the cafe 'back shops' became places where men gathered to play cards [Colpi 1991: 83]. By the 1930s shops developed to serve Italian households - selling oil, garlic, cheeses, olives, wine and other provisions - and became places where people could meet, gossip and maintain a sense of Italy [Rodgers 1982a: 17].

In America, Australia, and England 'Italian' churches were constructed and played a key role in the religious, social and cultural lives of immigrants and their descendants, but this was not the case in Scotland where Italian Catholics made use of the churches established for the predominantly Irish population. However, there were examples of Italian clergy attached to local churches: Don Pietro Rota was attached to the Holy Redeemers in Clydebank and travelled around to Italians in the area [Colpi 1991: 94]; and Gaetano Rossi, later Monsignore Rossi, served as an assistant priest and parish priest in Glasgow for 52 years [Rossi 1991].

Italian Catholics also made use of the schools established by the Irish population, where Italians were clearly a minority. This contributed to the likelihood that children born in Scotland would lose their 'mother tongue', and so Italian language classes were organised after school. By 1927 there were four such language schools in Glasgow [Colpi 1991: 95].

It was not until the *fascio* was founded in 1922 that Italian communal activity in Glasgow really developed. During the 1920s and 1930s many Italians in Britain embraced Fascism as a form of patriotism and *fascio* clubs were established as centres for social, cultural and educational activities. In 1935 Glasgow's *fascio* took over a new, prestigious Club House - the *Casa d'Italia*. The building had been acquired through subscriptions from Glasgow's Italian population and splendidly renovated by skilled craftsmen. The *Casa* accommodated a range of groups and organisations including the Scottish Italian Student Group, the Union of Italian Traders, and the College of Italian Hairdressers. Activities included Italian language classes and the promotion of Italian films, but, for many members, the *Casa* simply offered an opportunity to relax and socialise.

Mussolini's 1933 census of Italians abroad showed that almost 50% of those in Scotland were full members of the Fascist party. Although it is likely that this figure was inflated for propaganda purposes, there is little doubt that a significant proportion of Glasgow's Italian population were members of the *Casa d'Italia,* and that, for many of them, membership of the *fascio* represented pride in Italian achievement:

> It was not a question of being Fascists, Italy was now known internationally, and not because of fascism ... The Italians now occupied the front pages of the newspapers and not only in sport (although sport, perhaps, was the most common field). They could boast of Marconi (radio); Mascagni (music); Pirandello (literature).
> [Rossi 1991: 10]

It was as 'Fascists' and potential enemy agents that Italian men were interned when Mussolini declared war on the allies. Accounts of the activities in the internment camps give an insight into the feelings and preoccupations of the Italian internees, the majority of whom 'wished only to be free and reunited with their families' [Pieri 1997: 34]. While religion may not have been important to all of them, it seems that few doubted the importance of establishing a place of worship and this was permitted by camp authorities. In one camp the internees established a make-shift altar using a table covered in an army blanket and sheet.

> At the time I did not know that in the camp there was an artist, Severino Tremator. Only later I discovered his name. In a very short time a triptych appeared above the altar, in the middle the picture of Christ 'suffering' with, at his side, two adoring angels. It was almost life-size and it was painted with water colour on paper. The painting remained on the altar till the camp was closed with the departure of the Italian internees.[12] [Rossi 1991: 20]

As well as being an expression of faith, religious observance may have helped to break the monotony of camp life and boosted the morale of those who were worried about the future and their families. Other methods of keeping up morale were devised. It was not unusual to negotiate access to a field and a football, and one camp team included Dante Filippi who 'had a trial fixed for Glasgow Celtic just before he was interned' [Rossi 1991: 53]. The fact that Dante Filippi had a trial for Celtic suggests that as well as attending the schools and churches established by the Irish Catholics, there was an allegiance to their football team. Meanwhile the importance of food

---

[12] The artist, Severino Tremator, drowned with the sinking of the Arandora Star.

was highlighted by the care and ingenuity of Italian chefs, from some of the best restaurants and hotels in Britain, who were amongst the internees and who did their best to improve camp meals.

Very few of the Italians were Class A internees i.e. a potential security risk and so, towards the end of 1940, when farms and factories were short of labour, the military authorities began to invite internees to collaborate with the British war effort. The decision was not an easy one. Those who refused felt 'it was not a question of being Fascist or anti-Fascist, it was a question that we were Italians' [Rossi 1991: 59]; while those who did agree to collaborate did so because they 'finally decided to separate the image of their beloved Motherland from that of the Government which ruled it' [Sereni 1974: 58]. After the war it became clear that British soldiers and prisoners of war had been assisted by Italians, and they returned with stories of friendship and hospitality which contributed to a positive image of the Italian population.

An image had developed of a hospitable, family oriented population with a love of good food and wine. While this was inevitably a stereotype, there does appear to have been some justification for it. Even the Italians who worked for the Duke of Argyll in the 1950s formed themselves into a small delegation to broach the subject of the unpalatable food. An agreement was reached by which they were given the money normally spent on providing their meals so that they could do their own shopping and cooking. One Italian was withdrawn from the workforce and put in charge of the kitchen, and once a week he travelled to Glasgow for supplies [Sereni 1974: 43].

Maintaining Identity

During the 1940s and 1950s Italian activities in Scotland, particularly Glasgow, were regularly reported in the British Italian newspaper, *La Voce*, but the paper now struggles to maintain a Scottish page [Colpi 1991: 246]. Meanwhile, the *Casa d'Italia* became run down and shabby before its closure in 1989. But it would be difficult to spend time in Glasgow without realising that there is a significant population of Italian origin. Italian surnames are recognisable in a wide range of professions; some of the most popular and fashionable restaurants are Italian; Italian delicatessens, cafes, ice-cream parlours, and fish and chip shops abound; the Dante Alighieri Society organises language classes, lectures and visitors from Italy; and there is an active Scottish Italian Graduates Society based in the University of Glasgow.

Census figures indicate that the Italian-born population in Scotland is decreasing in size, with almost half of this population based in Glasgow and the surrounding areas. Since this is an ageing population, the numbers are likely to decline at an increasing rate, but it has been estimated that there are 23,000 'Italians' in Scotland [Ibid: 169]. This considerably larger figure includes the Scottish-born descendants of Italian immigrants and some of the ways in which their Italian identity is maintained are considered next.

Table 2.4 Italian-born Population in Scotland 1991

	Total	Male	Female
Scotland	3,947	1,995	1,952
Strathclyde	1,824	954	870
Glasgow City	656	326	330

[Source: Table 7 Census 1991 Report for Scotland]

Chain migration had established strong links with specific areas in Italy and *companilismo* is still evident in Glasgow today.[13] Italian family and regional links were particularly evident in employment and business life: through the process of chain migration, specific skilled crafts, shops, restaurants and delicatessens, and the 'back-shops' that became places for social gatherings. These links are still evident today and the move into the professions is not devoid of a notion of the family business so that, for example, it is not unusual for father and son to work together in the same law firm [Ibid: 197].

During the nineteenth and early twentieth centuries, the belief in an eventual return to the village of origin may have discouraged social interaction with the wider population.

> Your parents were very Italian, of course, all their thinking was Italian. Every Friday we used to have a whole congregation in our back shop and all the old ladies used to get together and have a good old gossip - I mean they missed the village life. They were very pleasant and polite to their customers but they didn't really mix with them ... They were very old fashioned and the girls were kept under a strict rule because they felt that everyone here was much too free and easy. [quoted in Rodgers 1982a: 17]

---

[13] *Campanilismo* can be translated as 'localism' and involves a shared, rather than individual, emotional loyalty to the place and people of the village of birth [Colpi 1991: 179].

The attempts to keep girls under strict control related to the issue of endogamy which was a favoured method of maintaining identity. It was through the family that Italian traditions and customs were preserved and the choice of a non-Italian spouse could result in 'a solemn wringing of hands' [Pieri 1997: 7]. The Scottish-born children of immigrants recall their parents attempts to make home-life as 'Italian' as possible with emphasis placed upon the choice of a suitable marriage partner:

> My father wanted us to be as much Italian as we possibly could. In the house it was definitely Italian, the food was Italian, we spoke Italian, we had Italian friends and we were brought up that we had to marry Italians. It wasn't only our family for that was a general thing with Italians. [quoted in Rodgers 1982a: 17]

Emphasis seems to have been placed upon Italian rather than Catholic identity. This may be because it was taken for granted that to be *Italian* was to be *Catholic*. Although in Scotland there is no 'ethnic church' as a focal point for the Italian population, many continue to attend local parish churches and schools and to be served by a missionary priest, based in Glasgow, who spends a great deal of time travelling around to 'Italians' throughout the whole of Scotland [Colpi 1991: 230-241].

The story of the Italians in Scotland is interspersed with references to food: their involvement with the catering industry; the establishment of delicatessens to initially supply the Italian population and later the population in general; the internees' attempts to keep up morale by improving the food in the camps; and the Duke of Argyle's forestry workers forming a delegation to complain about the food they were given. Unlike some ethnic groups, the significance of food to the Italian population is not related to religious doctrine but with specific ingredients and regional dishes, and with enduring notions of hospitality and family life.

External factors also served to reinforce identity. Italians were subjected to negative stereotyping and exclusionary practices because they were 'foreign' and they were Catholic. The indiscriminate way in which men of Italian origin were rounded up as 'the enemy' during the Second World War was a stark reminder that events well beyond the control of the individual could have considerable repercussions for those who are identified as 'Other'. But the experiences during the Second World War also appear to have had a positive effect on the wider population's view of Italy and its people, and in the post-war period Italian businesses expanded and thrived. This underlines the fact that integration is a non-linear, volatile process in which the Other may be accepted one moment and rejected the next.

Just as Irish immigrants and their descendants had contributed to the local environment, those of Italian origin did the same. In Govanhill the Unique Restaurant, that was eventually advertised as 'Second Home to the Irish Community' (see earlier), was also popular with the third migrant population to be considered in this study. The proprietors contributed a short history of their business to a local exhibition in which they described how their father, interned during the war, purchased this fish and chip shop in 1946 and developed it as a popular local venue:

> Mr Sichi liked it, visualised the potential, and took it over ... It was not long before school children started calling in at lunchtime. Sunday nights soon became a regular for the Jewish boys and girls going home from their club. [Larkfield Centre local history collection]

In the next chapter, consideration is given to the ancestors of these Jewish boys and girls.

3 Glasgow Jewry

Jewish Migration to Scotland

In 1812, when Isaac Cohen set up his business as a hatter in Glasgow, it appeared that he was the only Jew in the city [Edward 1993: 62]. The population gradually increased in size and by 1831 James Cleland included 47 Jews in his census of the population of Glasgow. His notes indicated a balance of age and gender, and the presence of children born in Glasgow: 28 males and 19 females; 19 under twenty years old and 28 over; 11 born in Prussian Poland, 12 in various parts of Germany, 3 in Holland, 5 in London, 10 in Sheerness, and 6 in Glasgow [Rodgers 1982b: 113]. They were mainly traders and merchants, and they were affluent enough to raise 100 guineas to purchase a small part of a new cemetery beside the cathedral for a Jewish burial ground [Edward 1993: 63]. Limited migration and family formation continued and by 1860 it was estimated that there were over 500 Jews in Glasgow, who consisted of only 26 families [Rodgers 1982b: 113]. The gradual development of this relatively prosperous community based in the north of the city continued, but towards the end of the nineteenth century events in Europe had a profound effect on the size and characteristics of Glasgow's Jewish population.

During the eighteenth century, parts of Poland, the home of many thousands of Jews, were brought under Russian rule. The Russian authorities adopted legal discrimination against Jews, restricting them to the Pale of Settlement and inflicting brutal pogroms.[14] In 1881 the brutality escalated when Jews were blamed for the death of Czar Alexander II and massive expulsions took place. Between 1881 and 1930 some four million Jews left Eastern Europe, most of them bound for America. As had been the case with Irish migrants, some of the Jews who had intended to pass through Britain on their way to America went no further. Thus the small Jewish population in Scotland was rapidly enlarged by the arrival of poor, Yiddish speaking refugees. By 1897 the Jewish population of Glasgow had reached 4,000 [Collins 1987: 6].

These poor and destitute refugees could not afford homes in the north of the city and they settled in the Gorbals area south of the River Clyde. They

---

[14] Hence a Jew 'beyond the Pale' was unacceptable.

gravitated towards occupations requiring skills they already possessed, or which could be easily learned, and where language problems could be minimised. The majority worked at home, or in backstreet workshops, in crafts such as cabinet making, tailoring, and shoe and hat making. Much of their employment came to be associated with sweatshops where they tolerated appalling conditions in the drive to overcome poverty in the early years.[15] Self employment often took the form of peddling and this continued into the twentieth century so that in 1906 there were an estimated 600 Jewish pedlars in Glasgow [Ibid: 9].

In 1858, when the population numbered about 500, the Glasgow Hebrew Philanthropic Society was set up to provide for the sick and needy. The system was based on the assumption that the amount of poverty was finite and could be fairly swiftly eradicated, but as the nineteenth century progressed it became clear that the numbers seeking assistance were increasing rapidly. By the end of the nineteenth century the Glasgow Hebrew Philanthropic Society had developed into the Glasgow Board of Guardians and attempts were made to systematise Jewish Poor Relief. Loans, medical relief, cash donations, the financing of apprenticeships and assistance to emigrate were made available with the emphasis firmly on promoting self help. In 1901 the Glasgow Hebrew Benevolent Society was founded and offered interest free loans to those who wished to set up in business [Rodgers 1982b: 114]. As immigration continued the burden on Jewish welfare organisations was considerable. Attempts were made by the British government, with the support of the Jewish Board of Guardians in London, to reduce the numbers entering the country and, in some cases, to repatriate [Collins 1987: 5]. The 1905 Aliens Act did reduce the numbers entering Britain but by 1921 the Jewish population in Glasgow had increased to 14,000 and was the fourth largest in Britain.

The 1930s were years of economic depression, high unemployment and the Nazi persecution of the Jews. Hundreds of thousands of German and Austrian Jews left their homes. About 60,000 came to Britain of whom over 1,000 entered Scotland directly from Germany [Edward 1993: 81]. In Glasgow they were initially received with sympathy, but as the Second World War approached, and Germans were increasingly seen as the enemy, even German Jews were treated with suspicion. The policy of male internment, which had such a profound impact on the Italian population, also resulted in the internment of German Jewish refugees before it was eventually abandoned [Kolmel 1987: 63]. As the Second World War progressed, Jewish aid organisations adopted a policy of dispersing refugees

---

[15] It should be noted that sweatshops predated Jewish immigration and existed outside of stereotypical Jewish occupations.

from London and several thousand of them constituted the last significant Jewish migration to Scotland.

Table 3.1 Jewish Population in UK and Glasgow 1955-1985

Year	UK	Glasgow
1955	450,000	15,000
1985	330,000	11,000

[Source: Alderman 1992: 323]

In 1948 the State of Israel was founded and some of Glasgow's Jews emigrated to the new homeland. This, together with a decline in the birth rate and increasing secularisation, contributed to a steady decline in the size of the Jewish population in Glasgow from the 1950s onwards [Alderman 1992: 326].

Attitudes Towards Jewish Immigrants

In 1923, Manny Shinwell, the first Jew to become an MP in Scotland, declared at a meeting of the Scottish United Council of Jewish Friendly Societies that there was 'no anti-Semitism in Scotland' [Collins 1987: 21]. Since there is always a danger of comparing deliberately brutal behaviour with lesser acts of hostility and pronouncing the latter as commendable, it is worth considering this issue in more detail.[16] During the nineteenth century the restrictions on Jews throughout Britain were gradually removed, but Scotland had led the way in relation to education and for a number of years 'Scottish universities, alone, allowed Jews to graduate as doctors' [Collins 1988: 11-12]. This had encouraged a significant number of Jewish students to read medicine at the University of Glasgow and they may well have regarded this opportunity as an aspect of Scottish egalitarianism. However, the majority of Jewish refugees in the 1880s and 1890s were less concerned with the right to read medicine at university than the ability to find a home, earn a living and practice their faith with the minimum of interference. In

---

[16] However, it is not the purpose to enter an analytical debate about whether anti-Semitism constitutes racism [Miles 1982: 100, Cox 1970]. Here anti-Semitism is taken as 'the conception of the Jews as an alien, hostile and undesirable group, and the practices that derive from, and support, such a conception' [Solomos & Back 1996: 50].

these areas they did experience prejudice couched in terms of their Jewish identity.

> Before the First World War it was very, very hard for a Jew to get a house. One landlord after another: 'No Jews!' If your name was Finkleberg then he'd say 'No'. So you just changed it to Faulkner or something and if you didn't have a Semitic nose then you might get it. [quoted Rodgers 1982b: 115]

These attitudes persisted and on 12 February 1935 a case was taken before the House of Commons concerning a leading firm of builders in Glasgow who refused to allocate a house in the Kings Park Estate on the grounds that the applicant 'belonged to the Jewish race' [Ibid: 119]. However, it should also be noted that this was declared unacceptable and the company was forced to change its policy.

Throughout the nineteenth and early twentieth centuries, the majority of Jews did not compete for jobs with the wider Scottish population, and by 1945 Jews in Britain remained concentrated in a small number of trades. This was especially apparent in Glasgow.

Table 3.2 Jewish Participation in Trade 1945

City	No of trades listed	Jewish participation
Glasgow	1,650	128 [8%]
Liverpool	1,200	155 [13%]
Manchester	1,040	250 [24%]

[Source: Dr N Barou *The Jews in Work and Trade 1945*, 3rd edition 1948, Trades Advisory Council, in Neustatter 1955: 129]

The lack of direct competition did not free them entirely from allegations made about other immigrant groups: that their presence undermined the struggle for improved wages and conditions. The Jewish Tailors Union was established in 1890, and, in 1921, a Jewish Workers' Union was formed [Collins 1987: 8]. But more widespread union activities were sporadic because of the immigrants' desperation for work, their predominance in small workshops, and wider trade union hostility that included anti-Semitism. The fight against excessively long working hours, incorporated into the campaign to prohibit Sunday Trading, was partly expressed as concern about the Jewish violation of the Christian Sabbath. The Glasgow and District Furniture Trades' Federation asserted in their submission to the Trades Council in June 1908:

> ... we think we ought to have secure protection that our valued Sunday shall not be broken down and trampled underfoot by the unthinking foreigner in his greedy pursuit of financial gain. [Rodgers 1982b: 116]

Although, in Scotland, Judaism was less likely to be described in the vitriolic tones reserved for Roman Catholicism, there was a concerted attempt to undermine the Jewish faith by making the immigrants in the Gorbals the target of considerable missionary activity [Collins 1987: 16]. In response, the Missionary Vigilance Society was founded in 1894 and the Chief Rabbi suggested that Christians should 'raise their own masses' to the level of 'the sober and virtuous conditions of the Jewish poor' [*Jewish Chronicle* 13/5/1896]. Attempts at conversion continued through the Glasgow Jewish Evangelical Mission, established in 1907, and through the Society for the Propagation of the Gospel to the Jews [Rodgers 1982b: 116]. In 1938 the *Glasgow Herald* reported that the Reverend James Black, a Church of Scotland minister, had made a speech in which he declared:

> ... there are only two ways to treat the Jews, and these are either to fight them or to convert them. Britain's desire is not to fight them but to see them converted to accepting the pure and unsophisticated principles of the Christian religion as their faith ... The problem which the Jews present is that they have a presence among other nationalities of a race of people with no land of their own who still wish to preserve their racial identity and remain unassimilated with the people amongst whom they dwell. [Edward 1993: 82]

This quotation highlights the way in which Jews were variously described as a religious group, a 'nation' and a 'race', with the potential to suffer exclusion on any or all of these accounts.

Poorer Jews were taunted because of their 'foreign' appearance and inability to speak English, but affluent Jews were also reminded of their unacceptable identity and were refused membership of golf, tennis and bowling clubs. A common response to this type of social exclusion was to set up separate institutions, and this was evident when Jewish golfers formed their own club in Glasgow in 1928 [Rodgers 1982b: 119]. A degree of prejudice was regarded as moderate compared with the Russian pogroms and the horrors of Nazi Germany, but examples of violent anti-Semitic behaviour were recognised and reported in the Jewish press. The *Jewish Echo* of November 1939 indicated:

> Malicious damage was done to a number of Jewish shops in Glasgow and extensive anti-Jewish propaganda appeared in Jewish owned property during the black-out at the weekend. About twenty windows or glass panels were cracked and swastikas were scratched with a diamond or metal tool on nearly eighty others. [Edward 1993: 83]

However, given their history, it was perhaps inevitable that older members of the Jewish population regarded their experiences in relative terms:

> I mind that when I had that experience here of being turfed out o' my job for bein' a Jew. I said to myself maybe I'd be better gettin' out of this country. Well, I haven't left yet 'cos I don't know a better one. [quoted Rodgers 1982b: 121]

The Jewish 'Community'

There is considerable debate amongst Jews about what constitutes Jewish identity. This was evident in a recent survey of British Jews which suggested that a number of factors were of varying importance to individuals: synagogue affiliation, religious belief, ritual observance, and participation in Jewish social or communal activities. With regard to religious practice the survey listed six categories: Strictly Orthodox, Traditional, Progressive, Just Jewish, Secular, and 'uninvolved Jews' who acknowledge their Jewish origin but take no part in religious or communal life [Miller et al 1996: 10]. But while individuals may define their Jewish identity in a variety of ways, a Jewish 'community' can be recognised through the establishment of key institutions including synagogues, cemeteries, *kosher* food outlets and schools.

The first synagogue in Glasgow was in a 'room and kitchen' in High Street in 1823 [Edward 1993: 63], and the movements of Glasgow's Jewish population can be charted through the subsequent establishment and closure of its synagogues [Collins 1993: 10-11]. In 1858, when the Jewish population in Glasgow numbered approximately 500, a synagogue opened in George Street to serve both the older established community and newer immigrants, followed by Garnethill Synagogue which opened in 1879. These synagogues were north of the River Clyde, some distance from the sizeable Jewish population that was beginning to settle in the Gorbals area. To serve this population more conveniently, a small synagogue was established in a converted workshop south of the river. Additional informal prayer houses were established during the 1880s, and larger places of worship were later located in a hall and converted Baptist Church. In 1901 the 'Great Synagogue' opened in the Gorbals with accommodation for over 1,000 worshippers. The building housed many of the major Jewish institutions in the city and was the only remaining Jewish building in the Gorbals at its closure in 1974.

Despite the significance of the Great Synagogue, Jews were already beginning to move out of the Gorbals at the beginning of the twentieth century. New synagogues were established at each stage as they gravitated towards the more affluent suburbs of the city: Queens Park 1906, Langside 1915, Pollokshields 1929, Giffnock and Newlands 1938, Netherlee and Clarkston 1940, and Newton Mearns 1954. Govanhill, immediately south of the Gorbals, was often the first stage in this movement and as early as 1901 a *Chevra* (fellowship) was formed there [*Jewish Chronicle* 6/9/01]. In 1932, as the Jewish population of Govanhill grew, Crosshill Synagogue opened, moving to larger premises in 1960 [Collins 1987: 26]. The poorest Jews remained in the Gorbals until the massive redevelopment in the 1960s when the Jewish Board of Guardians assisted some of these families through a special house purchase scheme. Today, the Jewish population is centred much further south around the Giffnock and Newlands synagogue complex in an area associated with the professional and business classes.

Not all of those who left the Gorbals moved south. Some moved north and increased the membership of Garnethill Synagogue. In 1898, with the formation of the United Synagogue of Glasgow, leadership of the Jewish population in Glasgow was effectively allocated to the Garnethill Synagogue despite the fact that there were far more Jews living south of the river. This 'unity' was always vulnerable and the United Synagogue broke up in 1906 following a number of disputes, including concerns about the cost of burials for poor immigrants [Collins 1993: 11]. The broad division of Glasgow's Jewish population was evident in the religious leaders of the two major synagogues: Rabbi Hillman from Russia had a traditional Orthodox approach and was appointed as religious leader in the Gorbals, while the Rev E P Phillips, with a more liberal approach, served the Jews in Garnethill.

Appropriate burial facilities are as important as the provision of a place of worship for a Jewish community. The earliest Jews in Glasgow had to take their dead to Edinburgh, but in 1830 a corner of ground was purchased at the Glasgow Necropolis with room for 50 plots. This was followed by the gradual acquisition of additional grounds across the city. The establishment of cemeteries tackled the issue of where to bury the dead, but the degree of poverty, and the high infant mortality rate, resulted in frequent requests to the Board of Guardians, and individual synagogues, for assistance with funeral expenses. These institutions were experiencing additional financial pressures as they struggled to meet the welfare needs of the expanding, and predominantly impoverished, Jewish population. In 1908 the Glasgow Hebrew Burial Society was formed and members were encouraged to contribute weekly sums to meet the costs of their family funerals. By 1937 the Society had 1,700 members and numbers continued to increase after the Second World War [Collins 1987: 18].

A further important concern of any Jewish community is the provision of *kosher* (ritually fit) food. The main dietary requirements are that meat and poultry must be appropriately slaughtered by a *shochet*, pork and shellfish are prohibited, and meat and dairy products must be separated. During Passover *matzo* (unleavened bread) is eaten and other bread and foods containing leaven are prohibited. A network of bakers, dairies, butcher shops and appropriate regulatory bodies was established so that within Jewish homes and institutions it was possible for practising Jews to observe these requirements.

The difficulty of adhering to dietary laws in a non-Jewish environment was illustrated by the problems that arose for Jews who required hospital treatment. In 1910 the Victoria Infirmary turned down requests to provide *kosher* food, and refused to allow food to be brought in by relatives, despite the hospital's proximity to a large Jewish population. The hospital authority was concerned about setting a precedent that might disrupt hospital routine, and this took priority over the distress caused to practising Jews. However, the Jewish population continued to assert their dietary requirements and Merryflatts Poorhouse (now the Southern General Hospital) did agree to open a *kosher* kitchen in 1914 [Collins 1993: 8].

The requirement for *kosher* food, and wider appreciation of Jewish sensitivities, resulted in the establishment of some separate institutional care. There were two unsuccessful attempts to set up suitable homes for the Jewish elderly, in the Gorbals in 1913 and in Govanhill in 1929, before the Jewish Old Age Home for Scotland was established in Pollokshields in 1949 [Ibid: 9]. Meanwhile, the upheaval entailed in fleeing persecution, and the incidence of tuberculosis amongst the inhabitants of Glasgow's slums, had resulted in a number of orphaned children. In 1913 Glasgow and Govan parish councils both gave support to the establishment of an orphanage where *kosher* food could be provided and children could take part in the life of the Jewish community. The increasing numbers of Jews fleeing Europe in the 1930s led to the opening of a children's hostel beside Garnethill Synagogue in 1938.

Education was another field in which special provision was required if the needs of practising Jewish children were to be met. The first Hebrew classes in Glasgow were probably available from Mr Moses Lisenheim, described by Cleland in the 1830s as the 'Priest, Hebrew Teacher and

Killer' (*shochet*) [Rodgers 1982b: 113]. But it was towards the end of the nineteenth century, as the Jewish population grew in size, that the educational needs of the children became more apparent. Classes were arranged after normal school hours in local primary schools and synagogue classrooms. The *Talmud Torah*, founded in the Gorbals in 1895 to provide a community wide educational structure, organised classes for three hours every evening except Friday, as well as on Saturday and Sunday [Collins 1993: 13]. Although the numbers registered to attend classes were high the actual level of attendance was only about 50%, reflecting the difficulties of expecting children to study for several hours beyond the normal school day [Collins 1987: 24].

The high concentration of Jewish children in the Gorbals area prompted unfruitful discussions in 1909 about the establishment of a separate Jewish school, as well as requests that Jewish children in existing schools be permitted to start the day with an hour of Hebrew and Jewish instruction while the other pupils undertook their Christian studies. The Jewish Representative Council, founded in 1914, continued to promote the idea of a Jewish day school similar to those which had already been established in London, Liverpool and Manchester. Some teaching of Jewish studies began in two Gorbals schools in 1917, but it was not until 1962 that a Jewish primary school was established, catering for over half of Glasgow's Jewish primary school children. The 1918 Education (Scotland) Act had paved the way for other denominations to seek parity with non-denominational schools over funding issues, and today the primary school is funded through the local authority while the Glasgow Board of Jewish Education is recognised in all Jewish educational matters at the school.

Despite the persistence of the struggle for a separate Jewish school, many Jews were not part of the campaign. Some had concerns that separate provision might draw attention to their Jewish identity and increase prejudice in the wider population; some had initial concerns that the standard of academic education might not compare favourably with local authority schools; and some wanted their children to mix with the wider school population. Academic achievement was prized, but for many children this involved confronting negative Jewish stereotypes within the school curriculum (including Shylock in Shakespeare's *The Merchant of Venice*, and Fagin in Dickens' *Oliver Twist*). Meanwhile the Jewish bible was referred to as the 'Old Testament' awaiting completion through the addition of the 'New Testament' [Cooper & Morrison 1991: 73, 81]. In spite of this, many parents preferred their children to attend existing local authority schools supplemented by the *chedar* system of Jewish instruction outside of the normal school day.

Extracts from the Log Book of Govanhill Primary School in the 1930s indicate that Jews were able to assert some of their requirements within mainstream schools, and that the local authority was willing to accommodate them:

> *19.4.33* The attendance during last week was 82.9. This low average was due to the incidence of the Jewish Passover, all the Jewish children being absent.
> *10.9.34* Today Miss E Carnovsky is absent owing of Jewish New Year holidays which fall on 10th and 11th Sept. Today 80 Jewish pupils are also absent.
> *19.9.34* Miss E Carnovsky was absent this day owing to Jewish Holiday - Day of Atonement.
> *1.10.34* Today Miss E Carnovsky is absent on account of Jewish Holiday - the Feast of Tabernacle. About 80 Jewish children are also absent. Jewish holidays have occurred this year on 10th, 11th, 19th, 24th, 25th September, 1st & 2nd October. These absences account for a loss of approximately 960 attendances.
> *16.11.34* Commencing today Jewish Pupils will be dismissed at 3.00pm on Friday afternoons until the New Year holidays. This order has been given by the E.A. on account of the Jewish Sabbath which begins at sunset.

The establishment of synagogues, cemeteries, *kosher* food outlets, and Jewish welfare and educational facilities, indicated the existence of a significant Jewish population in Glasgow. But for much of its history the 'community' was divided into two main groupings: the modern Orthodoxy of the Garnethill population who were relatively prosperous; and the poorer, more traditional, Yiddish speaking Jews of the Gorbals. The differences caused the collapse of the United Synagogue Council in 1906, followed by various unsuccessful attempts to re-establish a body representing communal unity. It was not until 1914, prompted by increasing anti-Semitism abroad, that the Glasgow Jewish Representative Council was finally formed. The Council immediately began to help unnaturalized Jews with the necessary registration documents to remain in Scotland. The Council also established a united board to regulate the provision of *kosher* meat which had also been a source of friction between the Garnethill and Gorbals congregations [Collins 1987: 23].

The 'united' community still showed a tendency to divide into separate groups, and this was evident when German and Austrian Jews escaping the holocaust arrived in Glasgow. They were educated, middle-class people who preferred to meet in each other's houses and they were considered aloof by the majority Jewish population [Kolmel 1987: 72]. The establishment of a separate Austrian Jewish Club in the University Union was severely criticised in the *Jewish Echo* as discouraging mixing with the wider Jewish population of Glasgow. In defence one of the refugees asserted:

> Most of the Glasgow Jews had come from Russia or Poland; their families had emigrated in the 1880s and 1890s at the time of the pogroms there. Earlier, German Jews had looked down on them; now they avenged themselves by being very reserved towards us. [Kolmel 1987: 74]

If this appears to be petty bickering in the light of the events in Nazi Germany, it nevertheless indicates how complex are notions of identity. Religious affiliation may unite in some circumstances, but be overruled by class distinctions or national origins in others. As the war progressed, and the full horror of the 'final solution' became clear, closer relationships did develop. The over-riding issue, even for non-practising Jews, became that of Jewish survival. The events of the Second World War generated considerable sympathy amongst non-Jews over claims to an internationally recognised Jewish homeland, and led to the foundation of the State of Israel in 1948. While a number of Jews emigrated from Glasgow to the new homeland, the majority did not. Glasgow remained the home of a significant population of Scottish Jews.

Maintaining Identity

The early history of the Jewish population in Glasgow illustrates how tensions can arise between Jews of different origins. This was exacerbated by the fact that a small, relatively prosperous Jewish population were 'outnumbered' by impoverished, immigrants from Eastern Europe. The tension that ensued was partly shaped by concerns about the advisability of being conspicuously Jewish in a potentially hostile environment. This was satirised, originally in Yiddish, by the poet-writer Israel Zangwall [Cooper 1991: 76]:

> My brothers, sisters newly here,
> Listen to my wise oration,
> You can live without the fear
> Of hatred and repatriation
> All you have to do, I bid,
> Is stop acting like a yid.

Yiddish was replaced by English in the *chedar* schools in Glasgow from about 1908 as it was increasingly felt that fluency in English was important for educational and social progress [Collins 1993: 13]. In 1914, in an attempt to preserve the language, the *Yiddishe Shtimme* [*Jewish Voice*] monthly newspaper was published in Yiddish, but the paper did not survive. It was eventually replaced in 1928 by the *Jewish Echo*, a weekly paper, published in English and covering local, national and international Jewish news until its closure in 1992.

The extreme poverty of many immigrants was tackled through Jewish welfare organisations which aimed to avoid excessive dependence on local Poor Relief, a potential source of hostility in the wider community. Jewish relief organisations emphasised the importance of self-respect and independence [Rodgers 1982b: 115]. In this, they appeared to have some success. From the First World War onwards members of Glasgow's Jewish population began to prosper, not only through successful businesses but also as children entered professions such as medicine, law and teaching (for example, Miss E Carnovsky at Govanhill Primary School who clearly asserted her Jewish identity). Their economic success was illustrated by the steady movement out of the Gorbals to more prosperous suburbs.

Today there continues to be clear evidence of a Jewish population in Glasgow [Collins 1993: 21-25]. The Glasgow Jewish Representative Council co-ordinates the activities of almost 50 organisations and works with both local and national statutory agencies to promote Jewish interests. There are seven synagogues, some maintaining their own burial grounds, while the Glasgow Hebrew Burial Society provides additional burial services. The Glasgow Board for *Schechita* and the Glasgow *Beth Din* provide *kosher* meat, and supervise local *kosher* bakeries, restaurants and caterers. The Glasgow Board of Jewish Education is responsible for Jewish education at the local authority primary school and *chedar* schools, and organises Hebrew Language lessons for teenagers and adults. Numerous welfare activities are co-ordinated by the Glasgow Jewish Welfare Board, and the Glasgow Jewish Housing Association provides a range of accommodation.

Yet, as in other parts of the world, there is concern about Jewish continuity. During the 1970s a study of Jews in a middle-class suburb of Glasgow found religious factors to be weakening as an aspect of Jewish identity, and concluded:

> ... it thus appears that, in order to be a good Jew, one has to pay some symbolic tribute to rituals and tradition, but more important, one has to support Israel and maintain the Jewish family system, as well as maintaining good neighbourly relations with non-Jews and

contributing to the civic improvement of the society in which one lives. [Benski 1981: 314]

Glasgow's Jews have remained predominantly Orthodox (six of the synagogues being Orthodox and one Reform) so that concerns about Jewish identity have focused on 'out-marriage' and secularisation rather than a strengthening of Liberal or Reform Judaism. As a counterbalance to these tendencies, there seems little doubt that the horrors of the holocaust strengthened a commitment to Zionism. These three factors – out-marriage, secularisation and Zionism - are considered in more detail.

The information available about early Jews in Glasgow indicates that the population was largely composed of families. The lack of a Jewish homeland for much of this period, together with persecution irrespective of age or gender, militated against notions of temporary migration followed by a return to the country of origin. In such circumstances the maintenance of family life, within a supportive Jewish community that made few demands on the wider population, was seen as essential for the survival of Jewish identity. Attempts to restrict out-marriage in Glasgow at the end of the nineteenth and early twentieth century appear to have been successful, but as the century progressed the rate of out-marriage increased:

> There's only one progressive synagogue in Glasgow that takes in the people who have mixed marriages - it's an easy outlet for them. I've never been in a progressive synagogue because I'm completely orthodox and I'd like ma family to follow me. Ma daughter is very orthodox but ma son's not so hot! [quoted Rodgers 1982b: 120]

Greater restrictions appear to have been placed on the social activities of girls than of boys. As with other immigrant populations, football appears to have been something of a male obsession, and played a part in both secularisation and integration. A Jewish football team, the Oxford Star, had been established but the majority of football matches in the wider population were played on a Saturday, the Jewish Sabbath.

> I was president then [1910] of the Oxford Star football team. You couldnae meet a nicer set o' boys, they were all Jewish boys who lived around Oxford Street in the Gorbals. I don't think we played on the Sabbath. Well, we never played near the Gorbals if we did play, we played in another district. I may tell you the candid truth we'd hundreds o' people used to come and watch us. [quoted Rodgers 1982b: 117]

By the 1920s and 1930s it was not unusual to find Jewish supporters on the terraces at Rangers and Celtic matches on Saturdays, while Third Lanark (a popular south side team that no longer exists) had a Jewish player:

> There was quite a good support for the Thirds, whether some of it was due to me being Jewish and playin' for them I don't know ... Even though I was playing' on the Sabbath I was sort of a wee tin god because I was playin' professional football and possibly enhancing the Jewish image as it were. [quoted Rodgers 1982b: 118]

'Lack of Jewish youth club experience' has been identified as a key factor influencing secularisation and out-marriage today [Miller et al 1996: 12] and it appears that this was already understood at the turn of the century. The Jewish Lads and Girls Brigade date back to 1903 in Glasgow when attempts were made to provide a range of sporting and recreational activities specifically for young Jews. But there was a lack of clarity about what constituted the 'Jewish' element of such provision and by 1930 the *Jewish World* newspaper was scathing when it reported that the Association of Jewish Youth conference had 'arrived at the sonorous and cleverly constructed definition that religion (Jewish religion bear in mind!) was "sportsmanship and good citizenship"' [Bunt 1975: 86]. Although the Jewish element remained unclear, it does appear that such clubs were popular until commercial clubs and activities proved to be a greater attraction (as was also asserted in relation to young Catholics). Today in Glasgow there are Jewish cubs, brownies, scouts and guides, while the Jewish Lads and Girls Brigade continue to provide 'disciplined participation in sport, drill, craft and social activities' [Collins 1993: 24]. The Glasgow Maccabi runs a sports and social centre in Giffnock, providing sporting and social activities but also fostering 'Jewish identity and an awareness of Israel' [Ibid].

The impact of Zionism on identity is complex and can only be briefly mentioned here as an illustration of the way in which events abroad continue to influence the identity of an immigrant population and its descendants. Glasgow's Jews had shown a commitment to Zionism in the 1890s when a branch of the *Chovevei Zion* (Lovers of Zion) was formed to give financial help to Jewish settlers in Palestine. The Russian pogroms gave strong impetus to the Zionist cause and before the First World War the Glasgow *Bnai Zion* held regular mass meetings of over 1,000 people. The movement was split over the acquisition of a Jewish homeland, with some members regarding Palestine as the only possible site while others were prepared to consider alternative territories, but only a small proportion of Glasgow's Jews rejected Zionism altogether [Collins 1987: 21]. The issue was settled with the formation of the State of Israel after the Second World War and a number of Glasgow's Jews emigrated to the new homeland.

Strong links have been maintained between Glasgow and Israel: numerous institutions sponsor educational, social and environmental projects in Israel; Israeli visitors and speakers are invited to inform Glasgow's Jewish population about contemporary issues; the Joint Israel Appeal assists new immigrants to Israel; and Glasgow is twinned with the Israeli town of Arad. Zionist youth groups are attached to both Orthodox and Reform synagogues, some emphasise the religious tradition of Judaism, while others provide links with the Israeli *kibbutzim* and labour movement [Collins 1993: 24]. But Jewish support for Israel has not been uncritical and the Glasgow Friends of Peace Now have held meetings with Palestinian representatives [Ibid: 25]. There seems little doubt that the Holocaust and the creation of the State of Israel have strengthened Jewish consciousness through notions of survival as a people, a faith and a nation. At the same time a Scottish dimension has been injected into the Jewish identity of those who were born in Scotland:

> I think that Jews very much identify themselves with the place of their birth. I feel very Scottish and I'm very happy to be in Scotland and I have a little foothold in Israel as well for my daughter was married there recently. [quoted Rodgers 1982b: 121]

Recent representations to the local authority in Glasgow summarised the aspirations of Scottish Jews in relation to public service provision. It was urged that 'employers, carers and teachers will be sensitive to the needs of Jewish people according them the opportunity to maintain their traditions while playing their full part in society'.[17] This essentially multicultural aim was evident amongst other immigrant populations and their descendants. It will been shown that it is also relevant to the more recent immigrant population of Pakistani origin. This population is considered next.

---

[17] From the *Resource Booklet on Jewish Issues* produced for circulation to the new Unitary Authorities. Ref: GPSIH912.SAM

4 Pakistanis in Glasgow

Recent migration to Scotland from Pakistan has its roots in the history of the British Empire and, in particular, the activities of the East India Company which was founded in England in 1599 [Maan 1992, McFarland 1991, Cain 1986, Parker 1985, Bryant 1985]. Scottish entrepreneurs attempted to set up an equivalent company but met with stiff opposition until, in 1707, the Act of Union gave them rights to equal trade opportunities throughout Great Britain and its dominions. These opportunities were readily exploited and by the second half of the eighteenth century there was a considerable Scottish presence in India. When Henry Dundas, Viscount Melville, was appointed Senior Commissioner of the Board of Control in 1784 it was alleged that 'there was scarcely a gentleman's family in Scotland ... that had not at some time received an Indian appointment or some act of kindness from Dundas' [Cain 1986: 16].

The East India Company dominated huge areas of the Indian subcontinent and dictated what was produced and sold, what wages were paid, and what prices were charged. Opportunities for corruption were great, and were exploited to the full, until the British Government assumed supremacy over the Company in 1858 and introduced reforms to limit the worst aspects of maladministration. However, government motives were not entirely altruistic and British industry prospered at the expense of the Indian economy. An impressive infrastructure was developed in India as roads, railways, waterworks and canals were constructed, but their primary purpose was to transport raw materials to Britain for her expanding manufacturing industries. Meanwhile industrialisation of the Indian economy was discouraged. This process was well illustrated through the development of the jute trade in the 1830s through which jute was shipped from India to the prosperous power looms of Dundee, while Bengali handweavers lost their livelihood.

Trading links may have motivated some of the wealthy Indian princes and noblemen who travelled to Scotland during the nineteenth and early twentieth centuries to be entertained by the Lord Provost of Glasgow [Maan 1992: 66-69]. But, as the twentieth century progressed, the uneven relationship led to increasing calls for Indian Home Rule. In 1919 the Hon V J Patel made a speech to a large gathering in St Andrews Halls in Glasgow in which he argued that after 150 years of British rule India had changed from being one of the richest countries in the world to one of the poorest [*Glasgow Herald* 27.9.1919].

While the British Raj had stimulated visits from some wealthy Indians, and had encouraged a number of students to study at both Glasgow and Edinburgh universities [Maan 1992: 76], the first real link in the process of chain migration to Scotland appears to have been the recruitment of Indian seamen by the East India Company [McFarland 1991, Dunlop & Miles 1990, Visram 1986]. They were paid less than a quarter of the wages of European sailors, and ship-owners often recruited them to boost profits [McFarland 1991: 496]. Harsh treatment resulted in some men jumping ship at British ports where they became temporary, and sometimes permanent, residents. References to lascar residents occur in the annual reports of Glasgow Sailors' Home, and in 1918 a home was opened especially for them at Queen's Dock.[18] It appears that there was some sympathy for these sailors and when Glasgow Corporation funded the construction of a new Lascar's Home in 1930 the *Glasgow Herald* reported that it had been thoughtfully designed 'to meet the special requirements and customs of the Eastern native' [Dunlop & Miles 1990: 151].

Following the First World War there was a slump in world shipping, and some of the Indian seamen looked for employment in collieries and iron and steel works. They met resistance from the existing workforce and, in an attempt to avoid direct competition for employment, a number became pedlars. At the same time poverty amongst peasant farmers in India was increasing. The traditional system of dividing land between sons resulted in attempts to sustain a living on ever decreasing plots of land.[19] This poverty prompted migration to a number of British colonies including the West Indies, Uganda, Kenya, South Africa, Malaya, Canada, Australia and New Zealand. Immigration controls were gradually implemented in these countries, but Great Britain remained open to her 'subjects' and the number of Indians entering Britain, including Scotland, gradually increased.

Maan's combination of oral history and academic research offers a plausible explanation of the way in which one man from a village in the Punjab contributed to the process of chain migration to Glasgow. His story also illustrates the transition many early immigrants made from seaman to pedlar [1992: 105-118]. Nathoo Mohammed left his fathers smallholding to become a seaman and arrived in Glasgow in about 1919 where he met up with the ex-valet of an army officer who introduced him to peddling. His

---

[18] The term 'lascar' probably comes from the Hindi or Persian for 'army' or 'camp' and was applied to seamen engaged on Indian articles. Its use was often extended to include Chinese sailors [McFarland 1991: 494].

[19] As had also prompted Italian migration.

success was such that he returned to India and impressed others with the opportunities available. Other temporary migrants sent letters and remittances from Glasgow to their villages in India, encouraging further migration and offering initial support to new arrivals in the city. The valuation rolls for Glasgow in the 1930s and 1940s show a continuous presence of Indian pedlars [Dunlop & Miles 1990: 153], and wholesale warehouses were gradually established to supply them with goods.

Numbers remained relatively small and by 1940 there were still only about 400 Indians living in Glasgow, with 50 houses owned or tenanted by Indians in the Gorbals area [Maan 1992: 150]. Although they formed a small 'community', a review of the pedlars' licences issued by the City of Glasgow Police between 1939 and 1940 indicated that they were not a homogeneous group: 35% were Sikh and 65% Muslim [McFarland 1991: 511]. Differences are likely to have become more apparent in 1947 as many of the 'Indians' in Glasgow became Pakistanis when the new state of Pakistan was established and India was granted independence. Initial celebrations were followed by concerns for the welfare of relatives as almost 15 million people were uprooted in mass migrations across the border: Muslims to Pakistan, and Sikhs and Hindus to India. The disruption was considerable, and at times brutal, prompting some to consider migrating further afield.

As Britain began to dismantle her Empire the 1948 British Nationality Act provided a framework which allowed citizens of Commonwealth countries to acquire United Kingdom citizenship through a relatively simple process of registration [Dummett & Nicol 1990, Cambridge & Feuchtwang 1992]. It seems probable that large-scale immigration to Britain from the New Commonwealth and Pakistan was not envisaged, but numbers did increase steadily. In 1950 the total number of South Asians in Scotland was about 600; by 1955 this had risen to 1,300; and by 1960 the figure was approximately 4,000 [Maan 1992: 162]. While economic and political circumstances in India and Pakistan stimulated emigration, there was no overall corresponding demand for labour to serve as an explanation for arrival in Scotland. In fact, net emigration from Scotland was evident throughout the 1950s and 1960s as a result of economic decline.

Evidence is scant but the main employment opportunities in Scotland at this time appear to have been in peddling, shopkeeping and wholesaling, less popular types of factory work, and in public transport. A survey of 700 Pakistani men in Glasgow in the mid-1960s indicated that 200 were employed as bus conductors and drivers, 100 worked in rubber factories, 30 in the chemical industry, and 30 in brick factories. 100 of this sample were retail grocers and a further 51 were involved in other retail outlets and services [Elahi 1967: 32]. Other figures for 1965 confirm a high representation in the public transport sector, indicating that Glasgow Transport Department employed 102 Indians and 405 Pakistanis, nearly all of whom were drivers and conductors [Beharrell 1965]. In contrast to West Indian recruitment patterns, there is no concrete evidence of direct recruitment from India and Pakistan [Dunlop 1988: 133]. It seems more likely that copies of advertisements placed in Scottish newspapers were sent to relatives and friends by men who were already settled in Glasgow. This had the effect of encouraging further migration to Scotland, both from the Indian subcontinent and 'internally' from England.

A popular conception had emerged that it was easier to establish a business in Scotland than in England. This may have been fuelled in Glasgow by some dramatic success stories through which enterprising migrants expanded small retail outlets into large wholesale businesses. One notable example was Yacub Ali who arrived in Glasgow in 1952 at the age of 19 and began working as a pedlar. He went on to develop wholesale and cash and carry businesses throughout the 1960s and 1970s, attained millionaire status, and was awarded the OBE in 1984 for his services to trade and industry [Maan 1992: 177-179]. While the vast majority of immigrants from India and Pakistan could not hope to become millionaires, there were enough examples of successful business expansion amongst the relatively small population to give credence to the idea that they might fare better in Scotland than in England.

A study of the Crosshill area of Glasgow suggested that during the 1950s and 1960s the majority of the South Asian population had migrated directly to Scotland from the Indian subcontinent, but during the 1970s and 1980s the pattern changed. 40 of the 65 families in the study had lived in England before moving to Glasgow [Watson 1984]. This evidence was supported by another study in Glasgow which found that almost half of those interviewed (16 of 35) had previously lived in England [Dunlop 1988]. Bearing in mind that economic recession had led to high unemployment levels in Glasgow, Dunlop asked what factors had influenced the move. Kinship networks were given as the major reason, but this cannot be seen as sufficient explanation since it might easily have worked in the opposite direction with people in Glasgow joining families in England. Additional reasons given included the perception that it was easier to set up a business in Glasgow than in England.

During the 1960s it became clear that the British government intended to impose restrictions on immigration from the New Commonwealth and Pakistan. Successive Acts in 1962, 1968 and 1971 engendered a feeling of 'now or never' that initially increased immigration figures [Dummett & Dummett 1982, Rees 1982]. This was reflected in figures for Glasgow where there was considerable growth in the population of South Asian origin at a time when there was a decline in the total population of the city. The overall effect of controls was to reinforce patterns of migration from particular areas and kinship groups so that, following the British system of numbering villages in the southern Punjab, it was suggested that 'almost everyone from villages 477 and 482 is in Glasgow' [Shaw 1988: 23].

Table 4.1 Population of Glasgow 1951-1971

Year	Population of Glasgow	Decline of Total Pop.n	Estimated Asian Pop.n	Growth of Asian Pop.n
1951	1,089,767		500	
1961	1,055,017	-3.1%	3,000	+ 500%
1966	978,250	-7.2%	10,000	+ 233%
1971	897,848	-8.0%	12,000	+ 20%

[Source: Srivastava 1975: 99]

The 1950s and early 1960s were characterised by the 'lodging house era' when single males initially looked for cheap rented accommodation, and then developed a system of pooling resources to purchase inexpensive housing. Most of the men regarded their migration as temporary, and aimed to minimise their expenses in order to send as much money as possible back to their villages and families. In contrast, the late 1960s and early 1970s were characterised by family reunion when wives and children, and to a lesser extent parents, joined the previously 'single' males. During this phase family homes were purchased close to the earlier settlement areas, a process which was accelerated in Glasgow by the policy of slum clearance in the Gorbals.

A study of the distribution of Indian and Pakistani settlement in Glasgow up to 1971 traced the movement of the small, concentrated settlement from the Gorbals area, south to Govanhill and Pollokshields, and north-west to Garnethill, Woodside and the West End [Kearsley & Srivastava 1974]. Further research noted a degree of separation between the various 'communities' with the majority of the Sikh population (73.7%) living north of the river, and the majority of Muslims (67.4%) concentrated south of the river in Pollokshields and Govanhill [Dalton & Daghlian 1989]. This supports the argument that an increase in the size of an immigrant population allows pre-existing divisions, which may have been temporarily set aside, to resurface [Dahya 1974: 87].

As with previous Catholic and Jewish populations, responsibility for establishing the necessary institutions to follow religious obligations was accepted by the immigrants themselves. The first Muslim Mission was set up in Glasgow in 1940 when hired premises in Gorbals Street were converted into a temporary mosque. This mosque was soon transferred into larger premises following the purchase of a billiard hall and six adjoining flats [Maan 1992: 150]. From the 1970s onwards, as numbers increased and it became clear that settlement was permanent, the Muslim population started to move into Govanhill, Pollokshields and Woodlands, and new mosques were established to serve these local communities. Then, in 1979, work began on Glasgow's Central Mosque which was to be one of the largest mosques in Europe. This prestigious building was officially opened in 1984 by the Imam of the Kabah in Mecca, Islam's holiest shrine [Ibid: 174].

With the establishment of family life came parental concerns about the religious education of children. Classes were organised in the central mosque, local mosques, schools and community centres. A Scottish Office survey found that of the 'ethnic minority' parents surveyed (categorised as Indian, Pakistani, Bangladeshi, African Asian, and Chinese), Pakistani Muslim parents were most likely to send their children to lessons outside of the normal school day:

Table 4.2   Lessons Outside of School (Householders with Children at School)

By national origin	*Indian* %	*Pakistani* %	
Asian religion	21	55	
Asian language/religious writings	24	57	
Other Asian language	8	21	
Any other subject	7	10	
None	65	34	
Unclear	1	-	
By religion	*Hinduism* %	*Sikhism* %	*Islam* %
Asian religion	6	22	55
Asian language/religious writings	11	19	58
Other Asian language	1	10	21
Any other subject	11	3	10
None	76	70	33
Unclear	3	-	-

[Source: Extracts from Tables 8.23 and 8.24, Smith 1991]

The influence of chain migration and family reunion on the settlement patterns of the South Asian population contrasts with the lack of success that the British government had in attempting to disperse East African Asians who had retained British citizenship when African colonies gained independence. During the 1960s and 1970s non-African citizens were removed from employment in Kenya and Uganda, and were eventually expelled [Cable 1969, Robinson 1986, Dummett & Nicol 1990]. By 1981 there were 155,000 East African Asians in Britain, and government policy concerning their settlement involved establishing 'red' (no go) and 'green' (go) areas. Glasgow was declared a green area, but the policy of dispersal was not successful and they constitute only 2% of Glasgow's total 'ethnic minority' population [Dalton & Daghlian 1989, Smith 1991].

Research during the 1980s estimated Glasgow's Indian/Pakistani population to be about 17,000. The vast majority of households who had moved within the previous two years had done so within Glasgow. Only 7.5% had moved from England, 2.1% from Pakistan and none from India, indicating that migration, whether 'internal' from England or from overseas, had reduced considerably [Bowes, McCluskey & Sim 1990].

The Current Pakistani Population

The 1991 Census data can be regarded, at best, as providing a statistical overview. The data was collected during the political struggle against the Poll Tax and there was a degree of deliberate non-registration and undercount. This was exacerbated by the difficulties some respondents experienced in completing the form. The Census Office estimated that 98.1% of residents and 99.9% of households in Scotland were included but the degree of undercount varied considerably [SRC 1994]. In Glasgow District the undercount for the total population was estimated to be 3.9%, rising to almost 20% among males in their 20s. In addition, because of the degree of self-assessment involved, discrepancies are evident between tables that appear to count the same thing.

The 'ethnic question' asked respondents to choose an identity from a given list: White, Black Caribbean, Black African, Black Other, Indian, Pakistani, Bangladeshi, Chinese, Other Asian and Other. These categories are problematic since 'White' can hardly be thought to constitute an 'ethnic group', and there is a consequent implication that only 'non-Whites' have 'ethnicity' [Ballard 1997]. In much the same way that the idea of 'race' has been legitimised through the terminology of 'race relations', the categories give credence to the notion of 'ethnicity' in Britain as something that distinguishes immigrants from the New Commonwealth and Pakistan, together with their descendants, from the rest of the population. Bearing these limitations in mind, relevant data concerning Scotland and Glasgow City are considered next.

Table 4.3 Census 1991: Population by Ethnic Group

Ethnic Group	Scotland No.	%	Glasgow City No.	%
White	4,935,933	98.75	641,336	96.75
Pakistani	21,192	0.42	10,945	1.65
Indian	10,050	0.20	3,374	0.51
Bangladeshi	1,134	0.02	191	0.03
Chinese	10,476	0.21	2,780	0.42
Other Asian	4,604	0.09	952	0.14
Black – African	2,773	0.06	726	0.11
Black – Caribbean	934	0.02	220	0.03
Black - Other	2,646	0.05	489	0.07
Other	8,825	0.18	1,840	0.28
Total	4,998,567	100	662,853	100

[Source: Table 6 Census 1991 Report for Scotland]

Using the Census categories, the total non-White population of Scotland is small, only 1.25% of the total population, although the figure is larger for Glasgow City (3.25%). To give an idea of scale, this can be compared with the total non-White population in English cities such as Birmingham (21.5%), Bradford (15.6%) and Manchester (12.6%). In Scotland, those identified as Pakistani form the largest 'ethnic group' with over 50% of Scotland's Pakistanis living in Glasgow where they constitute over 50% of the total non-White population.

The high percentage of Other respondents indicates that the ethnic question has not been entirely successful. Various Other categories were chosen by more than 25% of Scotland's minority ethnic groups, and more than 15% of those in Glasgow. If people do not identify with a suggested ethnic group it seems likely that the number of Others will reach a proportion where the categories become meaningless. However, for the Pakistanis who completed the 1991 Census form, this does not appear to have been too problematic. The proportion of Others in Glasgow is much less than for Scotland as a whole. The fact that the head of household tends to complete the form may indicate that older men were willing to identify themselves and their families as Pakistani, even though the majority of this population were not born in Pakistan.

Table 4.4 Census 1991: Ethnic Group of Non-White Population
(As % of Total Non-White Population)

	Scotland	Glasgow City
Pakistani	33.8	50.9
Indian	16.0	15.7
Chinese	16.7	12.9
Other	14.1	8.6
Other Asian	7.4	4.4
Black-African	4.4	3.4
Black-Other	4.2	2.3
Black Caribbean	1.5	1.0
Bangladeshi	1.8	0.9
Total	100	100

[Source: Table 6 Census 1991 Report for Scotland]

Table 4.5 Census 1991: Country of Birth of Pakistani Population

Country of Birth	Scotland No.	%	Glasgow City No.	%
Scotland	8,671	41.1	5,014	45.9
England	2,685	12.7	956	8.8
Other UK + Irish Republic	103	0.5	44	0.4
Pakistan	8,522	40.4	4,334	39.7
India	883	4.2	474	4.3
Bangladesh	6	<0.1	4	<0.1
East Africa	131	0.6	46	0.4
Other	98	0.5	41	0.4
Total	21,099		10,913	

[Source: Table 51 Census 1991 Report for Scotland]

A sizeable minority of the Pakistani population were born in England, which supports earlier small-scale studies suggesting that there has been internal migration from south of the border. About 4% were born in India and it is probable that these were the older immigrants whose nationality changed as a result of partition. But the largest proportion (over 45%) of Pakistanis in Glasgow was born in Scotland.

Table 4.6 Census 1991: Pakistani Population by Age and Gender

Age	Scotland Male %	Female %	Glasgow City Male %	Female %
0-4	12.3	12.5	12.9	13.0
5-15	26.3	27.4	26.9	27.5
16-19	7.2	8.0	7.2	7.9
20-39	34.8	36.1	34.3	36.4
40-49	6.8	7.9	6.5	7.1
50-64	10.9	7.1	10.3	7.1
65 and over	1.6	1.0	2.0	1.0
Total	100	100	100	100

[Source: Table 51 Census 1991 Report for Scotland]

The Pakistani population is broadly balanced in relation to gender, except in the older age bands. Amongst the over-65's in Glasgow there are twice as many men as women. This reflects different patterns of migration and indicates that not all of the earlier single men got married or were joined by wives and children from India and Pakistan [Bowes & Dar 1997: 83]. The gender imbalance in the older age-bands is in sharp contrast to the White population where the reverse is the case and there are almost twice as many women as men [Census 1991 Report for Scotland: 125].

Overall, the Pakistani population is noticeably young, with more than 80% under 39 years. It can be assumed that there will be an increase in the population size as new families are formed, and that they are likely to have particular concerns about child welfare and education (which are considered later). In contrast, the proportion of elderly is small. However, it is important to note that people aged 50 may be considered elderly amongst a Pakistani population, and research indicates an earlier onset of health problems [Bhalla & Blakemore 1981, Barker 1984, Askham et al 1995].

Figures for household composition suggest that the majority of elderly Pakistanis live with their families. Only 0.7% of Pakistani households in both Scotland and Glasgow City consist of a single adult of pensionable age (the figures for White households are 15.8% and 17.9% respectively). Even if some of the single adult households under pensionable age are assumed to be aged 50+ and included as elderly, the number of Pakistani elders living alone remains relatively small. The most common household size is that of two adults with one or more children i.e. a nuclear family. However, this does not necessarily mean that the nuclear family is replacing the 'extended family' as the preferred household. The age distribution of the population suggests that many of these households will consist of parents with older children. These children may be considering marriage, and whether or not their parents become part of an extended household will be observed over time. Over a quarter of current households consist of three or more adults with dependent children which does suggest that the extended family system is being maintained in some form. (Consideration will be given later to attitudes concerning the care of parents and elderly relatives which may influence future patterns of household composition.)

Table 4.7 Census 1991: Pakistani Household Composition

	Scotland		Glasgow City	
	No.	%	No.	%
1 adult of pensionable age				
0 children	30	0.7	16	0.7
1 adult under pensionable age				
0 children	350	7.7	172	7.5
1 adult any age				
1 or more children	189	4.2	99	4.3
2 adults (1 male + 1 female)				
0 children	332	7.3	156	6.8
1 or more children	1,869	41.4	957	41.7
2 adults (same sex)				
0 children	57	1.3	31	1.4
1 or more children	45	1.0	25	1.1
3 or more adults (males+females)				
0 children	359	7.9	180	7.8
1 or more children	1,267	27.9	632	27.5
3 or more adults (same sex)				
0 children	25	0.5	13	0.6
1 or more children	17	0.4	9	0.4

[Source: Table 43 Census 1991 Report for Scotland]

Information about household conditions indicates that the Pakistani population is far more likely to live in 'overcrowded' conditions than the White population.[20] Other measures suggest that the Pakistani population is living in poorer quality housing: they are more likely to share accommodation, to share bath and toilet facilities, and to lack central heating. Figures for households containing someone with a limiting long term illness were broadly similar for the Pakistani and White populations but, if this is taken in conjunction with the fact that the Pakistani population is considerably younger than the White population, there may be cause for concern. Care must also be taken in interpreting the figures relating to car ownership. Pakistanis are far more likely to be car owners than the White population, but this is not necessarily an indication of greater wealth or disposable income. Car ownership may be a means of avoiding difficulties with other forms of transport. It will be shown later that, during the fieldwork interviews, transport was considered to be a particular problem for the elderly.

Table 4.8 Census 1991: Household Conditions

	Scotland White %	Scotland Pakistani %	Glasgow City White %	Glasgow City Pakistani %
Over 1.5 persons per room	0.5	11.0	1.1	15.0
Lacking or sharing bath/shower and/or inside WC	0.6	1.6	0.8	1.7
No central heating	22.0	31.0	37.0	46.0
Not self-contained accommodation	0.3	0.9	0.9	1.0
No car	43.0	28.0	66.0	37.0
Containing person(s) with limiting long term illness	26.0	27.0	33.0	30.0

[Source: Table 49 Census 1991 Report for Scotland]

It is now broadly accepted that owner occupation is the 'preferred housing choice' of South Asian immigrants [Jones 1993: 140] and the 1991 Census data indicated that over 75% of Pakistanis in Glasgow were homeowners. Shared male owner occupation was used as a strategy to

---

[20] It is important to recognise that definitions of 'overcrowding' are relative.

minimise costs by the early immigrants, and was replaced by family home ownership when migration was perceived as permanent and families were united.

Almost 20% of Pakistanis in Glasgow own their homes outright which may indicate difficulties in acquiring a mortgage on some properties. The spatial pattern of the Pakistani population does indicate a concentration in older tenemented properties, and it will be shown later that serious problems with sub-soil conditions in Govanhill may have affected the possibility of obtaining a mortgage. However, the picture is complicated. Efforts have been made by the local authority and Govanhill Housing Association to maintain the residential status of the area (see later) and just as the move to Govanhill proved to be a stepping stone into more middle-class areas for previous immigrants, there are some signs that this may also be the case for the Pakistani population.

Table 4.9 Census 1991: Housing Tenure

	Scotland		Glasgow City	
	White %	Pakistani %	White %	Pakistani %
Owner occupied				
- owned outright	16.5	15.7	9.7	19.7
- buying	35.5	59.9	27.0	56.7
Rented				
- privately	4.8	10.5	5.0	12.3
- housing association	3.1	2.1	8.0	3.1
- local authority	34.3	10.0	44.0	7.5
- New Town/ Scottish Homes	3.8	0.9	5.2	0.5
Total	98.0	99.1	98.9	99.8

[Source: Table 49 Census 1991 Report for Scotland]

For those who are unable or unwilling to become home-owners, research has shown problems of access to social housing [Dalton & Daghlian 1989, Bowes et al 1989, MacEwen 1991, Bowes et al 1997, Third & MacEwen 1997]. In particular, institutional racism is thought to operate in both local authority and housing association allocations: the specific housing needs of larger families are not catered for; language difficulties have not been adequately addressed; potential clients are unaware of the procedures involved in making applications; and racism within specific housing schemes has been insufficiently challenged [Murray 1991a]. These factors contribute to the fact that those Pakistanis who are not homeowners are more likely to rent in the private sector, with the increased likelihood of paying higher rent for poorer quality accommodation.

Table 4.10 Census 1991: Economic Position by Ethnic Group (Males)

Males 16 and over	Scotland		Glasgow City	
	White %	Pakistani %	White %	Pakistani %
Employees				
- full time	51.8	24.3	42.5	25.4
- part time	1.9	4.1	1.7	3.5
Self-employed				
- with employees	3.5	19.3	1.7	14.7
- without employees	5.0	13.4	3.3	11.4
On government scheme	1.4	1.0	1.9	1.1
Unemployed	9.0	14.2	15.8	17.4
Economically inactive				
- students	3.6	12.9	3.4	13.3
- permanently sick	6.7	6.3	11.3	7.8
- retired	16.0	2.9	17.0	3.3
- other inactive	0.9	1.6	1.4	2.0

[Source: Table 9 Census 1991 Report for Scotland]

Research has also indicated that minority ethnic groups are more likely to experience poverty and unemployment [STUC 1992, Watt 1993, Strathclyde Poverty Alliance 1994, Hampton & Bain 1995, Save the Children & Glasgow Caledonian University 1995]. An indication of the economic progress of the Pakistani population can be discerned through statistics relating to employment, although interpretation is not straightforward. The differences between men and women are so great that they are considered here separately. Pakistani men in Glasgow are five times more likely than White men to be self-employed (the difference is greater in Glasgow City than in Scotland as a whole where the ratio is closer to 4:1). This contributes to over a third of Pakistanis being in the highest socio-economic groups as 'employers and managers' and further consideration of this point follows later.

The stereotype of the self employed shop-keeper is so strong in Glasgow that it is important to comment on the fact that three quarters of

Pakistani men in Glasgow are *not* self employed: a quarter are in full-time employment (some, of course, may be working in shops), and over 13% are students compared with just over 3% of White men. Unemployment rates are higher for Pakistani men than for White men, but the difference between the two categories is far less pronounced in Glasgow than in Scotland as a whole, reflecting the higher unemployment rates for all men in the city. The relative youth of the population means that the percentage of retired Pakistani men is small (3.3%) when compared to White men (17%).

Table 4.11 Census 1991: Economic Position by Ethnic Group (Females)

Females 16 and over	Scotland White %	Pakistani %	Glasgow City White %	Pakistani %
Employees				
- full time	26.7	8.9	24.9	7.9
- part time	15.9	5.4	11.6	3.8
Self-employed				
- with employees	1.0	3.6	0.4	1.7
- without employees	1.3	3.2	0.6	2.3
On government scheme	0.7	0.6	0.8	0.8
Unemployed	3.7	6.3	5.8	7.1
Economically inactive				
- students	3.4	12.0	2.9	11.9
- permanently sick	4.7	2.8	7.4	3.5
- retired	20.3	1.9	23.8	1.7
- other inactive	22.2	55.4	21.7	59.5

[Source: Table 9 Census 1991 Report for Scotland]

About three-quarters of Pakistani females are categorised as 'economically inactive', supporting the suggestion that they are traditionally discouraged from working outside of the home [Khan 1980, Lewis 1994: 184-5]. However, their rate of unemployment is higher than that of their White counterparts suggesting that other factors may be involved (such as language difficulties, lack of relevant skills or experience, and exclusionary practices in the labour market). Self employment is higher amongst Pakistani women than amongst White women which seems to indicate that a number of them are establishing businesses in their own right, although the numbers are small. This self employment may enable some women to avoid difficulties experienced through direct competition in the wider labour market. A relatively high percentage of Pakistani women are students and, although attendance at college is often thought to be used as a strategy to delay marriage, there is sufficient evidence of employment in secretarial and clerical occupations, as well as the professions, to suggest that some are making use of their qualifications in the labour market. But for the moment the percentage who are in employment is barely over 15% in Glasgow (21% in Scotland as a whole).

Table 4.12 Census 1991 Scotland (10% Sample):
Occupational Classification of Pakistani Population

	Male %	Female %
SOC Major Group		
1 Managers and administrators	58.1	32.8
2 Professional occupations	5.4	7.4
3 Associate professional & technical	1.8	5.7
4 Clerical and secretarial	5.2	17.2
5 Craft & related occupations	1.6	3.3
6 Personal & protective service	8.8	0.8
7 Sales	13.2	26.2
8 Plant & machine operatives	2.6	3.3
Other/inadequately described	3.3	3.3
Industry division		
6 Distribution, hotels, catering	78.5	64.8
9 Other services	7.0	18.0
8 Banking, finance	4.7	8.2
4 Other manufacturing	2.6	6.6
7 Transport & communication	3.1	0.8
5 Construction	1.0	0.0
Other/inadequately described	3.1	1.6

[Source: Table 93 Census 1991 Report for Scotland]

Both Pakistani males and females are heavily concentrated in 'distribution, hotels and catering' industries although men are more likely to be 'managers and administrators' which suggests a higher rate of business ownership, while women are twice as likely to work in 'sales'. It is tempting to speculate that a number of these women are employed in family businesses. However, women are also represented in banking and finance, and other services, suggesting that those females who are in employment are moving into a broader range of occupations than their male counterparts.

Table 4.13 Census 1991 Scotland (10% Sample): Employers and Managers

	Male White	Pakistani	Female White	Pakistani
As % of ethnic group				
1 Government/commerce/large organisations				
- Employers	<0.1	0.3	<0.1	-
- Managers	5.5	0.8	2.5	0.8
2 Industry/commerce/small organisations				
- Employers	3.5	31.8	1.6	18.9
- Managers	6.7	7.8	4.5	2.5
As % of all employers & managers				
1 Government/commerce/large organisations				
- Employers	70.4	1.4	25.4	-
- Managers	72.7	<0.1	27.0	<0.1
2 Industry/commerce/small organisations				
- Employers	68.1	2.1	26.3	0.4
- Managers	64.0	0.6	30.6	<0.1

[Source: Table 19 Census 1991 Report for Scotland]

The high representation of Pakistani men and women as 'managers and administrators' compared with the White population requires further investigation. When the type of organisation is specified it is clear that the vast majority hold these positions in small organisations. In fact, irrespective of gender or ethnic group, only a very small percentage of people are employers in large organisations. However, 0.3% of Pakistani men do reach this status. Bearing in mind the high emphasis on self employment it seems likely that these men are predominantly the owners of the wholesale, retail and catering business empires that were built up in the way described earlier [Maan 1992]. The figures for managers in large organisations show that a higher percentage of White males and females hold these positions than their Pakistani counterparts. This would suggest that Pakistanis are less likely to be promoted into top positions in large organisations that they have not established themselves. The figures for smaller institutions support the idea that Pakistani men and women are much more likely than their White counterparts to be employers. The differences are much less marked for managers. This reinforces the contention that their status as employers is due to the establishment of their own small businesses, and they are less likely to hold managerial positions in other organisations.

The different socio-economic status of White and Pakistani employers and managers is even more pronounced when the figures are calculated as a percentage of all employers and managers. This reveals that the 'top jobs' are clearly dominated by White males, with White females making some inroads. Pakistani males, and especially females, are barely represented in SEG1. Having said this, Pakistanis constitute 0.4% of the total population in Scotland and as such the men are over-represented (1.4%) in top employers positions (albeit that they appear to have created the opportunities themselves). It appears that progress has been achieved through considerable diligence since Pakistani men and women work much longer hours than the White working population, with over 22% of the men, and 9% of the women, working more than 60 hours per week.

Table 4.14 Census 1991 Scotland (10% sample): Hours Worked

Hours per week	Male White %	Pakistani %	Female White %	Pakistani %
15 and under	1.4	3.4	13.3	11.5
16-30	2.5	6.5	25.5	17.2
31-40	71.0	28.2	53.9	39.3
41-60	17.3	31.8	3.9	12.3
61 and over	4.3	22.2	0.8	9.0
Not stated	3.4	8.0	2.6	10.7

[Source: Table 19 Census 1991 Report for Scotland]

It has been shown that previous immigrant populations aspired for greater opportunities for their children and looked to academic education as a means of promoting social progress. There is evidence that the Pakistani population is following this pattern. While 10% of the White population in Glasgow hold a higher qualification, compared to 7% of the Pakistani population, the pattern seems likely to change. Amongst the Pakistani population there is a clear correlation between age and academic achievement: the younger the person, the more likely they have to have a higher qualification. This is less pronounced amongst the White population where the under-30s are slightly less likely to be qualified than the 30-44 age band. If these trends continue, Pakistani young people look set to be more qualified than their White peers.

Meanwhile, the data for social class based on occupation indicates that Pakistanis in Glasgow are more likely to enter the professions than their White counterparts, and are well represented in skilled non-manual work.

**Table 4.15 Census 1991 Glasgow City (10% Sample):
Ethnic Group and Qualified Manpower**

	White %	Pakistani %
Total persons qualified to a,b,c*	10.8	7.1
Aged 18-29	35.0	52.8
Aged 30-44	37.6	33.3
Aged 45-pensionable age	17.4	13.9
Pensionable age	10.0	-

* (a) Higher degree, (b) Degree, (c) Diploma etc
[Source: Table 85 Census 1991 Report for Scotland]

**Table 4.16 Census 1991 Scotland (10% Sample):
Social Class Based on Occupation**

	Scotland White %	Pakistani %	Glasgow City White %	Pakistani %
I Professional	4.7	4.7	5.0	6.3
II Managerial, technical	26.7	54.6	25.1	53.4
III(N) Skilled non-manual	22.7	24.0	24.0	21.6
III(M) Skilled manual	21.5	6.5	20.9	6.3
IV Partly skilled	15.5	7.1	15.1	6.8
V Unskilled	7.3	0.4	8.8	0.6
Armed forces	0.8	0.0	0.2	0.0
Inadequately described	0.9	2.8	1.0	5.1

[Source: Table 93 Census 1991 Report for Scotland]

Much of this data supports the notion of an immigrant population adopting a strategy of self-sufficiency and self-help during settlement with a view to establishing a base from which their descendants can take advantage of wider opportunities: purchasing property, establishing businesses, working long hours and encouraging children to seek academic qualifications as a means to enter the professions. In the next section consideration is given to the response of the wider population to the arrival and settlement of this population.

Attitudes Towards Lascars, Asians and Muslims

Material specifically relating to Scotland is sparse, but there is enough information to consider attitudes towards immigrants from the Indian sub-continent in three broad stages: the response to the employment of lascar seamen in the early twentieth century; attitudes towards larger numbers of South Asian immigrants from the 1960s onwards; and the anti-Muslim discourse which (re)emerged in Britain in the late 1980s.

In the early twentieth century, Scottish trade unionists showed resentment against Indian and Chinese workers who were accused of undermining White workers by accepting low wages and poor working conditions. While economic circumstances may have triggered this discourse, there was a perceived difference of 'race':

> A demonstration in furtherance of the agitation against the employment of Asiatic seamen was held last night in the City Hall, Glasgow, under the auspices of the Clyde District of the National Transport Workers' Federation. The attendance numbered about 2,000. The Chairman, Councillor F G Stewart, said that their objection to Indian and Chinese labour was not because they were a different race and colour, but because they lowered the standard of life for the white man. [*Glasgow Herald* 21.4.1914]

The perceived threat faded during the First World War when there was full employment, and, at the end of the war, the Lord Provost of Glasgow paid tribute to 'the sympathy and support which the Indian people had given to Great Britain in her hour of need' [Maan 1992: 96]. But protests soon resumed over the use of 'cheap lascar labour' when unemployed Indians attempted to find jobs in collieries and iron and steel works [Dunlop & Miles 1990: 159]. In response to such complaints the Coltness Iron Company admitted employing four lascars but emphasised:

> ... all four were British subjects, natives of Bombay; all had been on war service and possess medals; they were employed as casual labourers on surface; they were paid the same wages and worked the same hours; and they were not cheap labour. [*Glasgow Herald* 5.3.1920]

Nevertheless, the workers were sacked. The following year, a meeting of the Motherwell Trades and Labour Council included references to the employment of Indian workers while 'our own people' are unemployed, and to the supposed threat that the morals of Indian workers posed to the population of Lanarkshire [*Motherwell Times* 11.2.1921]. Such arguments were not unopposed and another speaker stated that it was not fair 'to decry them because of their colour'. A debate ensued in the *Motherwell Times* including letters defending the 'work and habits' of lascars and decrying these 'outrageous statements that come from our so-called Labour men in the Trades Council' [Dunlop & Miles 1990: 160]. But the hostility in and around British ports was such that, in 1925, the Special Restrictions (Coloured Alien Seamen) Order was enacted to refuse entry to 'coloured' seamen who were not British nationals or could not prove that they intended to return to their port of origin. Pressure was exerted by the police in Glasgow to have the city included in the list of areas covered by the Order [Ibid: 156], and the Secretary of State for Scotland instructed Chief Constables to take precautions over the issuing of pedlars licences to lascars and other 'coloured' seamen:

> ... the Police should be slow to grant certificates when there is good ground to suspect that the applicant is a deserter or has otherwise obtained entry to this country by irregular means. It is hoped that this course will tend to discourage desertions from Lascar articles and the irregular landing of coloured seamen. [Scottish Office Circular No 2440: June 1930]

However, some certificates were granted, and throughout the 1930s and 1940s there was a continuous presence of Indian pedlars in Glasgow. Numbers remained small, with an estimated 400 Indians in Glasgow in 1940, and racist discourse was at this time more likely to focus on Irish Catholics or Jews. It was not until the 1960s that the South Asian population significantly increased in size. Subsequent political debates about immigration and 'race relations' were particularly prominent in England, but are relevant here because the resulting legislation provided the framework for migration to Scotland. It has been noted that the 1948 British Nationality Act was comparatively liberal in relation to United Kingdom citizenship, but as the twentieth century progressed more far-reaching attempts were made to restrict 'coloured' immigration. Legislation increasingly differentiated between potential migrants who 'belonged' to the United Kingdom by birth or 'descent' and others who 'belonged' elsewhere. In 1971 the New Commonwealth (parts of Africa, Asia and the Caribbean) was distinguished from the Old Commonwealth (Australia, Canada and New Zealand):

> More and more openly it came to be admitted that the whole purpose of the immigration laws was to minimize the number of people of a different colour entering the country; indeed, the Government itself began to argue that this itself was a contribution to 'racial harmony', that it was in the interests of black people themselves that their numbers be kept to a minimum, because only thus would the native population find their presence tolerable ... [Dummett & Dummett 1982: 107].

Meanwhile racist discourse linked biological racism with notions of a cultural incompatibility that threatened social cohesion:

> To be integrated into a population means to become for all practical purposes indistinguishable from its other members. Now, at all times, where there are marked physical differences, especially of colour, integration is difficult though, over a period, not impossible. There are among the Commonwealth immigrants who have come to live here in the last 15 years many thousands whose wish and purpose is to be integrated and whose every thought and endeavour is bent in that direction. But to imagine that such a thing enters the heads of a great and growing majority of immigrants and their descendants is a ludicrous misconception, and a dangerous one. [Enoch Powell 1968, reproduced in *New Statesman* 17 April 1998]

Enoch Powell's infamous 'rivers of blood' speech in 1968 was publicly condemned, while legislation in the form of the Race Relations Acts 1965, 1968 and 1976 purported to offer redress against 'racial discrimination' on the basis of 'colour, race, nationality or ethnic or national origins'. But the policy framework developed by both Conservative and Labour governments during the 1960s and 1970s did give credence to a notion that New Commonwealth immigration was a problem. Yet, while immigration and 'race relations' policies applied to Britain as a whole, the dominant opinion north of the border was that racism was much more of a problem in England than in Scotland. Such ideas were reinforced by the absence in Scotland of inner city disturbances (frequently described as 'race riots') that occurred in England in the mid-1980s. At the same time, this apparent lack of racism was increasingly questioned [Miles & Muirhead 1986, Miles & Dunlop 1987], and examples of direct and indirect racism, including verbal threats, physical abuse, British Nationalist Party activity, and institutional racism, were documented [TCRC 1987, Walsh 1987, Armstrong 1989, Dalton & Daghlian 1989]. Police statistics showed a steady increase in the level of reported 'racial incidents' and confirmed that racism was a significant problem.[21]

Table 4.17 Reported 'Racial Incidents' in Scotland

Police Force	1988	1989	1990	1991	1992	1993	1994	1995/6
Total	299	376	636	678	663	756	791	832
Central	9	18	45	69	51	52	75	125
Dumfries & Galloway	-	-	-	-	-	4	6	2
Fife	-	-	3	35	30	20	40	44
Grampian	4	4	9	4	20	28	44	25
Lothian & Borders	89	91	178	213	184	229	266	288
Northern	-	-	-	-	-	1	-	1
Strathclyde	197	236	300	254	250	229	225	230
Tayside	-	27	101	103	128	193	135	117

[Source: Scottish Office correspondence 19/5/98]

It has been shown in relation to previous immigrant populations that negative stereotyping was often couched in terms of their religious identity and there is some evidence that this is the case for immigrants from Pakistan, the vast majority of whom are Muslim. But this does not appear to have been an important aspect of initial negative stereotyping. It seems doubtful if the religious identity of 'lascars', 'Indians' or 'Asians' was of particular interest to the wider population for many years. 'Colour' seems to have been a significant trigger for exclusionary practices, and, later, the term 'Paki' was applied indiscriminately to anyone whose origins were presumed to be in the Indian subcontinent, irrespective of their religious beliefs. More recently, the degree of antipathy towards Muslims has become prominent enough to be described as 'Islamophobia', and Muslims have been portrayed as espousing 'holy war and hatred, fanaticism and violence, intolerance and the oppression of women' [Esposito 1991: 5]. Much of this recent anti-Muslim fervour emanated from the events surrounding the publication in 1988 of Salman Rushdie's *The Satanic Verses*, and the subsequent *fatwa* issued by the Ayatollah Khomeini [Lewis 1994, Runnymede Trust 1997]. As the media focused on images of book burning,

---

[21] Although it should be noted that increased reporting may also indicate increased confidence that incidents will be dealt with.

even 'liberals' began to express intolerant and extreme views about Islam but again the affair seems to have been perceived as much more of a problem in England than in Scotland:

> If you remember following the Rushdie book being published, you had the *fatwa* and all the rest of it. The Muslim community here were clear that they were not getting involved in it. They weren't delighted with what was in the book and what Rushdie had done, but the leaders of the Muslim community here were very, very helpful, very calm and took a moderate stance. I strongly suspect that we never had anywhere near the problems that were witnessed in England at the time. [Convenor, Glasgow City Council Racial Equality Working Group]

But the affair also triggered more tolerant discourse about the place of Islam in British society [St Catherine's Conference 1991, Runnymede Trust 1997]. Concerns were raised about the way Muslims were being portrayed, particularly in the media, and the Commission for Racial Equality (CRE) in its *Second Review of the Race Relations Act 1976* recommended that 'a specific law against incitement to religious hatred should be introduced and a law against religious discrimination should be given further serious consideration' [EOR No.46: 1994]. The Government responded by asserting that 'as yet there is little hard evidence of discrimination against individuals on religious rather than racial grounds' [EOR No.57: 1994]. However, test cases under the Race Relations Act 1976 have established that, under certain circumstances, Jews and Sikhs are eligible for protection under the Act, while this is not the case for Muslims. In the face of this apparent lack of parity it might be argued that the majority of Muslims have shown remarkable patience in negotiating with British institutions [Joly 1986]. In Scotland there is evidence of such negotiation and this will be considered later through specific case studies. To contextualise the empirical research, the history and environment of Govanhill are considered next.

5 A History of Govanhill

The story of Govanhill is inextricably linked to the rise of Glasgow as Second City of the Empire; the subsequent demise of heavy industry in Scotland; and attempts to alleviate the worst aspects of deprivation in those areas most affected by economic decline. This story is outlined here to contextualise Pakistani migration to the locality in which the fieldwork was undertaken.

The Growth of Govanhill

Until the eighteenth century, the settlement of Glasgow was restricted to the north of the River Clyde and did not include the area now known as Govanhill on the south side of the river. The construction of a stone bridge in 1345 did provide a cross river link but when Mary Queen of Scots fought the Battle of Langside in 1568 it appears that much of the land was an unoccupied boggy mire [Eunson 1994: 2]. During the eighteenth century, Glasgow grew into a centre of trade and a major British port, and settlements to the south of the river started to expand. The small village of Gorbals developed as a weaving centre from about 1730 and the boggy land further south was drained to become rich farmland. But Govan Coal Works had already started to mine the area, and industrialisation soon diverted the history of Govanhill away from farming.

William Dixon, the first of three men by this name to influence the history of Govanhill, became lessee of the colliery which developed into one of the most productive in Scotland. When he died in 1822 his son, also William Dixon, followed in his footsteps. He founded Govan Iron Works in 1837 and used railway transport to move coal from the pits to the ironworks and to the River Clyde for shipment. Govan Iron Works became one of the largest manufacturers of iron in the world, and was known locally as 'Dixon's Blazes' because of the way the light from the blast furnaces lit up the night sky [Eunson 1994]. The increasing industrialisation of the area was reinforced by the arrival of another entrepreneur, Henry Dubs, who contributed to Glasgow's reputation as 'locomotive builder to the world' [Nicholson & O'Neil 1987]. In 1864 work began on the construction of Dubs Locomotive Works and two years later orders were taken to design locomotives for the East India Company.

Apart from a small settlement around Govan Colliery School, which had been established for the children of colliery workers, there were very few working class homes in the area during the first half of the nineteenth century. But in the 1860s the third William Dixon began feuing the ground to builders to construct homes for his workers and to cash in on a building boom in the expanding city. At this time the City Improvement Trust, in an attempt to tackle the desperate living conditions of the poor in the slums of Glasgow, imposed a number of regulations that resulted in the construction of buildings of a relatively high standard with a maximum height of four storeys. Today, Govanhill is characterised by the tenements built under these regulations, enhanced by William Dixon's paternalistic interest in the area and his insistence on wide streets [Worsdall 1979].

Under the Police Act of 1862, any settlement with a population of more than 700 people had the right to establish itself as a self regulating burgh with its own council, police force and fire service. The Burgh of Crosshill was formed in 1871, and that of neighbouring Govanhill in 1877 [Eunson 1994, Porter 1980]. Two years later William Dixon gifted a joint burgh hall to the residents of Govanhill and Crosshill. His health was failing and he was unable to attend the ceremony, but he sent a letter to be read out to those present. The letter made reference to the rapid population growth in the area:

> I need scarcely mention to those present the deep interest that I have all my life taken in this part of my property - the place in which I spent all the early years of my life and which I have seen change from green fields to two extensive and populous burghs. [*Glasgow Herald*, Dec 1879]

From a relatively small population in 1860, the population had grown to over 7,200 when the burgh of Govanhill was instituted in 1877. This figure increased to 10,000 in 1881 and 14,000 by 1891 [FitzPatrick 1986a: 8]. Between 1870 and 1891, over 3,000 new homes were built in the area. The majority were small homes for industrial workers and, although the original feuing restrictions placed on Govanhill had stipulated that all homes had to have a minimum of two rooms, some were sub-divided to form what was known as a 'single end' (literally a single room). It seems likely that some of these industrial workers were Irish Catholic immigrants and their descendants since Father O'Brien's congregation in the Parish of Holy Cross had grown to over 1,000 by 1889.[22]

---

[22] See Chapter 1.

By the 1920s schools, churches, a library and public baths had been built, trams ran along the major roads, and 'Dixon's Blazes' and 'Dubsies Iron Works' were the main employers. A prestigious Catholic church had been built to serve some 3,500 parishioners, and classes for Catholic school children were being accommodated in non-Catholic schools to ease congestion. Meanwhile, the Jewish population was also growing. In 1932 Crosshill synagogue opened and the log book of Govanhill Primary School indicated that some of the religious requirements of Jewish pupils were acknowledged by the authorities.[23]

More houses were constructed at this time by Glasgow Corporation who, between 1919 and 1939, were responsible for building 70,000 houses in the city, mainly for skilled and semi-skilled artisans and lower paid white collar workers [Bryant & Bryant 1982: 14, Glasgow Corporation 1973]. Today the north-west of Govanhill is dominated by housing constructed in the 1920s, and a 1930s development is evident in the south east corner of Govanhill. A slum clearance programme in the 1930s led to the introduction of a rehousing category with lower rents and fewer facilities. Such housing, evident in the north-east of Govanhill, became stigmatised as accommodating 'less respectable' tenants:

> It used to be separate and I think it will always be like that. People on this side always think of that side as the slum clearance. I think it is a stigma that will always be there. [Govanhill tenant quoted in Bryant & Bryant 1982: 14]

As the twentieth century progressed, there were signs that the reliance on heavy industry would have dire consequences for employment in Govanhill. Large-scale unemployment during the 1930s resulted in widespread poverty and many people in Govanhill were forced to rely on charity:

> By my mothers resolve and good housekeeping my brother and myself were saved from landing in the hands of the dreaded 'parish'. The hapless children who were on their books had to wear regulation rig-out. For the boys this was a horrible herring-bone pattern jacket and trousers with clumsy black boots. The recipients of this 'largesse' were tragic standouts in the school playgrounds as they paraded their poverty for all to see. [Murray 1991b: 4]

But the outbreak of the Second World War relieved the poverty of many. With war came full employment, and plenty of overtime for those who worked in munitions factories. For the residents of Govanhill:

---

[23] See Chapter 3.

Dubsies was just over the hill from where we stayed and was going at full production in the building of tanks. [Ibid: 31]

Economic Decline and the Development of the Local Plan

The Second World War gave only temporary respite in the decline of Glasgow's industrial base. Between 1961 and 1971 net employment in the city fell by 78,000 with the greatest loss in manufacturing and engineering [Bryant & Bryant 1982: 22]. Govanhill was hard hit when Govan Iron Works, the last blast furnace to operate within the city boundary, closed in 1959. The locomotive works closed soon after in 1962. Problems associated with unemployment were exacerbated by poor housing conditions as many tenements fell into disrepair. As early as 1960 part of Govanhill was approved by the Secretary of State for Scotland as an 'Outline Comprehensive Development Area', with the emphasis on clearance and redevelopment. Delays occurred but the 1971 Census data gave further evidence of the level of poverty and disadvantage in an area where 41% of dwellings were without exclusive use of hot water, bath and toilet.[24] Govanhill repeatedly figured in the official league tables of 'deprived' Glasgow communities and became the subject of a 'local plan'.

In June 1972 the Corporation of Glasgow identified factors considered to be 'indicative of serious deficiencies in the social and environmental well-being of the city'. Population trends, housing conditions and employment patterns in Glasgow showed worrying signs when compared with those for Scotland and Great Britain as a whole. Statistics indicated a high level of migration with a tendency towards an imbalance in the age structure of the population and a higher dependency rate. Those who were leaving Scotland were thought to be 'generally people who are economically active and of higher than average capability and ambition' [Glasgow Corporation 1972a]. The remaining male workforce was weighted towards semi-skilled and unskilled employment with fewer male professionals, managers and employers than in other parts of the country. Housing conditions were shown to be poorer in Glasgow than in Scotland as a whole and, when compared with those of Great Britain, the lack of basic amenities was striking (33% of households in Glasgow lacked a bath, compared with 15% in Great Britain as a whole).

In attempting to define and quantify the problems facing the city, the Scottish Development Department identified a number of 'social-physical'

---

[24] Many regard these delays as fortunate in that the wholesale demolition of tenements was averted and Govanhill retained much of its Victorian heritage.

factors and undertook a computer mapping exercise. The results suggested levels of multiple deprivation on a much larger scale than had previously been considered, leading to the conclusion that a well co-ordinated plan, involving large-scale expenditure, was required. The emphasis had moved away from a preoccupation with sanitary conditions towards recognising the wide range of environmental and social factors which defined an area as attractive or otherwise. It was argued that the loss of population would be slowed down, and economic growth encouraged, if the city was considered socially and physically attractive. The task in areas of multiple deprivation was enormous.

Within this wider context Govanhill was designated Planning District 41 and became the subject of a Preliminary District Study [Glasgow Corporation 1972b]. The aim was to collate available information about the area and identify issues for further study. The resultant report serves as a description of Govanhill one hundred years after William Dixon had orchestrated the wide streets and 'good quality' housing for his workers. The area was described as consisting of decaying tenement properties. Concern was expressed that most of the schools were on cramped congested sites and that Catholic schools were particularly badly off in relation to site requirements. Previous major employers in the area were gone and industrial and commercial activity was concentrated around Larkfield Bus Depot to the north-west, in small back court developments or infilled sites, and along the shopping thoroughfares.

At this stage local authority welfare and leisure provision in Govanhill was sparse. There was no nursery provision, no community centre, no youth centre and the swimming baths represented the only indoor sports facility. Yet the Report was able to describe a 'great diversity of social life' [Ibid: 8]. This social life was found in churches and associated halls, with additional activities taking place in school buildings. Such was the strength and diversity of provision that the Planning Department warned against undermining it through any comprehensive attempt to provide open space. Lessons had been learned from the planning disasters of the 1950s and 1960s to the extent that Govanhill's tightly packed and diverse population was seen as a strength rather than a weakness.

Facilities and organisations in the area included Crosshill Synagogue and the Hebrew Burial Society Hall; Clydedale Freemason Lodge Hall and Govanhill Unionist Club Rooms; and Holy Cross Roman Catholic Church and the Roman Catholic Diocese Hall. This gives a clear indication of the Jewish, Protestant and Catholic population mix that had developed as a result of nineteenth and early twentieth century migrations to Govanhill. The population was described as representing 'a wide cross-section of the social stratum in terms of class, religion and ethnic origin'. Specific reference was made to a 'well established Jewish community' and the site requirements of Catholic schools, but there was no mention of immigrants from India and Pakistan, some of whom had already moved south from Gorbals to Govanhill.

Five years after the Preliminary District Study had taken place, an internal memorandum was widely circulated at senior level within Glasgow District Council highlighting a problem that would affect future plans for the area [Hamilton 1977]. The memorandum outlined a number of characteristics of Govanhill that were said to contribute to its potential as a prime residential site: it was within one mile of the city centre, well served by public transport, with good local shopping facilities, and close to large industrial development sites. However, the *laissez-faire* industrial development of the early nineteenth century had left a maze of unmarked mining tunnels beneath the tenements and streets of Govanhill. It was argued that there were good reasons to maintain the community in such a favourable location whilst tackling the factors contributing to its disadvantaged status, but there was an urgent need for expensive ground consolidation works which the District Council could not afford to finance.

The unstable sub-soil conditions reduced the possibility of obtaining a mortgage on certain properties and hence lowered property prices. Under such circumstances new owner-occupiers were more likely to be those who considered purchasing outright. It has been shown that there is a higher rate of outright ownership amongst the Pakistani population in Glasgow, and it is tempting to speculate that problems over ground consolidation contributed to the pattern of Pakistani migration to Govanhill during the 1970s. In addition, research indicated a high representation of Indian and Pakistani men working as bus drivers and conductors. It may be that proximity to Larkfield Bus Depot contributed to the attractiveness of Govanhill as a residential area for these men and, later, their families [Beharrell 1965, Elahi 1967, Dunlop 1988].

The arguments in favour of supporting Govanhill as a prime residential area eventually won through and a considerable amount of ground consolidation work was co-ordinated by Govanhill Housing Association. However, it will be shown later that the growth of housing association activity, with an emphasis on tenancy rather than owner-occupation, subsequently restricted the settlement patterns of Pakistani immigrants and their descendants in the area.

It was not until June 1980 that the Written Statement of the Govanhill Local Plan was finally issued. Within the uncertain financial climate a number of proposals were made with an emphasis on preserving the character of Govanhill. Some 280 new houses were proposed, but wherever possible tenements were to be renovated and all new developments were required to be in keeping with the 'form, building line and materials used in adjacent buildings'. The District Council committed itself to essential repairs and environmental improvements, while Govanhill Housing Association was to implement the vast majority of tenement rehabilitation. It was envisaged that Govanhill would continue primarily as a residential area. Any development was required to be compatible with this, so that the Plan would have little impact on local economic activity and employment.

Govanhill in the 1990s

Before the implementation of the Local Plan, Govanhill had been characterised by a lack of local authority housing compared with other working class areas of the city. It had been predicted that the percentage of public housing would increase from 17% to 28% as a result of demolition and redevelopment [GDC 1979: 7]. This was not the case. The programme of improvement and repair of interwar District Council housing stock was implemented, but the proposed new-build projects were not undertaken by the local authority. Instead, limited redevelopment was undertaken by private contractors. This may have contributed to a slight increase in owner-occupation in the area, but the most significant change in housing tenure was from private rental to housing association rental.

Table 5.1 Housing Tenure 1971-1991

	Govanhill Local Plan Area		Glasgow District	
	1971 %	1991 %	1971 %	1991 %
District Council owned	17.0	18.6	54.0	43.7
Private rented	43.0	14.0	24.0	4.7
Owner occupied	40.0	41.6	22.0	37.4
Housing association	-	24.1	-	8.0
Other	-	1.7	-	6.2

[Source: GDC 1979, SRC 1994, and 1991 Census 1991 Report for Scotland Small Area Statistics]

By the 1990s Govanhill Housing Association had developed into one of the largest housing associations in Glasgow, managing a large stock of low-cost rented accommodation for low-income families [Dalton & Daghlian

1989, GHA 1994]. In addition the Association was addressing some of the specific requirements of elderly and disabled residents. However, research has shown considerable under-representation of minority ethnic groups in housing association homes, partly because of a preference for owner occupation and partly because of institutional racism [Dalton & Daghlian 1989, Third & MacEwen 1997].

A programme of extensive property rehabilitation contributed to disparity between the housing conditions of housing association tenants and those of low income owner occupiers. The 1991 Census data for Govanhill confirms that although Pakistanis are more likely to be owner occupiers they are also more likely to have lower income and poorer housing conditions (see later). In addition, the activities of the housing association included the refurbishment of back courts, and a programme of streetscaping involving pavement improvements and tree planting. A physical inspection of the area shows that this has had a positive impact on the environment in specific sections of Govanhill, but has also heightened the contrast between those streets with a predominance of housing association properties and those with a predominance of low income owner occupiers.

Much of the activity generated through the proposals in the Local Plan did not offer overt recognition to the increasing Pakistani population in the area. The commercial housing development consisted of small modern houses that are generally unsuitable for larger families, and the strong housing association activity did not favour those who preferred owner occupation. Meanwhile, community work research showed that local authority housing in north-east Govanhill was associated with the 'racial harassment' which was not adequately addressed [Murray 1991a].

> The day we put our things in the house, they got stolen. They made a mess, they spread flour all over the flat, they didn't leave anything, they broke everything. My children were young as well, so I got really scared and I left the house that day and rented a place [privately]. I asked them to give me another place - I still ask them - but they haven't yet. They said your points have been greatly reduced because you left that house. [quoted in Bowes, Dar & Sim 1997: 44]

Thus a number of factors contributed to the fact that the Pakistani population in Govanhill increased in size but became concentrated in those areas least affected by local authority and housing association activities.

By the 1990s the provision of community facilities had shifted away from churches and their associated halls. A physical inspection of the area indicated that several churches were demolished or converted for alternative use. The Hebrew Burial Society hall and Crosshill synagogue were closed, indicating that the 'thriving Jewish community' had moved away. But it would be wrong to assume that religious buildings were no longer significant in Govanhill. A new Roman Catholic Church, Our Lady of Consolation, had been erected, and the Freemason's Lodge had been converted into Govanhill's Central Mosque.

Meanwhile, the definition of Govanhill as an area of multiple deprivation gave access to an important source of funding for community groups and projects - Urban Programme Funding. Local activists, supported by community workers and local councillors, made a number of successful bids throughout the 1980s and early 1990s. Two projects established through this funding are considered later as case studies to examine the interaction between local service providers and Pakistani service users, but first the 1991 Census data will be examined to give a broad profile of the population.

The 1991 Census Data

In this section consideration is given to tables compiled using the SASPAC Census Analysis Package [Manchester Computing Centre 1992]. The limitations of the 1991 Census data, in relation to degrees of undercount and available choice of 'ethnic group', were outlined earlier and are equally pertinent to the following profile of Govanhill.

The total population of the area is approximately 9,800 and this represents a considerable decline from the estimated 13,600 in 1979. It appears that the reduction in population size has occurred through a decline in overcrowding and the demolition of some decaying tenement properties.

The country of birth of residents and their selected 'ethnic group' gives an idea of the mixed population in Govanhill. In order to justify the categories used for the rest of this profile, it is worth listing them in full (Table 5.3). The vast majority of the population (83%) were born in Scotland, while the other categories that constitute more than 1% of total population are those born in the Irish Republic (4.8%), Pakistan (4.1%) and England (3.6%). The relatively high percentage of those born in the Irish Republic points to the continued Irish Catholic presence in Govanhill. The high percentage of those born in Pakistan reinforces the significance of chain migration in settlement patterns, while the very small percentage for those born in East Africa supports the suggestion that the dispersal of East African Asians was unsuccessful. And the relatively small Indian population confirms a degree of separation of the Muslim and Sikh populations in Glasgow as numbers increased [Dalton & Daghlian 1989].

Table 5.2 Govanhill: Residents by Country of Birth

Country of Birth	Male	Female	Total	% of Total
All countries	4637	5221	9858	100
England	161	191	352	3.6
Scotland	3764	4425	8189	83.1
Wales	15	0	15	0.2
N. Ireland	19	51	70	0.7
Other UK	34	1	35	0.4
Irish Republic	242	227	469	4.8
Old Commonwealth	7	12	19	0.2
Eastern Africa	2	5	7	<0.1
Other Africa	1	4	5	<0.1
Caribbean	4	4	8	<0.1
Bangladesh	0	0	0	0
India	46	41	87	0.9
Pakistan	234	168	402	4.1
S E Asia	23	23	46	0.5
Cyprus	1	1	2	<0.1
Other New Commonwealth	2	3	5	<0.1
Other European Community	22	27	49	0.5
Other Europe	10	5	15	0.2
China	2	4	6	<0.1
Rest of World	48	29	77	0.8

[Source: Table SO7 Census 1991 Report for Scotland]

The figures give no indication of whether any of those born in England had parents of Indian or Pakistani origin, but previous research has shown that this is likely to be the case (and it will be shown later that 11% of those interviewed during the fieldwork were born in England).

When asked to ascribe ethnic origin, the picture changes and the percentage of people in a number of the minority ethnic group categories is higher than the percentage for country of origin. This is particularly evident in the case of the Pakistani population which increases from 4.1% to 10.6%. In contrast, the increase in the Indian ethnic group is very small (0.9% to 1.0% i.e. an increase of only 7 people). This could indicate that there are very few Scottish-born children of Indian parents in Govanhill, or that such children are less likely than their Pakistani peers to adopt an identity associated with their parents' country of origin. But such explanations are implausible. In practice, while the children of Indian parents are included in the Indian ethnic group, a number of the older people born in India before partition now identify themselves as Pakistani (see later).

Table 5.3 Govanhill: Residents by Ethnic Group

	Male	Female	Total	% of Total
All persons	4568	5244	9812	100
White (includes *)	3876	4566	8442	86.0
Black Caribbean	9	8	17	0.2
Black African	14	7	21	0.2
Black Other	8	4	12	0.1
Indian	52	42	94	1.0
Pakistani	523	521	1044	10.6
Bangladeshi	0	0	0	0
Chinese	38	38	76	0.8
Other Asian	13	17	30	0.3
Other	35	41	76	0.8
* Born in Ireland	220	285	505	5.2

[Source: Table SO6 Census 1991 Report for Scotland]

Only 5 of the 41 enumeration districts in Govanhill have no Pakistani presence at all, which might suggest a dispersed population. But Govanhill can be broadly divided into four sectors and, when the relevant enumeration districts are grouped together, it becomes clear that over 80% of Pakistanis live in the south-west sector where they form about a quarter of the total population.

Table 5.4 Govanhill: Distribution of Ethnic Groups by Sector

	Total	Pakistani	Pakistani *as % total pop.n in sector*	Pakistani *as % total Pakistani pop.n*
North-west	2405	75	3.1	7.2
North-east	1911	69	3.6	6.6
South-west	3463	848	24.5	81.2
South-east	2033	52	2.6	5.0

[Source: compiled using SASPAC 1991 Census Analysis Package]

The 1991 Census Small Area Statistics offer an opportunity to outline some of the characteristics of Govanhill's population and the general conditions affecting their lives. It should be remembered that Glasgow is especially disadvantaged when compared with both Scotland and Britain, so that higher measures of deprivation in Govanhill, such as unemployment and overcrowding, are an indication of the severity of problems affecting the area.

Where data is broken down by ethnic group the Census data often (though not always) combines the Indian, Pakistani and Bangladeshi categories. It was necessary to follow this system although a distinct Pakistani category would have been preferred. For such tables it is possible to remove 'Bangladeshi' because the data indicates that there are no Bangladeshi residents in Govanhill. Pakistani is used wherever separate figures are available, but when using Pakistani/Indian it can be noted that almost 92% of this category have identified themselves as Pakistani so that the data still provides a useful comparison with the White population.

Approximately 12% of the population of Govanhill had moved to their present address within the previous year. Over 20% of these migrants had moved within the postcode sector, reflecting the Housing Association's ongoing rehabilitation programme and policy of decanting residents within the local community. More than half of migrants had moved from other parts of Glasgow, suggesting that Govanhill was attractive as a residential area despite its 'deprived' status. This popularity is also supported by the fact that properties in the new private housing development were soon sold and only one 'new, never occupied' house was recorded in the Census data for Govanhill [Census 1999: Table S56].

Table 5.5 Govanhill: Migrants
(Residents with different address 1 year before Census)

	Persons	As % of total migrants
Migrants in households	1209	100
Within postcode sectors	252	20.8
Between postcode sector/within District	689	57.0
Between Districts/within Region	128	10.6
Between Regions/within Scotland	41	3.4
From England and Wales	45	3.7
From outside Great Britain	54	4.5

[Source: Table SS15 Census 1991 Report for Scotland]

Table 5.6 Govanhill: Ethnic Group of Migrants
(Residents with different address 1 year before Census)

	Persons	Total Migrants	As % of Migrants
Total persons	9720	1154	100
White	8334	1009	87.4
Pakistani/Indian	1138	92	8.2
Other	243	50	4.3
Born in Ireland	515	27	2.3

[Source: Table S17 Census 1991 Report for Scotland]

Most of the migrants are White (87.4%), with the largest minority ethnic group being Pakistani/Indian (8.2%). Some movement from England and Wales is evident, but it is not possible to tell from the statistics whether this includes people of Pakistani/Indian origin. Neither is the country of origin of migrants who came from outside Great Britain specified, but their presence suggests that overseas immigrants continue to be attracted to Govanhill.

Table 5.7 Govanhill: Age and Ethnic Group of Residents

Age	Total	White	Pakistani	Other
Total	9827	8382	1104	341
0-4	665	433	178	54
5-15	1187	820	295	72
16-29	2495	2137	272	48
30-pensionable age	3564	3117	328	119
Pensionable age & over	1916	1875	31	10

	White		Pakistani	
	As % of White pop.n	As % of total pop.n in age band	As % of Pakistani pop.n	As % of total pop.n in age band
Age				
0-4	5.2	65.1	16.1	26.8
5-15	9.8	69.1	26.7	24.9
16-29	25.5	85.7	24.6	10.9
30-pensionable age	37.2	87.5	29.7	9.2
Pensionable age & over	22.4	97.9	2.8	1.6

[Source: Table SO6 Census 1991 Report for Scotland]

The data concerned with age distribution confirms the national pattern that the Pakistani population is a young population, with over 40% aged under 16 years, 67% aged under 30 years, and less than 3% of pensionable age. When the figures are used to estimate the percentage of each 'ethnic group' within given age-bands of the total population, these trends are more evident. For example, while Pakistanis constitute about 10% of the total population, over a quarter of all school children in Govanhill are Pakistani. If their parents are keen for them to retain aspects of their cultural or religious identity then there are implications for the education system. At the opposite end of the age range, only 1.6% of all pensioners in Govanhill are Pakistani. If services cater for the vast majority of elderly, almost 98% of whom are White, then specific cultural or religious needs of the Pakistani elderly may be neglected. (These issues are explored in detail later.)

Table 5.8 Unemployment by Ethnic Group

Aged 16 & over	Govanhill White %	Govanhill Pakistani %	Glasgow City White %	Glasgow City Pakistani %	Scotland White %	Scotland Pakistani %
Male Unemployed	22.2	32.2	15.8	17.4	9.0	14.2
Female Unemployed	13.6	23.6	5.8	7.1	3.7	6.3

[Source: Table SO9 and Table 9 Census 1991 Report for Scotland]

Table 5.9 Govanhill: Economic Position by Sex and Ethnic Group

	All %	White %	Pakistani/Indian %
Males			
Economically active	68.0	67.0	76.0
Economically inactive	32.0	33.0	24.0
Unemployed	23.3	22.2	32.2
Females			
Economically active	42.4	44.0	26.0
Economically inactive	57.6	56.0	74.0
Unemployed	14.2	13.6	23.6

[Source: Table SO9 Census 1991 Report for Scotland]

The general rates of unemployment in Govanhill are high compared with those for Glasgow and Scotland, but the rates of Pakistani/Indian unemployment are significantly higher again than those for the White population. Over three-quarters of Pakistani/Indian men are categorised as economically active, but almost one third of them are unemployed. This is a disconcerting figure when taken in conjunction with the low female economic activity rate (26%), which suggests that male employment is regarded as the main source of family income. In addition, the unemployment rate for Pakistani/Indian females (23.6%) is much higher than for White females (13.6%), indicating that those women who are seeking work are less likely to find it than their White counterparts.

Table 5.10 Govanhill: Households with Dependent Children
(Ethnic Group of Head of Household)

	All	White	Pakistani/Indian
Total households	4719	4335	316
Total households with dependent children	1069	833	204
Ethnic group households with dependent children as % of all households with dependent children	100%	77.9%	19.1%
Households with dependent children as % of all households in ethnic group	22.7%	19.2%	64.6%

[Source: Table S43 Census 1991 Report for Scotland]

Of the total households in Govanhill, 22.7% have dependent children. The vast majority of these households have a White head of household, but over 19% of them are headed by adults who are Pakistani/Indian. The figures are more interesting when the table is turned around to calculate the percentage of households with dependent children within each ethnic group. This indicates that nearly 65% of all Pakistani/Indian households in Govanhill have dependent children compared to just over 19% of White households, and reinforces the notion that factors affecting the welfare and education of children are likely to be of considerable importance to Pakistani/Indian households in Govanhill.

Govanhill was not originally characterised by spacious accommodation, and the Victorian tenements included 'one apartment' homes and 'single ends'. Today such accommodation is more attractive to single people, and this may contribute to the relatively high percentage of single adult households (42%) compared with Glasgow (36%) and Scotland as a whole (29%). In addition, there are a number of local authority and housing association 'supported accommodation schemes' for single people in Govanhill. But single adult households tend to be uncommon amongst a Pakistani population (8.4% in Glasgow and 8.2% in Scotland). Thus the figure of 19% Pakistani single adult households in Govanhill is much higher than would be expected. It may be that some of the single men who moved to Govanhill as a result of slum clearance in the Gorbals did not marry and remained in the area, while those who formed families are beginning to move to more prosperous parts of the city.

Table 5.11 Single Adult Households

	Govanhill %	Glasgow %	Scotland %
All	42.2	35.9	28.6
White	44.1	36.3	28.7
Pakistani	19.0*	8.4	8.2

*Pakistani/Indian

[Source: Table S43 & Table 43 Census 1991 Report for Scotland]

Glasgow Corporation's Report *Areas of Need in Glasgow* [1972a] indicated that 11.8% of Glasgow's population lived in households with over 1.5 persons per room, 23.9% lacked hot water, 32.7% had no bath and 17.8% did not have exclusive use of a lavatory. Significant improvements have been made since then and this is reflected in the tables concerned with housing conditions. Over 98% of all households in Govanhill now have exclusive use of bath/shower and inside WC, although the figure of 1.9% lacking these basic amenities is more than twice that for Glasgow District [SRC 1994]. A breakdown of housing tenure indicates that people living in privately rented accommodation are the most vulnerable in relation to the standard of basic amenities: 12.7% of those renting private furnished accommodation lack or share a WC and bath or shower.[25]

---

[25] There appears to have been some confusion over the exact meaning of various housing tenures and some households were placed in more than one category.

Table 5.12 Govanhill: Housing Tenure and Household Amenities

	Total	Exclusive use bath/shower & inside WC	Lacking/sharing bath/shower & inside WC	% of tenure lacking basic amenities
All permanent households	4687	4599	88	1.9
Owned outright	605	602	3	0.5
Buying	1344	1336	8	0.6
Private rented:				
- furnished	353	308	45	12.7
- unfurnished	303	283	20	6.6
Rented:				
- with job/business	22	22	0	0
- housing association	1130	1125	5	0.4
- local authority	872	867	5	0.6
- new town/Scottish Homes	58	56	2	3.4

[Source: Table LS49 Census 1991 Report for Scotland]

The data confirm that the Pakistani/Indian population are more likely to be renting privately than the White population (17.4% compared with 14.0%). Although housing association activity has made a significant impact on housing conditions, the improved accommodation is four times more likely to be rented by the White population (25.5%) than the Pakistani/Indian population (5.6%).

Table 5.13 Govanhill: Housing Tenure by Ethnic Group
(Households by Ethnic Group of Head of Household)

	Total %	White %	Pakistani/Indian %
Owner occupied	41.4	38.7	76.0
Rented:			
- Privately	14.6	14.0	17.4
- Housing assn.	24.0	25.5	5.6
- Local authority	19.0	20.1	4.5
- Scottish Homes	0.9	0.9	0

[Source: Table SS49 Census 1991 Report for Scotland]

It was noted earlier that a much smaller percentage of Govanhill's residents (19.0%) are renting from the local authority than for Glasgow as a whole (43.7%), and Pakistani/Indian households the least likely to be doing so (4.5%). Percentages do not always give a clear impression, and so it is worth noting that in only 16 of the 288 Pakistani/Indian households rent from Govanhill Housing Association, and only 13 rent from the local authority. The Pakistani/Indian population are twice as likely to be owner occupiers (76.0%) than the White population (38.7%).

Pakistani/Indian households are over-represented in measures of overcrowding. Only 2.9% of households in Govanhill live in a dwelling with over 1.5 persons per room, but there are extreme variations within that figure (from 1.4% of the White population to 22.9% of the Pakistani/Indian population). Again, this figure is much higher than for Pakistanis in Scotland (11%) and Glasgow (15%). When considering all households with over 1 person per room, almost half of the Pakistani/Indian population (44.8%) are officially considered to live in overcrowded accommodation. Although the degree to which overcrowding is a problem may depend on the personal agendas of the occupants, this is a very high percentage when compared with the White population (6.6%).

Table 5.14 Govanhill: Occupancy Rates by Ethnic Group

	Total	White	Pakistani/Indian
All households	4652	4301	288
Over 1 and up to 1.5 persons per room	300 [6.4%]	225 [5.2%]	63 [21.9%]
Over 1.5 persons per room	136 [2.9%]	61 [1.4%]	66 [22.9%]

[Source: Table SS49 Census 1991 Report for Scotland]

General concerns about overcrowding were addressed during the rehabilitation programmes for the area, and the housing association combined some small units to make larger family homes (for example, by putting internal stairways between floors of tenement blocks to create maisonnettes). This contributed to a decrease in the total number of homes in Govanhill and a decline in the total population size. It seems unlikely that an average owner-occupier would gain planning permission for such radical structural alterations. The eventual solution to overcrowded conditions for most owner-occupiers is more likely to be movement to alternative accommodation. In the meantime, the south-west sector, where over 80% of the Pakistani population live, is the most densely populated part of Govanhill.

Table 5.15 Govanhill: Distribution of Population by Sector

	Total Population	Pakistani
Govanhill	9812 [100%]	1044 [100%]
North-west sector	2405 [24.5%]	75 [7.2%]
North-east sector	1911 [19.5%]	69 [6.6%]
South-west sector	3463 [35.3%]	848 [81.2%]
South-east sector	2033 [20.7%]	52 [5.0%]

[Source: compiled using SASPAC 1991 Census Analysis Package]

In the next chapter, some links between past and present are considered. Comparison is made between the migration and settlement of Irish, Italian, Jewish and Pakistani populations, and the qualitative fieldwork in Govanhill is introduced.

6 Past and Present

Govanhill developed with the industrialisation of Glasgow and the arrival of newcomers who were seeking to improve their economic circumstances. As such it has always been a multicultural and multi-faith area. In this chapter consideration is given to the ways in which cultural and religious identities have been asserted and acknowledged in the past, followed by an examination of issues relating to fieldwork in the Govanhill of the 1990s.

Attitudes Towards Immigrants and Their Descendants

Each of the immigrant populations considered in previous chapters was subjected to a degree of biological racism. References were made to the inferior 'race' and intelligence of the Irish; Jewish immigrants were described as people who wished to preserve their 'racial identity'; Italians immigrants were taunted for their 'foreign' appearance; and reference was made to the 'race' and colour of lascar seamen. Biological and cultural traits were connected in racist discourse and a key aspect of such discourse was the presumed reluctance of certain immigrants to conform to 'acceptable' standards of behaviour. Religious beliefs were cause for particular concern. Strenuous missionary efforts were made to convert Jews, while Scotland's strong Presbyterian tradition contributed to the anti-Catholic fervour that on occasions culminated in rioting. Religious affiliation influenced the employment opportunities of both Jews and Catholics as some firms openly promoted a Protestant ethos, and in the housing market there was clear evidence that Jews were subjected to exclusionary practices.

Negative stereotyping was exacerbated by economic circumstances. The vast majority of immigrants were impoverished on arrival and, despite the economic expansion that was taking place, employment was often erratic and poorly paid. Applications could be made for Poor Relief and the Irish in particular were accused of migrating to Scotland specifically to be kept by charity. In the labour market, Irish immigrants competed directly with the wider population and were frequently accused of undermining attempts to strengthen employment rights by their willingness to work hard for low wages. The majority of Italians and Jews were not involved in such direct competition for employment but, in establishing businesses and providing services, they were vulnerable to the accusation of profiting at the expense of the local population. Similar negative stereotypes were attributed to the population of South Asian origin: either prompted by direct competition for employment, as when lascar seamen sought industrial jobs in Glasgow; or through self employment, as shop-keepers were, and continue to be, subjected to 'racial incidents' including verbal abuse and damage to their property.

Events abroad had an impact on relationships between relative newcomers and the established population. In different ways, opinions about the Great Famine, Irish Home Rule, the persecution of Jews, Zionism, and the rise of fascism in Italy influenced attitudes towards immigrants and their descendants in Scotland. The volatile impact that events abroad can have on immigrant populations was particularly evident during the Second World War. Immigrants fleeing the holocaust were initially received with sympathy, but as the war progressed German origins resulted in the internment of a number of Jewish refugees. And when Mussolini declared war on the allies, Italians in Scotland were construed as potential enemy agents and a wave of anti-Italian rioting ensued.

In the 1980s the *Satanic Verses* affair highlighted the presence of a significant Muslim population in Britain.[26] The *fatwa* proclaimed by the Ayatollah Khomeini (notably in Iran, not Pakistan or Britain), prompted anti-Islamic fervour in many parts of Britain. Although this was said to be less pronounced in Scotland, the affair again illustrates how events abroad continue to have an impact on the lives of migrants and their descendants.

The results of negative attitudes can be particularly conspicuous, but it should also be noted that throughout the process of migration and settlement there were examples of sympathetic attitudes and notions of fair treatment. This was evident in policies allowing Jewish children to leave school in time for their Sabbath, the funding of Catholic schools, the establishment of homes for lascar seamen, the defence of Indian workers in the *Motherwell Times*, and the release of internees during the Second World War. It was also evident in the daily 'getting along' between neighbours, in the relationships that engendered 'mixed marriages', and in the transactions that

---

[26] It has been asserted that *The Satanic Verses*, seen through South Asian Muslim eyes, could hardly fail to trigger outrage [Lewis 1994: 155]. Bhiku Parekh, deputy chair of the Commission for Racial Equality, wrote of the book:

> Muhammad is called a 'smart bastard', a debauchee who after his wife's death, slept with so many women that his beard turned 'half white' in a year ... [his] three revered colleagues ... are 'those goons - those fucking clowns' ... *The Satanic Verses* reduces [the Koran] to a book 'spouting' rules about how to 'fart', 'fuck' and 'clean one's behind'. [*New Statesman and Society* 24 March 1989]

enabled some Jewish, Italian and Pakistani businesses to prosper. In these interactions, immigrants and their descendants played an active part in maintaining and promoting aspects of their identity. This process is considered next.

The Assertion of Identity by Immigrants and Their Descendants

The Irish, Italian, Jewish and Pakistani immigrants who played a part in the history of Govanhill did not define themselves solely as victims of a hostile wider population but asserted aspects of their identity in an interactive process. Their activities and opportunities may have been constrained by exclusionary practices, but they had work to do, children to nurture, weddings and funerals to attend, social lives to organise, and (for many of them) their God to worship. While they did encounter hostility in going about their everyday business, they also encountered notions of fair and equal treatment. They were able to assert some of their own priorities, to establish separate institutions and to negotiate with existing institutions over specific cultural and religious requirements.

Before considering the assertion of cultural and religious identity, it is important to acknowledge that some individuals regarded migration as an opportunity to 'shake off' their previous identity altogether. Furthermore, those who did assert aspects of a distinct identity could not be described as a united community. There were clear differences within categories such as Catholic, Irish, Jewish, Italian and Asian based on religious practices, class differences and geographical origins. At the same time there was evidence that these categories were used by the immigrants and their descendants to present a united front in a variety of circumstances.

As far as national origins were concerned, the struggle for Home Rule dominated both Catholic and Protestant Irish political loyalties in Scotland until at least 1922, and probably well beyond that. Similarly, Indians in Scotland joined the call for Home Rule, and many embraced a new Pakistani identity following partition. Italian immigrants showed the same strong interest in their place of origin but this tended to be expressed as emotional loyalty to a specific village or region. It was in the 1920s and 1930s that pride in a broader Italian identity was asserted through membership of the *fascio*. Jews on the other hand did not have a homeland for much of their history. Their 'national' loyalties were less likely to be to the country from which they had migrated, but to Zionism. This was initially expressed as support for the establishment of a Jewish homeland and later through contacts with the State of Israel.

Although religious identity could trigger hostility in the wider population, many immigrants and their Scottish born descendants showed considerable tenacity in asserting the right to practice their faith. While Irish Catholic parishioners engaged in sacramental activities to varying degrees, the importance they placed on Catholic rites of passage and their commitment to a Catholic identity was evident through financial and practical support for the establishment of churches and schools. Italian Catholics did not construct an 'ethnic church' in Scotland, but the importance of Catholicism to them was evident in their connections with Italian missionary priests, their attendance at existing Catholic schools and churches, and even the construction of places of worship during internment. The Jewish population, despite fears of attracting anti-Semitism, negotiated with the local authority about the religious education requirements of their children and established synagogues as the population settled in different parts of the city. Similarly, the first Muslim Mission was established in Glasgow in 1940 and as the population expanded and relocated, additional mosques were established.

However, suggestions that immigrants showed unquestioning religious commitment, or that religious leaders dominated their congregations, ignore the ways in which religious practice was negotiated. Both Irish and Italian Catholics were noted to be poor attenders of mass; only 50% of the children enrolled for Jewish education classes actually attended; priests resorted to adopting Irish symbols to attract parishioners; and socialist values were accepted by the Catholic hierarchy as a form of radical Christianity when it became clear that working class parishioners were increasingly drawn to the party reflecting their class interests.

The majority of immigrants believed that the social progress of their children would be enhanced by academic achievement, but there were concerns that attendance at existing schools would undermine their religious identity. Attempts to tackle this issue resulted in both concessions within local authority schools and the establishment of separate provision. Catholics steadfastly chose to remain outside of the local authority system until it was agreed that separate Catholic education could be provided. The campaign for a separate Jewish school was not as unified as that waged by the Catholic population. Specific concessions were negotiated within local authority schools, and a Jewish primary school was eventually established in 1962. But many Jewish parents preferred the *chedar* system of religious education classes outside of normal school hours. Similarly, classes were established outside of the school day to enable Muslim children to read the *Qur'an*.

Food can be imbued with notions of identity and this was particularly evident amongst Italian, Jewish and Muslim populations, albeit for different reasons. To the Italian population the importance of food was not related to religious doctrine but to specific ingredients, regional dishes and an Italian 'way of life'. The shops that developed to serve Italian households were also places where people congregated and enjoyed a sense of Italy. Moreover, from the early manufacture of ice-cream to the development of successful family businesses, food had enabled Italians in Scotland to support their families and even to become wealthy. For Jews the provision of *kosher* food was a religious requirement and appropriate regulatory bodies, bakers, dairies, and butcher shops were established as a priority. Concerns over the provision of *kosher* food led to negotiations with hospital authorities and the foundation of homes for elderly Jews and orphaned children. Similarly, for Muslims, *halal* food is a religious obligation and appropriate food outlets were established. In addition, the popularity of 'Indian' food has led to the establishment of numerous restaurants and takeaways.

In summary, aspects of national, cultural and religious identity were asserted by each of the immigrant populations, not just by religious or community 'leaders' but in the everyday lives of 'ordinary' people. Different aspects of identity were asserted in both the private and the public spheres, even where this might be thought to work to the disadvantage of the individuals concerned. In the longer term their descendants constituted part of the wider population into which other immigrants settled, but the process was that of integration rather than assimilation and this process is considered next.

The Process of Integration

Exclusionary practices were maintained well after the initial immigrants had settled in Glasgow, and were applied to their Scottish-born children. For example, some employers rejected applications for employment from those who indicated that they had attended a Catholic school, and membership of golf and tennis clubs was refused on grounds of religious, national or presumed 'racial' origins. These practices are now widely discredited or legally prohibited, but there is sufficient evidence to support the contention that a legacy remains. Today, all school handbooks are required to include a statement informing parents that certain forms of dress are not acceptable in school, including those which 'potentially encourage faction (such as football colours)' or 'could cause offence (such as anti-religious symbolism or political slogans)'.

To varying degrees, and in different ways, the physical and cultural environment was changed by the settlement of each new population. This was evident in the establishment of Catholic churches and schools, synagogues and mosques; in specialist crafts; in shops, cafes and restaurants; in Orange marches, political rallies and football rivalries; in legislation that attempted to control immigration and policies to assist immigrants.

Diasporic ties influenced the identity of immigrants and their descendants, and links are still maintained through familial, political, cultural and religious activities. At the same time some aspects of identity converged with those of the wider Scottish population. Despite attempts to preserve each 'mother tongue', English was given priority by the vast majority of immigrants. Increasing secularisation, particularly of the young, posed a problem for all religious groups, but attempts to encourage teenagers to engage in religiously or culturally based youth activities were undermined by the attraction of commercial activities.

While social mixing and 'marrying out' may dilute a specific identity, it is not necessarily eradicated and some cultural influences were reciprocal. Protestant parents may support Catholic education for their children, non-Jewish partners may be committed to 'Jewish continuity', and Scots who marry Italians may prefer pasta at the family table. Today, ecumenical and inter-faith work are important aspects of religious discourse in Glasgow. The Protestant tradition predominates but Catholics, Jews, Muslims and others have contributed to the religious discourse of the city.

The 'ethnic question' in the 1991 Census, albeit flawed, offered an opportunity to discern some characteristics of the current Pakistani population in Scotland. As with previous immigrants, there is evidence of poor housing conditions, overcrowding and higher rates of unemployment. This, together with a number of local studies, confirms that Pakistanis are victims of exclusionary practices, poverty and racism. There is evidence of low cost property ownership and self-employment involving working long hours in small businesses. But there is also evidence of business expansion, academic achievement, and entry into the professions. Thus, Pakistani immigrants are playing an active part in shaping their future (as was the case with previous immigrant populations). Aspects of this process were examined through qualitative research undertaken in Govanhill.

Combining Research Methods

There is increasing recognition amongst academics and political activists that a combination of research methods and material are required to understand issues as complex as racism and integration. In reconsidering thirty years of research relating to minority ethnic groups in Britain, the Policy Studies Institute acknowledged that different groups experience different degrees of disadvantage, and that both qualitative and quantitative research data are required to help explain the processes involved [Berthoud 1997: 146-7]. Others have asserted the importance of redressing the failure to link theoretical debates with substantive research [Solomos & Back 1996: 203]; and of developing anti-racist strategies that are informed by appropriate ethnic histories [Modood 1996: 96]. In accepting these arguments, this study incorporates historical comparison, analysis of quantitative data, and qualitative fieldwork.

Historical comparison of Irish, Italian, Jewish and Pakistani migration to Glasgow suggests some similarities in the assertion and acknowledgement of cultural and religious identity. With the arrival and settlement of each population, forms of multiculturalism were negotiated.

Analysis of quantitative data available through the Census 1991 Report for Scotland, allowed some broad conclusions to be drawn concerning the demographic and socio-economic characteristics of the current Pakistani population. However, this is not sufficient to understand the processes involved in the assertion and acknowledgement of identity. Quantitative data do not explain themselves. For example, the apparent over-representation of Pakistanis in the higher social classes based on occupation might be considered a triumph for anti-discriminatory legislation. But, when considered in conjunction with information from other tables, this is more convincingly attributed to the opportunities created through the business activities of members of the Pakistani population themselves. However, this is still not a satisfactory explanation. It does not, for example, explain how or why relatively impoverished immigrants established their businesses.

From the 1991 Census material it was also possible to speculate that a number of issues of concern to previous migrant groups, such as education, employment and marriage, were likely to be of importance to the relatively young Pakistani population. But such broad assumptions about an aggregate population provide very little information about the priorities of individuals *within* minority ethnic groups, and they tell us nothing about the ways in which cultural and religious identities are asserted and acknowledged in everyday life. Understanding such issues requires qualitative research.

Religious Identity

In this study a distinction is made between cultural and religious aspects of identity for a number of reasons. As with Christianity and Judaism, Islam is a 'world religion' and is not restricted to a particular geographical area. This offers the potential for differences to arise between the views of Muslims born in one country and their Muslim descendants born in another.[27] The source of such differences becomes clearer if cultural and religious factors are considered separately. In addition, the diasporic ties resulting from attachment to a country of origin may be quite different from those deriving from a shared religion. Thus, Catholic children may have something in common, but Italian and Irish children may not. Meanwhile, the significance ascribed by others to religious affiliation or ethnic identity can also vary. An Italian cafe might be a popular venue for someone who 'hates Catholics', while belief in equal opportunities for Asians might be accompanied by negative stereotyping of Muslims.

There is a tendency for social policy guidelines to omit religious terminology in relation to public service provision. This may imply that, with the obvious exception of denominational schools, services do not cater for the needs of specific religious groups. Therefore, in focusing on the local case studies in Govanhill, consideration was given to the ways in which religious identity was acknowledged in practice. Was there discrimination against practising Muslims because religious obligations could not be fulfilled? Were religious requirements catered for within a 'multicultural' environment? Or was there, in effect, separate provision on the grounds of religion, albeit couched in the language of multiculturalism e.g. a 'multicultural' group with an all Muslim membership?

It has already been noted that some theorists suggest Islam is impervious to secularisation. This argument has also been asserted through empirical work in which respondents were asked about their Muslim identity:

> ... it is because so much in the young people's lives is open to question, including many aspects of other sources of identity, that the certainties contained within Islam hold so much appeal. And thus Islam in Britain seems, for the time being at least, to be resisting the secularising trends that are manifest in wider society. [Jacobson 1998: 154]

But if individuals are asked questions about their identity *as Muslims*, it may be that their responses are skewed towards the ideal rather than the daily reality. Focusing attention towards situations which are not especially 'religious' can be a more realistic way of detecting whether secularising trends exist.

To gauge whether Muslim sensitivities are asserted or acknowledged it is important to have some understanding of the basic tenets of Islam [Esposito 1991, Schimmel 1992, Lewis 1994].

---

[27] It will be shown later that some younger respondents were keen to stress the difference between tenets of Islam and some aspects of their parents Pakistani culture.

Some Key Aspects of Islam

Wherever they live in the world, practising Muslims aspire to follow the Five Pillars of Islam:

The profession of faith. Muslims profess that there is only one God and Mohammed is His Prophet.
Prayer. The number of obligatory prayers is not specified in the *Qur'an* but five times a day is customary: an hour before sunrise, at noon, in the afternoon, after sunset and at night. Muslims may not always be able to follow this timetable in a non-Muslim society but attempts will be made to undertake Friday prayer which is a duty.
Alms giving. Charitable giving is an obligation for Muslims, with a requirement that the money be used 'in the way of God'.
Fasting during Ramadan. During *Ramadan,* the ninth month of the Islamic lunar year, Muslims are not permitted to eat or drink from dawn to dusk.[28] Travellers, pregnant and nursing women, the elderly and the sick are not required to keep the fast and may make up lost days at another time or make recompense through actions such as feeding the poor.
Pilgrimage to Mecca. All Muslims are encouraged to go on a Pilgrimage to Mecca at least once in their lifetime, but this should only be performed when the pilgrim is in good health and can participate without incurring debt.

The two most important Islamic celebrations are *Eid-ul-Adha* which marks the end of the Pilgrimage to Mecca and occurs in the 10th day of the 12th month of the Islamic calendar, and *Eid-ul-Fitr* which is celebrated at the end of *Ramadan. Eid* celebrations constitute family and social occasions as well as religious festivals.

The Muslim Holy Book is the *Qur'an* and pious Muslims believe that it is the unadulterated word of God. As such the *Qur'an* cannot be translated and its recitation in Arabic is considered to be an edifying experience. The majority of children, whatever their first language, are sent at an early age to recite the *Qur'an* in Arabic, and a *hafiz,* who can recite the *Qur'an* by heart, is highly respected.

Additional guidance comes from the *hadith* (the words and actions of Mohammed as told and retold from generation to generation), and the *ulama* (scholars of the law) are able to exert considerable influence. To some

---

[28] Because of its adherence to the lunar calendar, the season in which *Ramadan* falls gradually changes and fasting can require considerable commitment. During a Scottish summer the long hours of daylight can entail not eating or drinking from the early hours of the morning until late in the evening.

extent the *hadith* reflect the different currents which developed within Islam and some schools reject their authenticity. A *fatwa* is a legal opinion sought by Muslims on a wide range of issues, from simple queries about prayers and fasting to more complex concerns such as divorce and inheritance. Alcohol and pork are forbidden (*haram*) to Muslims, and permitted (*halal*) animal products must come from an animal that has been slaughtered according to religious rites.

Mosques play a key role in a Muslim community. Large mosques often accommodate children's religious instruction, language classes, a library and other community facilities. In a non-Muslim country it is not customary to hear the call to prayer and so literature produced by the mosque committee may include timetables for prayer and fasting times during *Ramadan*, as well as information about the contents of available food to distinguish between *halal* and *haram* components. Marriages are conducted by the *imam* (religious leader) although in Britain an additional civil ceremony is required (which is not the case for Christian or Jewish marriages). Major mosques also provide funeral facilities to enable burials to take place as soon as possible after death as is prescribed by Islam. As well as a large central mosque, Muslim populations are usually served by numerous small mosques which serve specific sects or regions of origin and enable children to attend lessons closer to home.

Local Services and the Acknowledgement of Cultural Identity

There are a number of concerns about the impact of emphasising cultural differences between minority ethnic groups and the wider population in service provision. It may be thought to undermine the universal principles once enshrined in a vision of the Welfare State. And there is an ever present danger of essentialism: the implication that there are distinct cultures, made up of bounded, unchanging beliefs and patterns of behaviour to which specific populations adhere. Such representations of culture in the provision of local services may be used to 'blame the victim' for lack of participation: 'They don't like mixing with us' or 'They take care of each other'. In addition, provision for minority cultures may oblige service users to publicly adhere to patterns of behaviour that they might prefer to limit to the private sphere, or even neglect altogether. For example, neglecting prayer is more noticeable where facilities have been especially provided and are not used.

On the other hand, there are problems inherent in ignoring cultural differences in the provision of services. Where cultural or religious requirements are not recognised, there is a very real possibility of indirect discrimination. Services that are optimistically described as 'open to all' may present barriers to members of minority ethnic groups. Thus, a lunch club, however friendly the atmosphere, would effectively exclude practising Jews and Muslims if consideration was not given to the menu. An important aim of the fieldwork was to detect the ways in which different aspects of identity were asserted and acknowledged in different situations, and how the repercussions of asserting identity were evaluated by the actors involved.

The Case Studies

Service providers who wish to acknowledge cultural and religious identity face the challenge of acknowledging specific requirements where appropriate, yet not conceiving of members of minority ethnic groups as purveyors of fixed cultures.

It will be shown that national and local government guidelines establish a framework within which multicultural services are possible, or encouraged, rather than prescribed. In interpreting and implementing these policy guidelines local services may adopt a range of approaches which fall broadly into three categories: positive action to attract and cater for the needs of users from minority ethnic groups; a less proactive stance while making concessions as specific needs are identified; or an 'open door' policy, suggesting that the service is 'available to all' without taking specific measures to accommodate minority cultural or religious requirements.[29] In the following chapters, these approaches are examined through specific case studies.

A number of criteria were used in selecting the general policy areas within which specific case studies were examined. It was important that the issue had been of concern to previous immigrants, and was relevant to the present Pakistani population, to enable some historical comparison. Areas were chosen in which concerns raised by individual respondents were likely to be of personal significance, but broad enough to have social policy implications. And, to assess the significance of religious and cultural identity in everyday activities, services were chosen which were not specifically 'religious' or 'cultural', but where aspects of cultural and religious identity were likely to be relevant (e.g. a lunch club rather than a prayer group or Urdu class).

---

[29] A hostile, exclusionary approach would not be permitted in public service provision although it would be naive to presume that this does not occur. Such an approach is more likely to be evident in private clubs or commercial organisations. However, it can be argued that the 'open door' approach to public services may permit such attitudes to exist and even flourish.

Education was an important issue for both Catholic and Jewish immigrants who had concerns that attendance at local authority schools would undermine the religious identity of their children. Analysis of the 1991 Census data indicated that nearly 65% of all the Pakistani/Indian households in Govanhill had dependent children, and over a quarter of local school children were Pakistani. The first case study, therefore, focused on the policies and procedures of local schools to examine the ways in which Pakistani children were accommodated within the education system.

Members of previous immigrant populations were, at least initially, apprehensive about their children being 'corrupted' by the new society in which they lived. Outside of formal education, the movements of young people were restricted and attempts were made to set up activities that would enable them to meet the 'right' friends. The 1991 Census data indicated that the Pakistani population is a young population and so it is likely that such concerns will also be pertinent to them. The second case study considered the ways in which the local youth project accommodated the needs of young people from the Pakistani population.

The majority of immigrants who settled in Glasgow in the nineteenth and early twentieth century established welfare organisations to care for the sick, frail and needy of their communities. After the Second World War, with the expansion of the Welfare State, a range of statutory services were developed to meet the welfare needs of the population of Britain 'from the cradle to the grave'. While charitable organisations continued to exist, their role tended to be regarded as peripheral. The political climate changed dramatically in the 1980s when the Conservative Government began its crusade to 'roll back the state' and the voluntary sector was encouraged to assume greater responsibility for welfare services. 'Care in the Community' was promoted and within this context services for the elderly were expanded in Govanhill. The third case study considered the ways in which the needs of elderly people from the Pakistani population were accommodated.

The Fieldwork Interviews

To gauge the importance to members of the Pakistani population of cultural and religious sensitivity in service provision, a series of detailed interviews were conducted with males and females from three age-bands: 14-24 years, 25-50 years, and 50+. These age-bands broadly coincided with three life stages: young and single; probably married with school-age children; and, elderly.[30] Respondents were selected according to a number of criteria: that they or their parents were of Pakistani origin; that they were actual or potential service users in Govanhill; and that they fell into the appropriate gender and age-bands. The aim was to gain the opinions of the 'man or woman in the street' rather than 'community leaders'.

Each topic was considered through a series of open ended questions to allow respondents to express their own opinions first, followed by multiple choice tick charts to test the importance they attributed to specific factors included in official policy guidelines.

The tick charts in each section of the interview schedule were compiled to detect the relative importance of 'mainstream', 'multicultural', 'culturally specific' and 'religiously specific' policy approaches. These approaches are outlined below, although it should be noted that they were used solely to assist analysis of the data and were not used during the interviews:

Mainstream. This term is often used to refer to standard services which are said to be available to all. In relation to the interview schedule the term 'mainstream' applies to those aspects of a service that are not specifically related to minority ethnic cultures or notions of multiculturalism.

Multicultural. This term is used to apply to those aspects of a service that suggest recognition of a number of different cultures.

Culturally specific. Because the research is focused on the priorities of Govanhill's Pakistani population, this term is used to refer to aspects of Pakistani culture.

Religiously specific. Again, because the research is focused in the priorities of Govanhill's Pakistani population, this term is used to refer to specific requirements of Islam.

The terms are not precise, and some points fell into more than one category. But when considered in conjunction with each other, and with the responses to the open ended questions, a picture of the preferred style of service did emerge.

As actual or potential service users, members of the Pakistani population have four main options: they may accept provision that makes no concessions to specific religious or cultural requirements; they may negotiate with services over some aspects of their religious or cultural identity; they may seek to establish separate provision appropriate to their needs; or they may reject provision altogether. The interview schedule was developed to test the importance placed on each of these options.

---

[30] It has already been noted that members of the Pakistani population tend to regard themselves, and to be regarded, as 'elderly' well before British retirement age.

The material is discussed in the following chapters. Each chapter begins with an overview of policies relating to service provision before examining a specific case study. This is followed by consideration of the interview material. A range of tables are presented and analysed in conjunction with quotations from the respondents themselves. The quotations are important because they vividly illustrate the language used, the priorities of individual respondents, and the ways in which different aspects of identity are asserted in different circumstances. It is not suggested that the respondents constitute a representative sample of the Pakistani population of Scotland. Nevertheless, their views and experiences are authentic and, combined with other sources of material, contribute to a broader understanding of the Scottish context which is frequently ignored in 'British' research.

7 School-age Education: a Pragmatic Approach

From the 1870s onwards some form of interaction between the education authorities and immigrants was inevitable because both had a legal obligation to ensure that children received school-age education. Through this interaction, different forms of accommodation were negotiated: the incorporation of separate denominational schools into the local authority education system; the establishment of religious education and language classes outside of the normal school day; and concessions within mainstream schooling such as allowing Jewish children to leave school early on Fridays in acknowledgement of the Jewish Sabbath. In this chapter the provision of school-age education to the Pakistani population is considered through an examination of the policy framework in Scotland and Glasgow within which education is provided to pupils from minority ethnic groups; the interpretation of these policies by schools in Govanhill; and the educational priorities of Pakistani immigrants and their descendants as identified through the fieldwork interviews in Govanhill. Finally, some conclusions are drawn concerning the interaction between the providers of school-age education and the Pakistani population as service users.

School-age Education in Scotland

In Scotland, parents or guardians are legally responsible for ensuring that their school-age children receive 'efficient education'. This duty is usually fulfilled by sending children to public schools which are comprehensive, co-educational and provided free of charge by education authorities [SOED 1995a].[31] School places are usually offered on the basis of designated catchment areas, and most children who attend public schools go to the one in whose catchment area they live. However, the Education (Scotland) Act 1980 does allow parents to submit 'placing requests' asking that their child attend a different school, and the education authority has a duty to grant the

---

[31] In Scotland the term 'public' refers to local authority schools, unlike in England where a 'public school' is, in effect, 'private'. In 1994, only 4% of the school population in Scotland attended fee paying schools [SOED 1995a: 1].

request unless there are legal reasons why it should not - usually when the school is full.

The School Boards (Scotland) Act 1988 gives every public school in Scotland the opportunity to form a School Board consisting of elected parent and staff members and members co-opted from the local community. The Scottish Office asserts that one of the most important duties of a School Board is to maintain contact with parents, but they also have a legal role in selecting Head Teachers, Deputy Head Teachers and Assistant Head Teachers, and may also be included in the selection panels for other teaching staff. During the early 1990s the Government issued further guidelines for the introduction of Devolved School Management through which education authorities retain a 'strategic, enabling and supportive role' while the day-to-day financial and managerial decisions may be taken by Head Teachers in consultation with their School Board [SOED 1993]. Thus a framework exists for local parents, through membership of the School Board, to assert some influence over the management and ethos of the school.

Also in 1988, the government launched its *5-14 Curriculum Development Programme* through which the school curriculum was divided into five broad areas: language, mathematics, environmental studies, expressive arts, and religious and moral education [SOED 1992a, 1995a]. The assertion and negotiation of religious identity is an important aspect of this study, and so consideration is given here to the arrangements for religious education.

National Curriculum guidelines state that no programme of work in religious education would be considered satisfactory if it did not contain elements of three 'attainment outcomes': Christianity, Other World Religions and Personal Search [SOED 1994]. The emphasis placed on each of the outcomes 'depends on the circumstances of the school, taking into account the religious background of the pupils and their families and the general educational principle of tolerance and respect for others' [SOED 1992]. The curriculum guidelines oscillate between emphasising that 'Christianity has shaped the history and traditions of Scotland and continues to exert an influence on national life', and acknowledging 'the many different beliefs and attitudes found in today's pluralistic Scotland'. Teachers are reminded of the importance of recognising Scotland's 'culturally diverse' society and this point is made in such a way as to challenge oversimplified arguments that the National Curriculum necessarily undermines multiculturalism:

> In dealing with world religions, Religious and Moral Education must be free from racial, cultural or religious bias and cater for the needs of all pupils, regardless of their background, gender or

culture. The school curriculum which values European culture must also value non-European cultures and their contribution to human knowledge and development. It is all too possible to teach about a world religion other than Christianity in a way that places it on the periphery of an individual child's experience or marginalises particular pupils, by focusing on the exotic or unusual. [Ibid: 52]

At the same time the guidelines acknowledge that in denominational schools the 'appropriate religious authorities' will have the final say:

> In Scotland, provision is made for publicly funded schools that are denominational; they are an integral part of the education system and they provide for particular religious communities. The religious education curriculum in these schools is determined by the appropriate religious authorities. [Ibid: x]

Formal lessons are not the only aspect of Religious and Moral Education covered in the guidelines. Schools are reminded that religious observance is a statutory requirement under the Education (Scotland) Act 1980, although parents do have the legal right to withdraw their children if they wish. The guidelines assert that in non-denominational schools religious observance, usually a morning assembly, should be 'of a broadly Christian character' without excluding the possibility of 'drawing on other religious traditions at times'. A further aspect of religious education is the appointment, in the majority of schools in Scotland, of a school chaplain. In denominational schools, they are appointed by the religious authorities and in non-denominational schools they may be invited by the Head Teacher with their appointment endorsed by the education authority. Once more the guidelines offer a degree of flexibility by pointing out that not all school chaplains are required to be Christian and some schools 'will wish to develop, a multi-faith chaplaincy service'.

The acknowledgement of religious and cultural identity in schools is underpinned by the Race Relations Act 1976 which, while not giving 'religious groups' direct recourse to the law, does set a framework within which education authorities have a general duty to provide all their services without unlawful direct or indirect discrimination. Thus:

> Uniform and dress regulations that result in the rejection of a pupil who cannot comply with them for cultural or religious reasons are generally indirectly discriminatory ... This would be unlawful, unless it could be justified on objective grounds. S.1(1)(b) & 17 [CRE 1991: 17]

> The placement of English as a Second Language (ESL) pupils in separate language classes for extended periods, or denying them access to mainstream curriculum opportunities, may be discriminatory, depending on the circumstances. S.17(c)(i) [CRE 1991: 25]

Also under the Race Relations Act 1976, no application for a minority faith school should be given less favourable treatment than any other application [CRE 1990: 22]. In Scotland, where publicly funded denominational schools form part of the education system, it would be difficult to reject a viable application for a separate Muslim school that could offer 'efficient education'.

Within this framework the Scottish Office has issued instructions for the collection of 'ethnically-based statistics' on school pupils as a means of 'identifying need and thus helping ensure fair and equal treatment for all' [SED 1989: 1]. The specified minimum requirement is the annual collection of information on all first year entrants to primary schools, and all pupils in secondary schools, concerning ethnic background, religion, and languages used at home, in order to:

> ... respond to the pupil's educational and pastoral needs ... be aware of their religious beliefs and the implications these may have for the curriculum, for the provision of school meals, and for the observance of religious festivals ... calculate what provision is needed for those for whom English is not their main language; what the likely demand for community language teaching might be; and how best to deploy available staff and materials [Ibid: 3]

Thus, a policy framework exists within which some specific religious and cultural requirements are acknowledged; where parents can exercise a degree of choice; and where some parental involvement in the day-to-day management of schools is permitted, even encouraged. The way in which this operates in practice, however, requires consideration of specific education authorities and, more importantly, the opinions and actions of service providers and their clients.

Multicultural and Anti-racist Education in Glasgow

Discourse concerning the educational needs of minority ethnic groups in Glasgow has been shaped by the legacy of the 1918 Education (Scotland) Act. It is unofficially acknowledged that many local councillors feel 'stuck' over the issue of publicly funded Catholic schools and this has contributed to the development of multicultural and anti-racist policies as a strategy to minimise demand for additional minority religious schools.

> The local authority funds Catholic schools. It's not ideal but we have to put up with it. In theory any religious denomination can set up a school, run it, then ask the local authority to take it over, and appeal to the government if their application is rejected. But if there was a request for a separate Muslim school we would do everything we could to dissuade them. [Labour Councillor and Education Committee member]

> Most liberal minded people hate separate Catholic schools. Children are together when they are very young and are separated when they go to school. This feeds stereotypes. People who are aware of this are not keen to see it further substantiated by adding new communities to it. [Senior Community Relations Officer]

Reluctance to support the idea of separate Muslim schools also stemmed from a belief that Catholic schools were established under very different conditions from those of the late twentieth century:

> We have to remember that conditions are very, very different from those which prevailed when Catholic schools were set up. The discrimination and bigotry that existed against Catholic people, and the sheer numbers involved, were why Catholics had to have separate schools. That kind of discrimination, certainly in public life, the way the Council operates and the way the state operates, doesn't exist in my opinion as far as Muslim people are concerned. The discrimination that they suffer in terms of the community at large is greater, but in terms of education and so on I don't believe it to be so. So therefore I think we are not comparing like with like. [Convenor Racial Equality Working Group]

In Glasgow, early recognition of the needs of the children of South Asian immigrants focused on language classes. The Immigrant Reception and Language Centre was set up in 1970 to provide intensive courses in English and then return pupils to mainstream education. Ten years later the focus remained on teaching English, and Urban Aid funding was used to create a number of new posts. These included a home visiting team, two specialist psychologists, three peripatetic English as a Second Language (ESL) teachers, and four adult ESL teachers.

It was not until 1986 that a broader policy document, *Education in a Multicultural Society,* was produced by Strathclyde Regional Council. It was acknowledged that some local schools had already shown considerable commitment to the concept of multicultural education, particularly the celebration of a variety of festivals, and the development of topics concerned with religious and cultural differences. It was suggested that the needs of a multicultural society 'do not include the assimilation or elimination of minority cultures but instead conscious support for diversity'. It was argued that ESL teaching should continue, but specialised provision should be reviewed and extended to include bilingual approaches to learning, guidelines on dietary requirements and participation in physical education, and support to voluntary language schools run by minority ethnic communities. In line with local authority concern to minimise the demand for minority religious schools, a broad view was taken over the definition of 'language' schools:

> The local authority will accommodate anything that is reasonable within the law. Local authority money contributes towards *Qur'an* schools run by the UK Islamic Mission. This is funded as 'language and culture' rather than religion, but in Muslim society religion and culture shade into one another. [Labour Councillor and Education Committee Member]

The importance of challenging racism at school was formally acknowledged in 1990 when Strathclyde Regional Council produced a manual entitled *Tackling Racist Incidents within the Education Service* [SRC 1990: 7]. The manual was circulated for use in schools and contained guidelines on recognising racist incidents, what to do, and who was responsible for taking action. Areas covered included physical assault, derogatory name calling, insults, racist jokes, graffiti, wearing racist badges or insignia, bringing racist materials to school, verbal abuse, racist comments, attempts to recruit to racist organisations, ridicule of cultural differences, refusal to co-operate with others because of their colour, ethnicity or language, and written derogatory remarks.

Thus, in Glasgow during the 1990s, there was formal commitment to multicultural and anti-racist education, reinforced by political concerns to minimise demand for additional denominational schools. Within this context, responsibility for implementing multicultural and anti-racist education was delegated to local schools.

Schools in Govanhill

The approach taken by different schools can be considered through an examination of the school handbooks which are issued to parents to inform them of school procedures. The 1996 handbooks of five primary schools and two secondary schools serving Govanhill are considered here.

All schools are required by the Scottish Office to inform parents of certain national and educational authority policies, but there is also an opportunity for individual schools to signal a more specific ethos. The degree of variation suggests that Head Teachers and School Boards have a degree of autonomy over the ethos of individual schools and the way in which this is signalled to the local population.

School Aims/Mission Statement

The education authority's mission statement included a commitment 'to promote equal opportunity and social justice' and this was included as a minimum requirement in all handbooks. But individual schools were able to make additional comments when describing their general aims. Catholic schools made it clear that their general ethos was rooted in the Catholic Church, but there were differences of emphasis. In Govanhill one Catholic primary school made specific reference to developing in pupils 'a caring attitude which will reflect the cultural diversity of our area' and 'fostering respect, tolerance and understanding of other faiths and cultures'. Each of the non-denominational schools made reference to a variety of cultures and faiths when referring to the aims of the school, but one included very clear multicultural signals:

> Children from many faiths attend our school and the ethos of our school is such that we encourage the children to understand and to tolerate the beliefs of others. We also encourage our bi-lingual pupils to develop their mother tongue which will be respected by all staff, pupils and visitors to our school.

This was the only handbook with a 'welcome' statement written in several languages including Punjabi, Urdu and Arabic.

Religious Education and Observance

Under Section 9 of the Education (Scotland) Act 1980, parents have the right to withdraw their children from Religious Education and Observance whether a school is denominational or non-denominational and this was indicated in all the school handbooks. However, each of the Catholic schools included a reminder that they were established to provide Catholic education for their pupils. For example:

> Parents who elect to send their child to this school are expected to accept the religious tradition and ethos of the school and their children should therefore attend all religious instruction and observance.

The Catholic secondary school handbook referred to the 'normal' practice of beginning classes with a short prayer and encouraging pupils to take part in daily mass. Meanwhile the non-denominational schools tended to focus on the importance of understanding and respecting a range of faiths:

> Our aims will be to teach the children about Christianity and other World Religions and to foster positive attitudes of open enquiry and attitudes of awareness of prejudice towards the beliefs and cultures of different religions.

> As well as learning about different religions it is important that children learn to value and respect all religions equally, irrespective of their own beliefs.

Two non-denominational primary schools indicated that religious observance took the form of celebrating all of the main religious festivals including Eid, Christmas, Hanukkah (Jewish festival of light) and Divali (Hindu and Sikh festival of light). The non-denominational secondary school indicated that the school chaplain conducted services at Christmas and Easter 'but alternative facilities are available for the many pupils of other faiths who may not wish to attend'.

Equal Opportunities

At one non-denominational primary school the importance of equal opportunities was described in relation to religion, 'race', ethnicity, gender, social background and special needs. The policy included an acknowledgement of 'the positive nature of bilingualism' and the importance of tackling racist incidents. In a similar vein, the non-denominational secondary school asserted pride in its status 'as a leading Scottish multicultural school'. This school handbook was the only one that included direct reference to the Race Relations Act 1976 and to the education authority document *Tacking Racist Incidents Within the Education System*. It was asserted that 'the adoption of a multicultural and antiracist approach should be seen as one part of the continuing attempt to improve the quality of education'. It seems likely that some of these statements were prompted by events in 1992 when media reports of violence between White and Asian youths outside the school gates prompted public debate about the state of 'race relations' within the school [*Community Voice*, December 1992].

In contrast, at the Catholic secondary school, although one Assistant Head Teacher was listed as having responsibility for equal opportunities and multicultural education, the small section outlining the school's stance on equal opportunities made no mention of multiculturalism or anti-racism, but concentrated on the fact that 'the school curriculum is reviewed regularly to ensure that it offers equal opportunities to boys and girls'.

Authorised Absence

The required statements concerned with authorised absence from school included two important points with specific relevance to immigrants and their descendants, and to minority faith communities:

> Parents may request that their children be permitted to be absent from school to make an extended visit to relatives.
>
> Parents from ethnic minority religious communities may request that their children be permitted to be absent from school in order to celebrate recognised religious events.

Beyond this, only two non-denominational primary schools made additional comments. One indicated that 'it would be helpful if parents inform the school if the child is going to be absent from school for some time e.g. if she/he is going to Pakistan on holiday'. The other included additional notes reflecting the school's role in accommodating children from a wide range of backgrounds:

> 1] A number of our pupils go on extended visits to their families abroad and are marked absent during their time abroad.
> 2] Our Iranian pupils only attend our school for part of each week. As they are marked absent for the remainder of the week, our absent rate increases weekly by a considerable amount.

Staff

The composition of staff teams varied considerably. There were no teaching staff of Pakistani origin at any of the Catholic schools serving Govanhill.[32]

---

[32] It might be argued that this is because of an obvious preference for teachers of the Roman Catholic faith, but this cannot be a complete explanation since Catholic schools frequently employ non-Catholic staff in subjects other than religious education.

However, one Catholic primary school did have an English as a Second Language teacher, indicating that this school was responding to some of the needs of the significant Pakistani population living in the catchment area. Meanwhile, the non-denominational schools had both bilingual teachers and language support staff, and two also had bilingual Home Link Assistants who took positive action in encouraging contact between the school and minority ethnic groups.

School Boards

Of the seven school boards, only one non-denominational primary school had parent members of Pakistani origin. However, at the non-denominational secondary school, two staff members and one co-optee, although not parent members, were of Pakistani origin. There are often difficulties in recruiting parents who wish to accept responsibility for the management of schools, but it would appear that both of these schools had taken positive action to ensure some representation of minority ethnic groups on the School Board.

School Uniform

Schools were permitted to encourage the wearing of school uniform, but were obliged to inform parents that pupils should not be denied education as a result of not wearing uniform. Furthermore, Scottish Office guidelines indicate that 'account must be taken in any proposals to prevent any direct or indirect discrimination on the grounds of race or gender'. Each of the Catholic schools included the obligatory statements concerning dress codes, but beyond this there were no signals that the uniform had been adapted to accommodate specific cultural needs.[33] In contrast, the non-denominational schools all made it clear that trousers or jogging bottoms could be worn by girls, thus signalling that it is possible for them to cover their legs. Only one primary school included *shalwar kamiz* as part of the uniform.

Meals

Each of the schools operated a cafeteria meals service, as well as allowing pupils to take their own packed lunches or to go home for lunch. Thus it was possible for pupils to eat *halal* food without additional arrangements.

---

[33] However, observations made through working with local families and schools suggested that there were no problems for female pupils who wished to wear trousers to cover their legs.

However, some schools indicated more specific recognition of dietary requirements. One Catholic primary school specified that vegetarian meals were available, and all three non-denominational primary schools made reference to the availability of vegetarian and *halal* meals.

The Curriculum

Much of the curriculum information in school handbooks referred to the subject content and the skills developed at various stages. However, some schools did include references to the specific needs of minority ethnic groups. One non-denominational primary school informed parents that 'boys and girls are taught separately for swimming'. Another indicated that 'we try to draw on the cultural heritage of all our pupils to make learning more relevant and interesting, including a tabla (Indian drums) instructor, and Indian dance'. The non-denominational secondary school was the only school to teach Urdu as a subject, and pupils were able to study GCSE and 'A' level Urdu.[34]

But the curriculum issue that concerned many parents and pupils, irrespective of ethnic origin, was that of examination results. It is a Scottish Office requirement that examination results be printed in school handbooks.[35] Those for the Catholic secondary school were notably 'better' than those for the non-denominational school, and for Scotland as a whole. This was a key reason why the school was regarded locally as a 'good' school and had no difficulty in attracting pupils.

> Observing festivals and so on cuts little ice compared with achieving academic results. Parents may be pleased if their religion is accommodated, but this would not deter them from sending their child to a school where they felt the academic education was better. [Labour Councillor and Education Committee Member]

It will be shown later that this observation was supported by the comments of some fieldwork respondents. The words 'as an individual' are significant. This councillor suggested that in talking to people as 'representatives' of a Muslim population they might feel an obligation to assert a specifically Muslim perspective. But as individual parents, they

---

[34] It is interesting to note that these are not Scottish examinations. Pupils normally take Standard Grades and Highers at Scottish schools, while GCSEs and 'A' levels are associated with schools in England and Wales.

[35] Teachers express concern about what are effectively academic league tables. It is argued that lists of results do not give an indication of the progress made by individual pupils of a range of abilities.

were as likely as anyone else to turn to the back of a handbook to check the qualifications gained by pupils at the school.

All of the primary schools in Govanhill were operating below capacity and this does seem to have played a part in shaping a multicultural ethos at those schools competing for pupils in sectors with the largest concentration of Pakistani residents. The non-denominational primary school that signalled greatest sensitivity to cultural and religious requirements was popular, and had the healthiest school roll of the non-denominational schools. But choice of primary school was also influenced by strategic decisions concerning future secondary school education. Parents, irrespective of ethnicity, were aware that children who attended local Catholic primary schools were eligible to attend the prestigious local Catholic secondary school. Consequently, the most popular local primary school was a Catholic school that signalled some recognition of the needs of minority ethnic groups.

To assess how much importance members of the Pakistani population placed on cultural and religious sensitivity in a school setting, the fieldwork interviews are considered next.

The Priorities of Pakistani Immigrants and Their Descendants

Denominational Schools

When the table of points considered 'very important' for a 'good' education was sorted, the three least important points were whether the school was Muslim, non-denominational or Catholic. Elderly respondents were much more likely to see a Muslim school as 'very important' although it will be shown later that this appeared to be more of a commitment to the idea that Muslim schools should be available for those who want them, than a desire to send their own children to such schools. Other aspects of education were given greater priority by all age-groups. Even when responding to later questions about reading the *Qur'an*, a separate Muslim school was the least favoured location. The arguments against a separate school reflected a number of issues which are considered below. The most common response highlighted a commitment to the idea that children should 'mix' and learn to respect each other's beliefs.

> If we segregate ourselves then we won't be mixing with other people and that's the main way to stop racism, by mixing with people. At my school I had friends that were Christian and I learned a bit about

> their religion and they learned a bit about my religion. [Female, aged 19]

> You talk about a school that is just Muslim, right, no Christian people, not Jewish, that causes racism. You should be all together. You should learn each other's religion, right. [Male, aged 33]

These quotations also illustrate that there was a clear connection in the minds of some respondents between religious intolerance and racism (i.e. that racism was not seen simply as deriving from perceived phenotypical differences). Other respondents felt that to ask for a separate school was expecting too much in a non-Muslim country.

> It's just that I feel living in this country you can't ask for too much. D'you know what I mean? [Female, aged 26]

> I think of, like, when in Rome do as the Romans do, you know. I mean it's OK for Pakistan, you can do those things, right, that's fine. But here you should get along with one another. [Female, aged 33]

A major concern was whether a Muslim school would be able to provide as good an academic education as the existing schools. This lack of confidence over the viability of a separate Muslim school appeared to stem from a previous unsuccessful venture:

> There was an Islamic School opening up so I spent a good four years there. It was the Central Mosque that had organised it. Originally they said everything would be the same as the normal state schools with obviously the addition of Islamic Studies in it, but I just think it was the lack of resources. Although we were paying them, it was a fee paying school, it just never took off. It wasted our years really. The education was really minimal - English, Arithmetic, a bit of Urdu and a bit of Islamic studies. I mean, no offence, they are teaching the right things regarding Islam and all that but it has put me off. [Female, aged 29]

> I don't know if you remember once there was a Muslim school and it didn't really do well. At the end it closed down. People remember that school and that it had to close down. [Female, aged 50]

These views contrast with the more positive attitude to the existing educational system.

> I still believe that this country is one of the best countries in the world for education. [Male, aged 28]

> I personally wouldn't go for a separate school because they wouldn't have the facilities that my child had in school. Maybe after twenty years, if they are financed by the local government or countries like Saudi Arabia or Libya who are friendly to Britain, to supply the finance and have a Muslim school with all the facilities, apparatus, everything from the computers to whatever, then it would work. But at this stage I don't think so. [Male, aged 68]

Young people were concerned that a Muslim school would involve single sex education.

> I don't think a Muslim school is a good idea because then you start to talk about single sex schools as well and I don't agree with it. [Female, aged 19]

There were also concerns about the overall ethos of the school:

> It would be really strict. I mean I just went to that mosque for one and a half hours, Monday to Thursday, and sometimes I found it really scary. If you got things wrong they would hit your hand, you know. So if that was school! Nine 'til four! [laughs]. [Male, aged 20]

> I think some schools can go over to the extreme. I don't believe in that. They twist the *Qur'an* round and make it very, very strict but it isn't very strict at all. [Female, aged 38]

Arguments in favour of a Muslim school were less emphatic, and were concerned with notions of equality.

> A Muslim school is a possibility. The Jewish people have them so why don't we? [Male, 59 years]

A small minority of respondents felt that religion should be kept out of schools altogether.

> I was brought up Muslim you know but I don't agree with any faiths being taught because of all the quarrels there are because of it around the world. And not just around the world, but round here as well. [Male, aged 29]

Table 7.1 Govanhill Sample: Which of the Following Points are 'Very Important' for a 'Good' Education?

	14-24		25-50		50+		Total
	f	m	f	m	f	m	
Total respondents	10	10	11	11	10	10	62
School has anti-racist policy	10	8	10	10	10	9	57
Equal opportunities boys/girls	10	7	10	10	10	8	55
Parents kept informed	8	6	10	10	10	10	54
Halal food is available	7	7	8	9	10	9	50
Staff are friendly to parents	7	6	10	7	10	10	50
Exam results are good	4	8	9	8	10	9	48
Firm discipline	7	6	8	6	10	10	47
Prayer facilities are available	7	6	5	6	10	7	41
Different religions/cultures	6	3	7	8	10	7	41
Wide range of abilities	6	6	8	9	5	7	41
School does not charge fees	7	3	2	7	7	7	33
There is a school uniform	3	3	6	3	10	6	31
There are Muslim staff	2	2	4	1	10	7	26
Girls can wear *shalwar kamiz*	4	4	1	4	5	7	25
Social events for parents	1	0	5	5	7	6	24
Translation into Urdu	3	3	5	2	8	2	23
Some staff speak Urdu	1	2	5	0	9	6	23
School is close to home	0	0	4	3	8	7	22
Translation into Punjabi	3	3	4	2	7	1	20
Some staff speak Punjabi	1	2	5	0	7	4	19
School is 'single sex'	1	1	1	0	8	7	18
The school is a Muslim school	0	1	1	0	7	6	15
Not a religious school	2	1	2	1	1	1	8
The school is a Catholic school	0	0	0	0	0	1	1

Before moving on from the issue of denominational schools, it is interesting to note that, despite the popularity of local Catholic schools, 'the school is a Catholic school' was regarded as the least important point in the list. Insofar as Catholic schools were believed to take a firmer line in matters of discipline, and to stress the importance of 'moral values', it might be argued that some members of Govanhill's Pakistani population preferred Catholic schools by default.

> I think there's more discipline in the Catholic schools. So I think they are brought up more strict, similar to the Asians. [Male, aged 37]

> My youngest son went to a Catholic school. It was a good school. Catholics and Muslims are close in some ways. There must be some religion in education. [Male, aged 50]

It has already been noted that Catholic schools appeared to make fewer concessions to other cultures and faiths than non-denominational schools, but for some parents this was outweighed by the potential for academic achievement at the local Catholic secondary school.

> [The school] has got a good reputation for qualifications and people going on to do better things. There are more qualifications gained by school leavers leaving there than from other schools in this area, and that's what you want, isn't it? [Female, aged 30]

And there were signs that, despite the school's apparently low commitment to multiculturalism in comparison with other schools in the area, a pragmatic approach was adopted by both staff and pupils:

> They are religious. I mean we do have mass quite often. I don't find that necessary for me but it's a good school. I don't feel uncomfortable. Sometimes I've actually said to the teachers 'Can I go to the library instead of mass?' because I've got an assignment due the next period. They say 'No problem'. [Female, aged 15]

Religious Requirements

The interview schedule included questions about the importance of *halal* food, prayer facilities, Islamic studies, and Muslim staff. Irrespective of age or gender respondents gave high priority to the availability of *halal* food. Slightly less importance was placed on prayer facilities, and Muslim staff were only seen as 'very important' by older respondents. One man's comments encapsulated this hierarchy of views:

> *Halal* food is important for Muslims. I am very strict for that. I would restrict my children. They must eat *halal*. Sometimes prayer facilities are important for children. It would be good if this was available for all children. But I don't mind at all about Muslim staff. It doesn't matter if it is Christian, Jewish, Muslim, Sikh, Hindu - it is not important to me at all. [Male, aged 29]

For many older Muslims, observing dietary requirements was fundamental to daily life.

> I cannot take meat into my stomach if it is not *halal*. [Male, aged 56]

But, although there are clear restrictions in relation to meat and products containing animal fat, it should be noted that fish is *halal*, as is a vegetarian diet. Thus fish and chips (cooked in vegetable oil), a jacket potato with beans, or vegetarian pizza are all *halal*. The cafeteria style of school meals, the popularity of packed lunches, and the tendency of many young people to leave the school premises to go home or to buy their own lunch, enable Muslim and non-Muslim friends to eat together without making any specific reference to religious requirements. This may explain why respondents did not express any particular concerns about school catering arrangements.

Ideally, a Muslim prays five times a day at set times. But it was acknowledged that this may not always be possible, and a more pragmatic approach was taken. Some respondents were reluctant to demand facilities that may not be available to other faiths, particularly if alternative arrangements would suffice.

> I suppose it is quite important, but they can pray in the house. [Female, aged 19]

> If there was a place in the school I don't think I would have gone to pray. There are all sorts of reasons behind it I suppose. You want to be accepted in your peer group. It would be like 'What's she away to do?' you know. And even though I am a fairly religious person, I believe in the religion, but I don't really pray so often. You know it's probably during *Eid* or during *Ramadan* that I do it more so. [Female, aged 26]

> Well, we have our own facilities and Christians have Sunday schools, so it doesn't matter. [Male, aged 67]

Respondents in the younger age-bands placed very little importance on the presence of Muslim staff. Older respondents were much more likely to believe that Muslim staff were 'very important', but even they expressed very mixed opinions.

> It is very important to have Muslim staff because the children won't know which religion they believe. When they are married they cannot bring their children to the proper religion as we had done twenty years earlier. [Male, aged 68]

> Children should understand Easter and Passover, and Muslim staff could explain about Ramadan. [Male, aged 59]

If they can do the job they should get the job. It doesn't matter whether they are Muslim or not. [Male, aged 67]

Islamic studies were included in a list of possible curriculum subjects, and it was clear that the older the respondent the more likely they were to consider this to be 'very important'. But young people did not reject Islamic studies altogether, and were more likely to regard this as 'quite important' than 'not important'.

Table 7.2 Govanhill Sample: How Important is it to Teach Islamic Studies in School?

	14-24		25-49		50+		Total
	f	m	f	m	f	m	
Total respondents	10	10	11	11	10	10	62
Very important	2	2	4	5	9	6	28
Quite important	5	6	2	4	1	1	19
Not important	2	1	4	0	0	3	10
Don't know	1	1	1	2	0	0	5

But when asked to choose the two most important subjects, the majority of respondents prioritised other subjects, particularly English and mathematics.

Table 7.3 Govanhill Sample: Which are the Two Most Important School Subjects?

	14-24		25-49		50+		Total
	f	m	f	m	f	m	
Total respondents	10	10	11	11	10	10	62
(top 6 subjects chosen)							
English	9	9	10	9	9	5	51
Mathematics	6	8	6	7	5	5	37
Sciences	3	1	0	3	1	4	12
Islamic studies	0	1	2	1	4	1	9
Computers	1	1	1	2	1	2	8
Urdu	1	0	0	0	0	1	2

Of the factors included to gauge the importance of religiously specific concessions in school, the availability of *halal food* was rated as the most important, irrespective of age or gender. Prayer facilities were considered important by two thirds of respondents. But Muslim staff, Islamic studies, and a separate Muslim school, were not favoured by the majority of respondents and were particularly unpopular with the youngest age-band.

Cultural Requirements

A number of the younger respondents stressed that their older relatives confused Pakistani culture and 'Muslim' obligations. They also suggested, as is often asserted about expatriates irrespective of nationality, that the older generation had not kept pace with changes in their country of origin. To gauge the importance respondents placed on culturally specific factors, the interview schedule included questions concerning bilingual staff, translation of information into Urdu and Punjabi, and the right of young women to wear *shalwar kamiz* to school. The preference for a single sex school is often regarded as a cultural requirement and is also included in this section, although it should be noted that some young people raised this in relation to Muslim schools. Table 7.1 indicates that, after sorting, all of these points were placed in the bottom half of the table.

Table 7.4 Govanhill Sample: How Important is it to Teach Urdu (and English*) at School?

	14-24		25-49		50+		Total
	f	m	f	m	f	m	
Total respondents	10	10	11	11	10	10	62
Very important	3[9]	3[9]	4[11]	2[11]	9[10]	5[10]	26[60]
Quite important	5[1]	5[1]	5	9	1	2	27[2]
Not important	1	2	2	0	0	3	8
Don't know	1	0	0	0	0	0	1

* figures in brackets indicate response in relation to English as a school subject

Respondents considered bilingual staff and translated material as important for parents rather than children, with women more likely than men to regard them as 'very important'.

> It would be useful for parents because a lot of parents speak Punjabi.
> [Female, aged 15]

> That wouldn't be important to me because I speak English but there may be some parents who maybe can't read English so it would be important for them. [Female, aged 32]

Some older respondents were less sympathetic, taking pride in the fact that they were proficient in English and showing little concern for those who were not.

> Most of my generation are able to read and write English so translation isn't needed. [Female, aged 50]

> Urdu and Punjabi are not important in school. They should be speaking English. [Male, aged 59]

The assertion that most of the older Pakistani women in Govanhill could read and write English was inaccurate. The majority of older women had very little formal education and could not speak, read or write English fluently. Neither could many of them read or write fluently in any other language, so that written material translated into Urdu or Punjabi would not be helpful either. However, their own needs were not given priority when considering languages taught to their children. This was made clear, not only in relation to English, but by the fact that Urdu was given priority when almost all of the respondents spoke Punjabi.

> Punjabi is not important but Urdu is very important because it is the mother tongue of Pakistan. [Female, aged 50+][36]

> Punjabi is not important at school. It is not a book language. It is a language for the home. [Male, aged 56]

Despite the importance placed upon Urdu as a book language, when asked to choose the two most important school subjects, the vast majority of respondents felt English must take precedence. Choice of subjects was influenced by potential employment opportunities.

> I suppose I am trying to think what subjects are useful if you want to go on to do other things. In that sense I would say English is important. I can't separate them out in terms of what I think are valuable. I can only think of them in terms of future opportunities. [Female, aged 26]

---

[36] Some of the older women indicated that they did not know exactly how old they were since they were born in rural areas and had no birth certificate. Age was often calculated in relation to significant events such as the partition of India.

> It varies according to the demand of the market. When I came to this country, most of the Pakistanis liked to go into medicine. At the stage of my boys and girls going to the schools and university the market changed to the engineering side. Then it came that all the jobs were in computers. So I'll put the subjects for today's market. At this stage I think English and computers. [Male, aged 68]

Shalwar kamiz (essentially trousers and a tunic) are the most common style of dress worn by Pakistani women in Govanhill. For many women this provides an appropriate standard of modesty, but to describe *shalwar kamiz* as 'traditional' dress would be misleading. Styles vary considerably from year to year, and many young women are extremely fashion conscious. Those who do not meet fashion standards can be subjected to the same ridicule from their peer group as young people might be if they are not wearing the 'right' training shoes:

> We say TPish. In Pakistan there are bright things, really colourful things. Sometimes you see a girl with red socks and gold sandals, you say it's very TPish. We mean it's very, very typical of a girl to dress like that in the villages in Pakistan. I know we shouldn't say it, but we do, our generation [giggles]. [Female, aged 24]

Respondents of all ages had mixed opinions about whether schools should incorporate *shalwar kamiz* into their dress codes. Those who felt it was 'not important' were more outspoken:

> As long as girls cover their body it is not important that *shalwar kamiz* is worn. A lot of people do that when they come from Pakistan. They are adamant that their daughter should wear *shalwar kamiz* to school because they did in Pakistan. They don't realise it is completely different. *Shalwar kamiz* is not Scotland's traditional outfit, it is Pakistan's. [Female, aged 50+]

It did not appear to be the case that young women were pressurised into wearing 'traditional' clothing by parents and grandparents.

> I wear English and *shalwar kamiz*, whatever I feel comfortable with on certain days. [Female, aged 15]

> *Shalwar kamiz* are not important. I was worried with my eldest daughter but by the time you get to the fifth you don't care [laughs]. [Female, aged 53]

> I think girls should wear *shalwar kamiz*, even though my daughter did not! [laughs] [Male, aged 56]

Table 7.5 Govanhill Sample: How Important is it for Girls to Wear *Shalwar Kamiz* to School?

	14-24 f m	25-49 f m	50+ f m	Total
Very important	4 4	1 4	5 7	25
Quite important	2 2	4 4	0 3	15
Not important	3 3	6 3	5 0	20
Don't know	1 1	0 0	0 0	2
Total	10 10	11 11	10 10	62

Nevertheless, during the process of interviewing, and during participant observation in a range of community projects over six years in the area, it was extremely unusual to see a young woman of Pakistani background wearing a skirt that revealed her legs. Trousers and jeans were often worn, and long skirts were sometimes evident, so that in finding alternatives to *shalwar kamiz* the vast majority of young women observed the requirement to cover their legs. Meanwhile, one young woman raised the question of the *hijab*, not in terms of modesty or parental coercion, but of courage and empowerment.[37] This supports the idea that some young women are deliberately engaging in 'conscious and public projections of identity'[38] [Modood 1997: 337].

> I think for me and my friends it's not a strict thing but we would like to wear the *hijab*. Some of my friends have got guts and they have actually done that, wearing it to school. They do get some racism from people and that's something I don't really want to happen to me. So I think there should be knowledge about the *hijab*. Girls should be given the courage by parents and by other people. [Female, aged 15]

---

[37] Scarf securely covering the head and hair. This is distinct from the *dupatta*, a long scarf worn with *shalwar kamiz* which covers the head and shoulders when required, but may also be loosely draped as part of a fashionable outfit.

[38] It will be shown later that a part-time youth worker in Govanhill also chose to wear the *hijab* as an assertion of her Muslim identity.

Most younger respondents preferred co-educational schools, although there were some concerns relating to physical education which again related to modesty requirements.

> I don't think there should be single sex schools. But if it's a mixed school would Muslim girls be allowed to have a PE class where only girls participate? It would be better if it was a mixed school with an understanding of cultures whereby separate facilities are available when required. [Male, aged 26]

The majority of older respondents regarded single sex schools as 'very important', but even here there were signs of pragmatism:

> It is not important that boys and girls go to separate schools because if you do that then they will go wild anyway [laughs]. [Female, aged 50+]

> Single sex schools are not that important in this society. I mean, here they are integrated and there you are [laughs]. [Male, aged 72]

Overall, less importance was placed on specific 'cultural requirements' than might be popularly assumed. Language, dress and gender separation were all placed in the bottom half of the table, although there was a tendency for older respondents to regard these points as more important than younger people. This is not surprising since they were more likely to have been brought up in the Indian subcontinent. But it is important to note that even older respondents adopted a pragmatic approach as far as schooling is concerned.

Multiculturalism, Anti-racism and Equal Opportunities

The importance of equal opportunities to the respondents was considered in relation to teaching children about different religions and cultures, the school having an anti-racist policy, and the belief in equal opportunities for boys and girls. These were all ranked in the top half of the table. However, the comments made during the interviews indicate diverse interpretations of these issues. The majority of respondents felt children should have some understanding of other religions and cultures, although the predominant attitude was perhaps best encapsulated by one of the older women.

> The old saying is, it's an Urdu saying, don't taunt anybody's religion and don't leave your own. [Female, aged 64]

This attitude was confirmed by the relative importance placed upon Christianity and Islamic studies as school subjects. 13 of the 62 respondents felt it was 'very important' to learn about Christianity, while 28 felt Islamic studies were 'very important'. When asked more specifically which were the two most important subjects, no-one chose Christianity while 9 people continued to choose Islamic Studies.

> It's going to be awkward. You've got Christianity and you've got your own. I think everybody would go for their own. [Female, aged 39]

The existence of a school anti-racist policy was ranked top of the table of points for a 'good' education. Throughout the interviewing process respondents were free to expand on particular points as they wished, but were not prompted in any particular direction by the interviewer. However, in answer to the general question 'What did you dislike about the school?' respondents volunteered information about racism:

> Some people at school, well, you get a lot of prejudice and all that. Racism, but it's only some people, not all. [Female, aged 15]

> There were incidents of racism. Not harassment really, just comments. Nothing was actually done, it was just comments. [Male, aged 20]

> The Head Teacher was a wee bit biased you know. I had to write a strong letter to him. Then he called me for interview. I said this is all wrong what you are doing. He understood what I was saying. He was a wee bit racist. Not much but a wee bit above the average. [Male, aged 72]

Phrases such as 'only some people', 'not harassment really' and 'a wee bit above the average' indicate a degree of resignation to the existence of racism. This was articulated by one of the older men.

> You see the way I look at racism, there are two different aspects. There is racial hatred and there's racial harassment. Racial hatred you'll never stop. Catholics hate Protestants, Arabs hate Jews and vice versa. Rangers hate Celtic [laughs].[39] It's always to be. Racial harassment is the thing we should do something about. I would have a policy against that. [Male, aged 67]

---

[39] This quotation again illustrates how racism is perceived in terms of religious antagonism.

Almost everyone agreed that a school should have an anti-racist policy. And it will be shown later, when considering youth service provision, that racism was regarded as a problem facing most young men and women of Pakistani origin living in Govanhill. But there was a sense in which the existence of racism was taken for granted and other issues took precedence as individuals went about their everyday business. Schools that had taken the most positive action to counter racism and cater for specific needs of minority ethnic groups were not necessarily regarded as 'better' schools.

> There is a lot of Asian people going there. I was walking past the playground one day and all you could hear was wee children swearing in my own language and I was totally gob-smacked. I thought 'No way am I sending my child there'. [Female, aged 26]

Another young mother gave several reasons why she had chosen not to send her child to the same primary school:

> It's too overpopulated with the Asian ethnic minority and I've seen children speak their own language. There is a girl that has been going there for a few years and I feel her English is still not up to standard ... I just thought they have got to learn to mix with other races. I mean they are with our people all the time anyway. My son's school is mostly dominated with White people and a small minority of Asians go there. I thought he's got to have White friends as well as Asian friends and at the moment when I see him in school he's got both races that he's friendly with ... And I was just put off one day because there were three boys that I know go there, and they came out and the language they were using! Actually they were swearing in our own language. I thought he is probably going to pick this up. [Female, aged 29]

Fifty-five of the 62 respondents indicated it was 'very important' that a school believes in equal opportunities for boys and girls. This does not conform to a popular stereotype of a Muslim population and so it is worth spending time considering how this aspect of equal opportunities was interpreted. Each age-band is considered in turn to detect generational and gender differences. Within the 14-24 age-band there were only minor differences between males and females at most qualification levels.

The numbers are small but one difference shown in Table 7.6 may be significant i.e. that three young men had finished their education at Standard grade while none of the young women had done so. A possible explanation for this was given by an older man when speaking about his son who left school without any qualifications.

He wasn't keen on school and he didn't get any qualifications. When he left school he helped me in the business. That is the problem with our children. They can work in the business and they don't try at school. [Male, aged 50]

Table 7.6 Govanhill Sample: Qualifications of 14-24 Age-band

	Male	Female	Total
Still at school	2	3	5
Standard grade or equivalent	3	0	3
Highers or equivalent	4	5	9
Undergraduate	1	2	3
Total	10	10	20

Young women, on the other hand, may be encouraged to take another course.

> I had to force my daughter to do a small course and after this she was married because she didn't want to further her studies. [Female, aged 50+]

One explanation for 'forcing' a daughter to undertake a course was put forward by a younger respondent.

> They want the daughter maybe just to do a small course. At least when they are looking for a son-in-law they can say she's done a course in such-and-such. They want an educated husband for their daughter but if she is not educated herself how can they expect her husband to be? [Female, aged 24]

Whatever the motivation, the young men and women in the youngest age-band appeared to be given equal encouragement at school. The majority were still at school or at college and so it might be assumed that the next age-band would give a clearer indication of the longer term prospects of young people. Again, there were only minor differences in academic attainment between male and female respondents. The occupations of the men largely conformed to a popular stereotype, with seven of the eleven involved in shop work, while the majority of women were part-time workers in voluntary sector projects.

Table 7.7 Govanhill Sample: Qualifications of 25-50 Age-band

	Male	Female	Total
No qualifications	1	2	3
Standard grade or equivalent	6	5	11
Highers or equivalent	2	3	5
Degree	2	1	3
Total	11	11	22

It is interesting to note that, of the graduates, a male Community Resource Worker had a degree in Management with Mathematics and a female Community Worker had a degree in Biology. This suggests that some people were gaining qualifications but not finding jobs in their subject area. A number of youth, community and social care projects in Govanhill had taken positive action to recruit bilingual staff and this may account for the changes in career choice, as well as the apparently high representation of local females in part-time positions in the voluntary sector.

Table 7.8 Govanhill Sample: Qualifications of Children of 25-50 Age-band

	Male	Female	Total
Too young to take examinations	10	12	22
No qualifications	1	0	1
Standard grade or equivalent	2	1	3
Highers or equivalent	1	2	3
Undergraduate	3	1	4
Total	17	16	33

The respondents in the middle age-band had a total of 33 children between them, and there was no indication of significant differences in qualifications based on gender. Once again this suggests that young women were being given equal encouragement at school. It was only in the oldest age-band that significant differences were apparent.

Most of the older women had little or no formal education, had no qualifications and had never worked outside of the home. When asked about their personal ambitions, the majority made it clear that they 'did not think about that' because they knew they would be married at a young age.

> I can't remember the name of my school. I completed five classes and I left school when I was ten. I never thought of doing any kind of job when I was in Pakistan. I left school at a young age and then I learned to do the housework. [Female, aged 50+]

> In my village girls were not allowed to go to school. They did not think of that. We grew up and got married. [Female, aged 64]

Table 7.9 Govanhill Sample: Qualifications of 50+ Age band

	Male	Female	Total
No qualifications	3	7	10
'Metric' [10 classes]	2	2	5
Further education	1	1	1
Degree	4	0	4
Total	10	10	20

The men in this age-band received more formal education than the women. They were also more likely to have had career ambitions when they were young, including engineering and medicine. But their actual occupations did not match their ambitions or utilise their qualifications. Nine of the ten men either had been, or were still, shopkeepers, of whom five had worked 'on the buses' for Glasgow Corporation before becoming self employed.

It was only in this older age-band that there was strong evidence of unequal access to education according to gender. This related to the situation prevailing in the Indian sub-continent at the time. In order to detect whether their experience influenced their aspirations for their own children in Scotland, consideration was given to the qualifications and employment of their children. Between them they had 40 sons and 34 daughters. They were remarkably well qualified, with approximately half of the males and a quarter of the females attaining degrees. The pattern of qualifications suggests that daughters were encouraged to achieve at school, but less likely to go on to university. Comments made during the interviews revealed that five of the twelve women who passed Highers went on to take non-degree courses at local colleges, adding weight to the earlier suggestion that a shorter course was more acceptable to some parents who wished to promote their daughter as 'educated' while looking for a marriage partner. The fact that more than twice as many males as females left school with no qualifications also supports the earlier suggestion that some young men looked to family businesses for employment and were less worried about academic achievement.

Table 7.10 Govanhill Sample: Qualifications of Children of 50+ Age band

	Male	Female	Total
No qualifications	14	6	20
Standard grade or equivalent	1	7	8
Highers or equivalent	6	12	18
First degree	13	8	21
Higher degree	6	1	7
Total	40	34	74

When asked about the ambitions they had for their children, there was very clear evidence that the priority for daughters was to arrange a 'good' marriage. Four of the older women and six of the older men specifically mentioned marriage when asked 'What did you want her to do when she left school?' No-one mentioned marriage in response to this question about their sons.

> She went to college to do a business course but she didn't finish. It was a good family that came for her hand in marriage and I decided that the boy was decent, respectable. [Female, aged 50]

> My youngest daughter was like me. She tried hard but she didn't get qualifications. I said to her 'There is your house and your mum. You can help her out'. Now she is married and she has a baby. Her older sister is going to University in the autumn. She loves studying. She is very keen. She has ambition, but one day she will be married and that will be left behind. [Male, aged 54]

There was a suggestion that 'good offers' could not be turned down or delayed, but there was also evidence that some daughters were asserting their own agenda.

> She has a degree from Glasgow University and then she went to York for a masters degree. I wanted her to get married and settle down but she has her own priorities. [Male, aged 56]

> She is not married. She is working away from home. If you are strict with your children they will go the opposite way. [Female, aged 50]

In summary, despite the fact that most of the older respondents grew up where girls had little or no schooling, few appeared to believe that their daughters schooling should be inferior to that of their sons. They were, however, likely to see a woman's role after completing her education as that of wife and mother. The middle and younger age-bands were less likely to describe a woman's role solely in terms of marriage and motherhood, but it remains to be seen whether they will utilise their qualifications in the labour market.

Qur'an School

It has been shown that respondents did not regard Islamic studies as an important subject for the public school curriculum, but this did not mean that Islam was regarded as unimportant in the education of the young. Outside of the normal school day extensive arrangements were made to ensure that children undertook the important religious obligation of reading the *Qur'an*. Children usually went straight from school to a local mosque or to a house where there was a suitable teacher, but some were taught at home. The most common arrangement was to teach the Arabic alphabet to children as soon as they started to read and write, and then progress to reading and reciting the *Qur'an* from the age of about seven until completion. There was an element of competition concerning the age of completion and the ability to recite with the correct accent.

> My children all read the *Qur'an*. They were primary school age. They all finished before they were twelve. They went to three different teachers to have the proper Arabic accent. Two of the teachers were women and one was a man. He was *hafiz*, a person who knows the Holy *Qur'an* by heart, so they would have the proper accent and pronounce it properly. [Male, aged 59]

This can be a long and difficult process for young children but, irrespective of age or gender, it was widely acknowledged as essential.

> Well, as a Muslim youngster I knew I had to read the *Qur'an*. It is something we have to do and the best time is in your childhood when you can't say 'I am tied down with work' or whatever. And what you learn as a child stays with you for the rest of your life. I know that now, and I wish I could go back and thank my mum for teaching me. [Female, aged 19]

> It is important for all Muslims to learn at some stage in their lives. I mean it is our faith. Even the ones who aren't too orthodox, even they send their children. [Female, aged 29]

> It is hard to explain to you. For me it is everything. [Male, aged 39]

A number of reasons were given for the importance of *Qur'an* school. The most important for the older respondents was that the *Qur'an* is the Word of God.

> The *Qur'an* is the final Word of God you see. If you read Arabic as it is, without the translation, you are reading the Word of God. [Male, aged 72]

A number of younger respondents spoke of the importance of understanding their parents and their religion. The vocabulary here is important, because many respondents talked of learning about 'my religion' or 'our religion'. There was a sense in which religious identity was accepted as given.

> It taught me to know what my religion is about. When I was young if someone had a child or something, someone would say things in Arabic and I wouldn't understand. And with traditions, like when someone dies you have to do this and do that, and I wouldn't have a clue, but they taught us. [Male, aged 20]

> That is my religion. You don't have a choice in that. I wouldn't like to change my religion. Even though I am a Muslim and I don't follow it, I wouldn't change it. [Female, aged 26]

Even young people who were reluctant learners felt a sense of loyalty to their parents and of achievement when it was complete.

> See me, myself, I've actually learned it all by heart. I finished last year. To tell you the truth, right, I never actually wanted to do it myself. It was my dad. He was like 'I want you to do it'. I did it for my dad. [Male, aged 17]

Those who were critical of *Qur'an* school directed their criticisms at the style of teaching, rather than the obligation to read the *Qur'an*. The *Qur'an* is a book of guidance for Muslims, and so the translation and interpretation can be critical. Some felt they were given no insight into what they were reading, while others were concerned that they were being given the teacher's personal opinions. This does not suggest a lack of interest or commitment, but rather that young people were demanding higher standards of teaching. Some young people indicated that *Qur'an* school and Islamic studies helped them to differentiate between cultural constraints imposed upon them by elders from Pakistan, and the actual teachings of the *Qur'an*.

> Too many *Imams* do not teach the *Qur'an* in the light it should be taught. For example you're taught to learn in rote fashion, and can recite it beautifully but not fully understanding what it means. I think nowadays it's changing slowly so the new *Imams*, younger *Imams*, who have been raised in this country are realising that. They are now teaching young children the passage and translating the words and saying 'Well this is what that passage means'. [Male, aged 26]

> It teaches you about the *Qur'an* and about Islam as it should be, and not Islam as society has made it. [Female, aged 30]

One of the difficulties for children is that they are going to school all day and then undertaking one or two hours of *Qur'an* school. This was generally acknowledged to be hard work.

> I did it after school but that way you don't get any free time at all, straight after school you are there. So it is a lot of pressure. Your head spins a bit. [Male, aged 17]

> Sometimes I think after school is too much. I found it myself, you know. It's really hard going to school, you've got homework, you've got housework, helping out. It's just all too much coming home and then going, especially in the winter. [Female, aged 25]

The option of reading the *Qur'an* at a local authority school during the normal school day proved to be quite popular, although there was some surprise that it was suggested. None of the respondents expected local authority schools to make such an arrangement (and indeed none of the schools did). Some young people felt that it might make teachers more aware of how hard they were working.

> Yes, I think that would have been better because then the teacher would have known that yes, he's got to work on the *Qur'an* and he's got his own education to work with. Otherwise teachers do not understand that, wait a minute, he's doing the *Qur'an* in his own time. [Male, aged 17]

Mothers, who normally accept responsibility for making sure that their children attend *Qur'an* school, felt it would have benefits for family life in general.

> The normal school day would be best because on a school day you hardly have time to see your children anyway. You know what I mean, they've got to go to bed early so you don't have a lot of time to spend with them. [Female, aged 26]

> *Qur'an* during the school day? That would be brilliant. Oh, that would be brilliant. None of the rush. Getting them to eat something, change their clothes and take them down the road, and the traffic! [Female, aged 38]

But not everyone thought this was a good idea. Some had concerns that it would not be done correctly:

> As long as the etiquettes are adhered to. For example, that the *Qur'an* is opened with the understanding that this is a Holy Book just like any other Holy Book and should be treated as such, not just thrown around, or scribbled on. [Male, aged 26]

Others suggested that children would not attend (clearly assuming it was easier to avoid lessons at a local authority school than at *Qur'an* school).

> No that wouldn't work. I wouldn't have gone [laughs]. That's true. When you're small you don't want to do that kind of stuff. I mean I was forced at times to go to the mosque. [Male, aged 20]

> I don't think many children would go if it was up to the school authorities. You need the right atmosphere. [Male, aged 56]

It was also suggested that to ask for such an arrangement would be unreasonable and could cause friction.

> If we demanded that from an ordinary school, that someone should teach my child Islam, other parents would want that as well. Christian people, and Sikhs, and Hindus as well so it would be quite a big demand and the system couldn't cope with it. [Female, aged 19]

> We are living in a White society. How can we expect children to read *Qur'an* during the school day? That's asking for too much

really. We can't come here and take over because it's not our country. [Female, aged 50+]

In summary, respondents felt that sufficient concessions had been made to their specific cultural and religious requirements. They were aware of racism in schools and an anti-racist policy was considered very important. Beyond this, both pupils and parents wanted schools to concentrate on providing an academic education that would equip pupils with the qualifications necessary to compete in the labour market and enhance social status (including marriage prospects). Meanwhile, in local mosques and houses they continued to make their own arrangements for the religious education of their children.

Interaction Between Service Providers and Service Users

Some form of interaction between education authorities and the Pakistani population in Scotland was inevitable because of the legal requirement for children to receive 'efficient education'. In the mid-1980s, following concerns about the education of minority ethnic groups in Britain, the Swann Report had asserted:

> We cannot favour a 'solution' to the supposed 'problems' which ethnic minority communities face, which tacitly seems to accept that these 'problems' are beyond the capacity and imagination of existing schools to meet and that the only answer is therefore to provide 'alternative' education for ethnic minority pupils, thus in effect absolving existing schools from even making an attempt to reappraise and revise their practices. [Swann 1985: 510]

A degree of reappraisal and revision did take place and by the 1990s increased emphasis on the legal obligation to avoid indirect discrimination, combined with the grass roots practices developed through the day-to-day realities of teaching children from minority ethnic groups, influenced the environment for the majority of pupils, irrespective of ethnic origin. Some specific religious and cultural requirements had been asserted by the Pakistani population, and the education authority had largely catered for them. School uniforms and school meals were adapted, authorised absence was permitted for *Eid* celebrations and extended trips abroad, the National Curriculum asserted the importance of respect for 'Other World Religions', and members of minority ethnic groups were evident in some staff teams.

While concessions were made for the religious needs of Muslim children in Glasgow, there was some opposition amongst politicians to the establishment of separate Muslim schools. This was not necessarily born of antipathy towards Islam. There was increasing concern that sectarianism in Scotland was perpetuated by the separation of children on religious grounds for educational purposes. To avoid an increase in the number of denominational schools, local councillors showed commitment to the accommodation of non-Christian religious requirements within existing schools. In addition, a pragmatic approach was taken over financial assistance for *Qur'an* schools under the education authority's 'language and culture' budget. Ironically, the presence of the Muslim population was having an impact on both non-denominational and Catholic schools in Govanhill. While there may have been some resistance to a dilution of the Catholic ethos, the pressure to recruit local children at a time of falling school rolls led to increasing religious diversity within the Catholic primary school population.[40]

There was very little support amongst Pakistani respondents for the establishment of separate Muslim schools. Neither was it generally considered appropriate to teach Islamic studies or read the *Qur'an* in local authority schools. This was thought to be making unnecessary demands on the system. The majority of respondents asserted that Islamic education was the responsibility of the Muslim population themselves, and young people were willing to undertake studies after school and at the weekends in order to retain the opportunity to mix as widely as possible at school. They asserted, as their parents did, that schools should promote tolerance and understanding between different faiths.

As far as religious identity is concerned, differences were emerging between Muslim parents brought up in Pakistan and their Scottish-born children and grandchildren. Young people expressed commitment to Islam, but argued for changes in the quality and style of their religious education as they negotiated a Scottish-Muslim identity.

During the interviews it was clear that the repercussions of asserting identity were evaluated by respondents. In a school setting, conspicuous concessions to Pakistani or Muslim identity were given lower priority than English language development, academic achievement and mixing with the wider peer group. Thus, with policies in place to ensure that essential religious and cultural obligations were not violated, the choice of school was more likely to depend on local perceptions of a school's reputation and academic results. Indeed some respondents deliberately avoided schools making the greatest provision for minority ethnic groups.

---

[40] One Catholic primary school in neighbouring Pollokshields has a school population described as 21% Roman Catholic, 62% Muslim and 8% Sikh [SOED 1995b: 1].

Respondents were aware of racism in schools and felt that it was important to have an anti-racist policy. But a difference was perceived between holding racist attitudes and cases of overt racial harassment: the former might be tolerated in the short term if there were compensating factors such as good examination results. There were even some signs that the schools making the greatest provision for minority ethnic groups were not always regarded as 'good' schools. In the pursuit of academic success some respondents were prepared to tolerate less committed multicultural and anti-racist policies. However uncritical this might appear, there is some evidence to suggest that Pakistani academic achievement in Glasgow is higher than in other parts of Britain [Runnymede Trust 1997b: 44]. It cannot be assumed that a pragmatic approach works to the disadvantage of those who adopt it.

On 14 February 1996, in an article in *The Independent* newspaper, Polly Toynbee expressed a commonly held opinion that in accommodating Muslim sensitivities 'the state will acquiesce in the repression of young girls, putting their parents' cultural rights above the duty to educate British girls equally' But, having considered the attitudes and qualifications of the respondents in Govanhill, there is little if any evidence to suggest that the girls were being repressed in relation to their school-age education. It was clear that daughters born and educated in Scotland received considerably more formal education than their mothers born in the Indian sub-continent. The degree to which these young women, having gained the necessary qualifications at school, will go on to higher education and pursue career ambitions remains to be seen. There were signs that marriage and family life continued to take precedence over career aspirations, but this cannot be seen as a specifically Muslim dilemma. How to combine the responsibilities of family and career is likely to be a problem they share with many women, regardless of religious affiliation.

Broad agreement amongst the Pakistani population about the acceptability of public, co-educational schools may have resulted from a belief that the school day was sufficiently structured and supervised to minimise inappropriate behaviour. Furthermore, the potential benefits of academic achievement may outweigh the possible disadvantages of inappropriate social contact. The next chapter considers youth services, where participation is not a legal requirement, activities are less structured, and the 'benefits' are less clear.

8 Youth Services: the Socialisation Model

Irish Catholic, Italian and Jewish immigrants in Scotland all showed concern about social and recreational activities outside of the home that might lead their adolescent children to reject the values of their parents. Each population attempted to establish activities that encouraged children to socialise with 'appropriate' friends and retain aspects of their cultural heritage. In this chapter these concerns are examined in relation to the Pakistani population through consideration of relevant national and local policies that shape the framework within which youth services are provided; the implementation of these policies by the main youth service provider in Govanhill; and, the priorities of the Pakistani population in relation to services for young people. Finally, some conclusions are drawn concerning the interaction between youth service providers and the Pakistani population as service users.

Youth Work in Scotland

In a report entitled *Youth Work in Scotland,* the Scottish Office Education Department attempted to identify and analyse what constituted good practice in youth work. It was asserted that the main aim was 'to assist young people, in an informal setting, to grow towards responsible adulthood' [SOED 1992b: 5]. Whilst the setting was informal, it was argued that high quality youth work should have a clear educational content. Five key dimensions were identified: learning through social contact, involvement in decision-making, guidance and counselling, the imparting of knowledge and information, and the teaching of skills. However, concern was expressed that the public image of youth work was poor:

> Seldom are the educational objectives of youth work fully appreciated by the wider public ... Too often the public perception of youth work is out of focus: youth provision is regarded as a minding service for older children and teenagers which is available while the rest of the community goes about its business. [Ibid: 32]

But consideration of previous immigrant populations suggests that, as parents, they did recognise the 'educational objectives' of youth work, which is why they had concerns about its potential to undermine the religious and cultural values they hoped to pass on to their children. Following on from the report, the Scottish Office commissioned research into the social and educational benefits of youth work which culminated in a document entitled *Measuring the Benefits of Youth Work* [University of Aberdeen 1991]. The influence that youth work could have on young people was confirmed in the list of 'benefits' which were couched in terms of a 'socialisation model'. These included testing and developing new ideas, examining issues in a non-threatening environment, and working out a personal code of values. Although parents were not involved in the survey, reference was made to the importance of parental influence. It was asserted:

> A young person's home background plays an important role in the choices of youth group chosen. In particular, it gives a predisposition to join a particular 'like-minded' group, which enhances the opportunities and values the parents would like their son/daughter to grow up with. [Ibid: 70]

There was very little evidence of consultation with minority ethnic groups, so that the predisposition for 'like-minded' groups appeared to be a general parenting concern rather than a characteristic of immigrants who 'refuse to mix'. An important aspect of the fieldwork undertaken in Govanhill was to consider the extent to which the style and content of existing youth service provision reinforced or conflicted with the values of Pakistani parents.

Youth Work Policies in Glasgow and Govanhill

Young people were classified as a target group in Strathclyde Regional Council's *Social Strategy for the Nineties* document. The main policy objectives were: to improve the situation in which young people live; to reduce discrimination against particular groups of young people; to empower young people by seeking to increase the control that they have over their own lives; to increase the involvement young people have individually and collectively in the decision-making process of services and agencies which affect them; and to encourage departments and agencies to develop flexible responses which are centred on the needs of young people and young adults [SRC 1993: 14]. Areas of concern included youth unemployment, homelessness, poor housing and environmental conditions, and the risk of exposure to alcohol, drug and solvent abuse. Particular reference was made to the provision of services for vulnerable girls and young women. This broad agenda made very little reference to minority ethnic groups, although it might be argued that the issues raised affected young people across all ethnic groups.

In the autumn of 1993 the Council implemented a review of the Community Education Service, revising team boundaries and placing renewed focus on youth work. Within this context the *Area 10 Development Plan 1994-1997* was produced [CES 1994a]. Area 10 incorporated Govanhill and it was argued that in order to ensure youth provision properly reflected the needs of the young people from 'black and ethnic minority groups' a number of elements were to be built into the youth programme:

> Single sex groups will be established which will offer provision for both boys and girls from particular communities e.g. Asian Boys Group. Recruitment of sessional youth work staff will actively seek people from these communities and training of all sessional youth work staff will include racism awareness. The programme offered in general youth groups will offer a range of activities which will attract participation from a fair representation of the geographical community the group is aimed at. [Ibid: para 2.3]

Concern was expressed that accommodation for youth services was limited and that the youth wing at a local secondary school was to be withdrawn for conversion to classrooms. The youth wing accommodated an Asian Boys Group which was effectively disbanded. Thus at the outset of the Plan there was a reduction in provision for Asian boys in the Govanhill area. Meanwhile, in 1994 Govanhill Area Liaison Committee established a Sub-Group on Youth which undertook a survey of 'the views and opinions of Govanhill young people with regard to youth facilities in the area' [Govanhill ALC 1995].

Govanhill Youth Survey

During the survey 287 young people were interviewed, of whom 72 were of Asian origin.[41] The data was predominantly analysed in relation to age and gender, and the resulting report made few direct references to the views of young people from minority ethnic groups. In order to determine whether more specific information could be discerned from the data collected, the 72 Asian responses are considered here. When asked whether they had used any

---

[41] In the survey the figure is given as 71. Analysis of the data revealed that there were 71 'Asian' + 1 'Scottish Asian' respondent.

local youth groups or facilities in the last five years, two-thirds of young men and half of the young women said that they had done so.

Table 8.1 Govanhill Youth Survey: Use of Youth Facilities in Last 5 Years

	Male	Female
Yes	22	20
No	11	19
Total	33	39

School venues were particularly prominent in the list of facilities used and it was clear that the Asian Boys Club in the school youth wing had been popular with young men before its closure.

Table 8.2 Govanhill Youth Survey: Youth Facilities Used

Male	Female
Asian Boys Club (school wing) [16]	Urdu Class [8]
Karate(community centre) [2]	Asian Girls Club (primary school)[4]
Karate (secondary school)	Asian Girls Club (community centre)[2]
Swimming	School Drama group [2]
Temple	Swimming (swimming baths)
Boys Brigade	Dancing (primary school)
Urdu Class (primary school)	Karate
School Club	Mosque

It appeared that there was much greater enthusiasm on the part of young people from minority ethnic groups than their White counterparts for a range of suggested services.[42]

---

[42] The figures for 'All' include those of minority ethnic groups so that the difference is greater than first suggested by the table. The difference was especially evident in relation to young Asian women seeking information and advice, but this was partly in contrast to the remarkably small figure for all young women. Unfortunately there was no additional information to indicate why this was the case.

Table 8.3 Govanhill Youth Survey: Youth Facility Preferences

	Male		Female	
	Asian %	All %	Asian %	All %
Youth Club	76	47	85	61
Youth Centre	63	20	46	22
Info/Advice	36	10	62	4
Youth Cafe	48	40	54	22

It will be shown later that there was likely to be resistance to some of these services on the part of Pakistani elders, particularly where young women were concerned, unless religious and cultural obligations were acknowledged. Nevertheless it was clear that young people from minority ethnic groups were keen to access a range of youth services.

Table 8.4 Govanhill Youth Survey: Reason for Facilities (Order of Preference)

	Male				Female			
	1	2	3	4	1	2	3	4
Somewhere to meet friends	18	2	4	2	25	9	1	0
Access to info/advice	2	6	2	9	7	4	8	7
Play pool etc	8	10	6	1	4	11	5	4
Somewhere to hold groups	3	5	8	8	4	6	9	6
Other:								
Football	5							
Sports	1							

Most of these young people said they would use the facility as 'somewhere to meet friends'. Some young men added their own preference for football and sport, and it seems likely that if these options had been included in the original list of choices the figures would have been much higher.[43] In the event, no new facilities were established as a result of the survey and an existing youth project continued as the main youth service provider in the area. In the next section consideration is given to the development of this project, with particular emphasis on the period covered by the *Area 10 Development Plan 1994-97*.

---

[43] See later fieldwork responses concerning sport, especially football.

The Youth Project in Govanhill

In 1989 an Urban Programme funding application for the establishment of a youth project in Govanhill was submitted to the Scottish Office. It was asserted in the application that considerable gaps existed in youth provision in Govanhill and that issues of concern included drug and solvent abuse, theft, violence, truancy, homelessness, unemployment, apathy, debt and difficult family relationships. In addition, incidents of racial harassment were said to be increasing so that positive action was required to combat racism. It was argued that the proposed youth project would work progressively with young people and the resulting benefits would include 'a reduction of racist based incidents and the foundations laid for the fostering of a more tolerant multi-cultural community' [Urban Programme Project 1327/90].

Evidence of racism in the area was fragmented but nevertheless tenable. Local community workers regularly dealt with cases of racial harassment, and research indicated that North Govanhill was considered an undesirable area by members of minority ethnic groups because of racial harassment [SCVO 1988, Bowes, McCluskey & Sim 1990]. The Urban Programme application indicated that the proposed youth project would tackle racism and foster multiculturalism in two ways: by working with 'numerous ethnic minority young people' and by taking positive action against racism in pursuing 'strategies that build positive, tolerant and co-operative attitudes among young people of all races'.

The application was successful and during 1992 the permanent staff team was recruited: a project leader, an assistant youth worker and a clerical assistant, all of whom were White. (The composition of the staff team is significant because it would be argued later that the project lacked workers with the experience and skills to work with minority ethnic groups.)

Having established the permanent staff team, six part-time staff were recruited to undertake street work: three White males, two White females and one Pakistani male [Strategy Report 1993]. The street work took place in the evenings when staff made contact with young people, informing them about the new youth project and encouraging them to form themselves into manageable sized groups who would meet on a weekly basis at the project's base or in one of the two community centres in the area. It was not long before shortcomings were recognised in relation to the stated aim of working with young people from minority ethnic groups:

> Very little contact has been made with black youth mainly due to their lack of activity on the streets of Govanhill at night.[44] Some observations have been made, centred particularly around the Asian video shops and shops with video game machines but generally it is true to say that young Asian people don't hang around street corners or walk around the streets at night. This is no doubt a reflection of the different social and cultural emphasis of the Asian Community ... contact has proven to be difficult and this issue warrants greater consideration and perhaps a rethink on contact strategies. [Ibid]

It will be shown later that this explanation for lack of contact was relevant to young women, but that their male peers *were* hanging around the streets and becoming involved with gangs. The fact that the youth project was not making contact with them suggests that other factors were relevant. This was acknowledged in an application for additional Urban Programme funding submitted in September 1993:

> The ethnic minorities population in the area (who currently make up 25-30% of the total population)[45] are inadequately served by the youth project. This is mainly due to two facts. At the present level of staffing even with work with ethnic minorities young people given the highest priority, it would not be possible to effectively progress work in this area, due to the considerations of time, staff availability and commitments to existing groups. Secondly, it has become clear that the project lacks the cultural sensitivity, awareness and experience to further work in this particularly important but difficult area. [Supplementary Application 1327/90]

In the meantime, the youth project continued to develop. Emphasis shifted away from street work to 'a mix of social/recreational activities as well as group work oriented discussion groups' [Annual Report 1994]. By the time the Community Education Service undertook its interim evaluation of the project, nine groups had been established but there was still no involvement of young people from minority ethnic groups. The evaluation was largely favourable but recommended that if the application for supplementary funding was successful 'there should be a re-assessment of the work currently being carried out with a far clearer input into working with the ethnic minority communities within Govanhill' [CES 1994b]. Meanwhile the project leader asserted:

---

[44] Throughout the Project's literature 'Asian', 'Black' and 'Ethnic Minorities Community' are used interchangeably.
[45] This estimate is well above the figure indicated in the 1991 Census data.

> If the application is unsuccessful then the project staff will have to reassess its priorities and work to allow it to address the issues associated with developing work with young people from ethnic minorities backgrounds. If this is the case then it is likely that working practices will have to be altered to take into account the cultural and social needs of young black people in Govanhill.
> [Annual Report 1994]

The application was unsuccessful but in September 1994 a second supplementary application was made requesting funding for an experienced specialist worker to work with 'ethnic minorities young people' plus additional sessional hours and clerical support. This bid also proved unsuccessful and the 1995 Annual Report indicated that there were still no young people from minority ethnic groups attending the project, although a commitment to tackle racism was apparent in relation to one boys group:

> Some members of the group have recently given indications of racist behaviour and associations and for this reason a programme of anti-racist work has been established with the group. The response to this input will be closely observed and further programmes will reflect the required level of ongoing response.

By 1996 an Asian Girls Group had been established (see later). However, no work was being undertaken with young men from minority ethnic groups and it was asserted that particular emphasis would now be given 'to establishing contact with boys and young men from Ethnic Minorities' [Annual Report 1996]. In February 1996 an application was made to the National Lottery requesting funds to expand services in order to employ a full time worker who would be 'culturally sensitive and bilingual and will be the focus of a programme targeting the needs of the young Ethnic Minorities who are vulnerable or at risk'. This application was also unsuccessful but the project leader signalled an intention to re-apply:

> It is our intention to apply to the Lottery again under an appropriate theme to fund this type of work and we are also considering investigation of other potential funding sources for this and other work. It is clear however that the project is fully occupied with the volume of work relating to the development of established and newer groups and to develop more innovative work it would be necessary to either re-prioritise significantly or to attract funding.
> [Annual Report 1997]

Although it was suggested that 'this type of work' would be difficult without additional funds, it was also acknowledged that new groups had been established. These groups were made up of:

> ... the siblings and younger associates of the 16-18 year olds currently with the project and represent the 'new wave' of young people who may benefit from a long term involvement with the project and its programmes. [Ibid]

It was stated that they were 'presenting themselves to the project' and that the staff looked forward to 'giving them the benefit of experience and service delivery tried and tested on those who have gone before'.

Table 8.5 Youth Project: Involvement of Minority Ethnic Groups

	1994	1995	1996	1997
Management committee members	0	0	1	1
Permanent staff	0	0	0	0
Male sessional staff	1	1	1	0
Female sessional staff	1	2	2	3
Asian Girls Groups	0	0	1	1
Asian Boys Groups	0	0	0	0
Multicultural groups	0	0	0	0

In relation to the Youth Project's remit to work with minority ethnic groups, the above table indicates some progress between 1994 and 1997 in the composition of the management committee and the female sessional staff team. However, there were no permanent staff from minority ethnic groups, and no work had been undertaken with young men from minority ethnic groups. By 1997 the male sessional worker was no longer employed by the project, and the three female staff were working solely with the Asian Girls Group. This suggests limited interaction between young people from minority ethnic groups and White staff and young people. To examine the interaction that was taking place between the youth project (as a service provider) and the Pakistani population (as service users), the development of the Asian Girl's Group is considered next.[46]

---

[46] The story of the development of this group was recorded through a series of interviews with the project leader and key workers and the project's Annual Reports 1994-1997.

The Asian Girls Group

In the youth project's 1995 Annual Report the project leader stated:

> The Asian Girls Group is currently an idea rather than a group. It has been the intention of the project to target specific groups for positive intervention and high in the projects priority are young women from the Ethnic Minorities community.

Two female workers of Pakistani background were recruited and proved essential in the establishment of the group: one had experience of setting up an Asian Girls Group in another area but was not bilingual; the other spoke English, Urdu and Punjabi and, to the approval of a number of parents, wore the *hijab*.[47] In addition, two White workers were assigned to the group, one of whom was allocated responsibility as a driver.

The Asian Girls Group was different from other groups at the project in a number of ways. The young women met at an earlier time (5.00-7.00pm instead of the more usual 7.00-9.00pm) and were offered transport to and from the meetings. Members were recruited through an Open Day to which 'all the family'[48] were invited, rather than through street work contact. Posters and leaflets to advertise the Open Day were produced in English and Urdu, and were distributed in local schools and around the area. The translation of information into Urdu attracted young women from a Pakistani background, and the presence of a worker wearing the *hijab* indicated to parents that Muslim values would be respected. These factors were significant because, although the group was described as an 'Asian' girls group, it was made up of young women of Pakistani backgrounds. This became particularly pertinent when planning the group programme.

It was customary at the youth project for young people to plan their own activities, and the Asian Girls Group followed this pattern. Their ideas included ten pin bowling, Indian dance, hairdressing, and netball. But a controversy arose when interest was expressed in Islamic studies. This was mentioned at a team meeting of all project staff and prompted a negative response from the majority of White workers (including those originally assigned to the group). Most were against the idea of religion being discussed, and one worker compared this with promoting the Orange Order. Opinions became heated and the project leader stopped the discussion saying

---

[47] This young woman chose to wear the *hijab* to assert her Muslim identity. Her sisters did not do so.

[48] In practice the Open Day was an attended by young women and their female relatives.

he would arrange a separate meeting with the workers designated to the group.

At the subsequent meeting the project leader explained that the youth project could not be linked with any specific religion and it was important that non-Muslim girls should also feel the group was open to them. However, the two workers of Pakistani background (one of whom indicated that she was not a practising Muslim) had been upset by the reaction at the staff team meeting. They felt some workers had automatically linked religion with sectarianism and appeared to believe that Muslims were fanatical. They suggested that issue-based discussions about contraception and sex were less appropriate for young Muslim women while there was interest in discussing women's rights within Islam.[49] The issue was settled through the project leader's suggestion that they could have a discussion about Islam, whilst not 'teaching' Islam.[50]

The project leader later asserted that 'a mountain had been made out of a molehill' and described the Asian Girls Group as a success for the youth project. He felt that one of the reasons for this success was that he had allowed workers considerable autonomy, although in the 1997 Annual Report it was clear that this approach could also make the group vulnerable:

> The [Asian Girls Group] overall have had a successful and eventful year affected only by a break of two and a half months at the start of this year while the project secured new staff for the group ... There was perhaps an issue that the group operated semi-autonimously [sic] from the project which was not necessarily a problem until the key worker with the group left when she got full time employment.

This illustrated the extent to which specific workers, rather than a coherent policy, had influenced the development of the group. The implications of the approach taken by the youth project as service providers to the local Pakistani population are discussed later, but first consideration is given to the priorities of Pakistani immigrants and their descendants.

Youth Work Priorities of the Pakistani Population

Four key areas were considered during the interviews to determine the priorities of parents and young people as actual or potential service users. What were the main problems facing young people? What was the level of

---

[49] This was confirmed by respondents during the interviews (see later).
[50] It might be argued that this was what had been requested originally.

participation in existing youth groups and organisations? How much importance was placed on religiously or culturally specific provision, and on multicultural, anti-racist and equal opportunities policies? And what sorts of activities were considered acceptable in a youth work curriculum?

Problems Affecting Young Men and Women

The majority of respondents felt 'racism' and 'finding a good job' were key problems for both young men and young women, but these were given different emphasis when respondents were asked to choose the two worst problems. Table 8.6 lists the three highest scoring problems in each category.

Table 8.6a Govanhill Sample: Which of the Following Problems Affect Young People?

	14-24 f	14-24 m	25-50 f	25-50 m	50+ f	50+ m	Total
Total respondents	10	10	11	11	10	11	62
For young men:							
Racism	10	8	9	11	10	9	57
Finding a good job	9	8	11	11	8	9	56
Getting involved in gangs	9	9	9	8	10	9	54
For young women:							
Racism	8	7	10	8	9	8	50
Finding a good job	9	8	9	9	6	8	49
Finding a suitable husband	7	3	10	8	10	9	47

Table 8.6b Which are the Two Worst Problems Affecting Young People?

	14-24 f	14-24 m	25-50 f	25-50 m	50+ f	50+ m	Total
For young men:							
Finding a good job	4	3	5	2	0	4	18
Drugs	0	4	2	3	4	1	14
lack of respect for parents/adults	1	1	1	3	4	2	12
For young women:							
Finding a suitable husband	3	2	5	3	6	5	24
Parents too strict	5	5	5	5	0	2	22
Finding a good job	1	1	4	2	2	3	13

Racism was often linked with employment difficulties. It was suggested that in formal education the success of young people depended on their own effort and achievement, but that this was not the case in the world of work.

> Your life is different when you come out of education and start a job. You need to be twice as good as White boys and girls. Asian kids have got it hard. [Male, aged 56]

A number of respondents were uncertain whether racism or the general lack of employment opportunities was the most significant factor in limiting job prospects.

> I mean, I don't know how you would define a good job. Even Scottish people are finding it difficult to get jobs here. I think finding a job is difficult anyway. [Female, aged 24]

> I see it working in the shop here. School leavers, and leaving college and university, they seem to have a lot of problems with employment. A lot of them do talk about racism especially with the jobs. They think they are getting blocked. I think it is more to do with how you feel. You build up that fear. It is perhaps not as bad as they make out, but there are problems there. [Male, aged 35]

One young woman referred to gender expectations within the family which placed pressure on young men to find employment quickly, while young women were not expected to work.

> The guys get a lot of pressure because from the age of about sixteen they are supposed to help to support the family, especially the eldest son. 'We have no money and we have to wed off your sisters. We have to start saving money.' Males have a lot of pressure, but at the same time I am the eldest in my family and I wanted to go out to work but my parents said it is not the females who go out to bring bread into the family. I said 'I want to go out to work, I have the ability to do it and I want to do it'. But my parents said 'We don't want the support of our daughter. You are going to get married, you are going to go away, so these are the years you should enjoy in the house'. [Female, aged 19]

When asked to pick out the two worst problems, racism was often omitted. Again, as was apparent when discussing education, there was a perception that racism was so difficult to eradicate that it formed a context within which other, more immediate problems had to be addressed. These often related to the gender specific social spheres of young men and women. There was general concern that young men were becoming involved with gangs.

> A lot of guys have actually made up their own gangs. A certain area becomes their area, you know, like the Young Govanhill Boys or something like that. I think that's something that affects them. If they are walking in another area, guys say 'Oh that's a Govanhiller' or 'They are in our area, what are they doing?' you know. [Female, aged 15]

> Young Asian men are fighting against each other when they shouldn't be, right. That's the worst point. They watch too many films and they think they're heroes. They don't realise they are doing damage to other people's parents and families, attacking people and thinking 'We are bigger than you. We organise'. [Male, aged 33]

Respondents in each age-band also expressed concern that young men were involved with drugs.

> With my generation there was a problem with alcohol. Alcohol is playing a lower part now than dance drugs and cannabis and all that. [Female, aged 30]

> Nowadays drugs is a problem. I think it is a really big problem in the Govanhill area. It is going on so much. I don't know if the police don't know about it, or do know about it but they are not doing anything. Just by working in the shop you see a lot. [Male, aged 37]

Some respondents expressed concern about declining respect for parents and elders, but others suggested that the situation was more complex. The long hours worked by fathers in order to provide for their families, and the contrast between growing up in Pakistan and Scotland, contributed to poor communication between father and son. Thus, some difficulties appeared to be inherent to the process of migration and settlement during which both parents and young people struggled to negotiate boundaries of acceptable behaviour and discipline.

> Not having our parents guiding us the right way. I think that tends to be most of the problem. We were basically the first generation between East and West. We were learning everything East at home, but everything that was West appealed to us. Trying to balance that I think. There was nobody there. I never had an older brother to guide me. We want to do everything that our non-Asian friends are doing but we can't. So that makes us do things on the side. I have been there, seen it and done it! [laughs] [Male, aged 28]

> I think parents, especially fathers, don't give enough time to their sons. There is a barrier between them now, you know. I mean I feel in my house my son talks to me rather than his father. I think the father should play more of a role and advise them. [Female, aged 39]

Despite these concerns, young men continued to have a good deal of freedom in their social lives. Meanwhile, there was broad agreement between both sexes in the younger age-bands that parents were 'too strict' with young women. It appeared that the main motivation for restricting the social lives of young women was to preserve modesty and safeguard their prospects for a 'good' marriage. The questionnaire was specifically designed to avoid focusing on 'arranged marriages' which can be a source of fascination for researchers but are not necessarily pertinent to youth work. However, the topic of marriage did generate further comment with relevance to youth service provision since it involved consideration of appropriate social contact as well as the type of agency that would be best placed to deal with any difficulties that arose. It became clear, irrespective of age or gender, that there were major concerns about the effect on the immediate and extended family if young people married 'unsuitable' partners. Marriages arranged with the support of the family were considered to offer greater long-term security.

> If you're going to go out and find a husband how do you know if he is going to be suitable? I mean if I went out and found a man for myself he might like me now but in five years he might say 'You're not the same person you were five years ago, you're fat and bulging', and he might dump you. [Female, aged 19]

> I hope the system will stay, and I think it will because it is a good system in that the families get to meet and they think 'Is the family good? Is my daughter going to be happy in this household if she lives with the other parents?' And all these issues are taken on board. [Male, aged 26]

Clear attempts were made to enforce endogamy and a number of young people stated that if they chose a marriage partner without the approval of their parents, they could not expect support if things went wrong.[51]

---

[51] Such warnings are not always put into practice. It appeared that where problems arose parents and children did their best to build bridges and maintain family relationships.

> My dad would just say 'Well if you want to marry so-and-so, go on, but you won't come back in this house'. You know, he wouldn't lock me up in the house or send me over to Pakistan for an arranged marriage, he wouldn't do that. He'd just kick me out of the house! [laughs] [Female, aged 23]

> I had a very open mum that said 'You can have a love marriage, but you'll be on your own. If you want to marry someone that's fine, but if anything goes wrong we won't stand by you. If not, if you have an arranged marriage, I'll stand by you all the way.' Meaning that you're going to have to make a very good decision. He's going to have to be worth it. So I agreed to an arranged marriage. [Female, aged 26]

There were some examples of more direct pressure being applied, but even where problems arose young people were anxious to maintain close relationships with their parents and were reluctant to appear disloyal.

> When I finished secondary school I was taken to Pakistan because my mum wanted me to get engaged to my cousin. I wanted to come back to Scotland to go to university. I kept telling my mum and she finally agreed to let me come back to Scotland so long as I got engaged to my cousin before I left. It was awful. We had a big engagement party the day before I left. I had to do it. It was the only way I could come back to Scotland. The first thing I did when I got on the plane was to take my engagement ring off. I've got a love marriage now but it has been very hard. We have finally brought our parents round. [Female, aged 23]

> My marriage didn't work out. I got married to my first cousin. I got married because my mum had spoken to her sister and said 'Yes, fine she'll marry him' and then afterwards, after they had arranged it all, then came to me and said 'You're marrying this guy and that is it'. They had set the date and everything and then came and told me. I just burst into tears and said 'No way'. My mother started crying. It was like emotional blackmail. But you have to have that bit of responsibility inside you and that bit of respect, so I had to say yes. The way she was crying, you could hardly sit there. D'you know what I mean? I couldn't do it to her. I love my mum. At the end of the day I still love my mum. [Female, aged 26]

Although issues relating to marriage were often considered to be more significant for young women than young men, there were aspects that clearly affected both genders. Parents were keen to arrange a marriage to someone who shared their values and did not have a 'reputation'. This meant that some young people born or brought up in Scotland were judged to be too 'westernised' and partners were sought from Pakistan.

> The boy's family would want someone from Pakistan. They don't think of girls here, they think of them as too westernised. I don't think a mother would want her daughter-in-law from here. [Female, aged 33]

> They find out the history. It doesn't matter where they are, in London or another part of the country. They will try to get information from somebody else. 'You see this boy, can you tell us how he is?' And they get the stories and most of the time it is 'He's done this' and 'He's done that' so it makes it quite difficult. So then they go back to Pakistan. [Male, aged 37]

However, there were signs that young Muslims were challenging some of their parents cultural expectations by referring to the *Qur'an*.

> Although some families, you know, will only say 'That's the person you are going to marry', those are backward cultural values. They are not religious values. In Islam, the two people do meet and talk and sit down. If you look at the young people now, the young Muslims who marry now, they are much more outspoken than they were before. [Male, aged 26]

Having outlined some of the difficulties it is important to acknowledge that marriage and family life were valued by the vast majority of those interviewed and, although some aspects of 'arranged' marriages were criticised, 'love' marriages were not necessarily seen as preferable.

> More and more parents in this day and age are giving their children the choice. They go and meet him and his family. Arranged marriages like that are fantastic. [Female, aged 30]

> It's not as it used to be when the families got together and decided who was going to marry who. They thought they knew better, well maybe they did. They knew the circumstances of both families and the problems with the children. It wasn't the same as two strangers meeting and saying 'Let's get married next week' [laughs]. Love at first sight and all that daft talk. I think there's more divorces on the pick your own side than there is on the other side. Having said that, I think it's getting more to be now of picking your own. [Male, aged 67]

Participation in Youth Groups and Activities

Issues of marriage and appropriate social contact were major concerns for previous immigrants who responded by attempting to restrict informal social interaction between their children and the wider population. To examine this in relation to the current Pakistani population, consideration was given to the attitudes of respondents towards youth service participation. Only 3 of the 62 respondents disapproved of youth groups altogether. These (older) respondents tended to perceive a youth 'club' as a place for young people who had nothing better to do with their time:

> If they go to a club they won't do anything good. They should stay away from clubs. [Male, aged 50]

> Clubs and discos are for if you have nothing to do. I don't want my children to get occupied in that. [Male, aged 56]

Table 8.7 Govanhill Sample: Participation in Youth Groups

	14-24		
	f	m	Total
Total respondents	10	10	20
'Mainstream' youth group	0	0	0
Asian Girls/Boys group	3	2	5
Commercial club e.g. gym, snooker	1	2	3
Muslim group	2	0	2
Other e.g. school club	0	2	2
Total participating in youth groups	6	6	12

However, the vast majority indicated that young men and women could take part in youth groups and organisations. The fact that none of the youngest age-band had actually attended any 'mainstream' youth group required an explanation and this is discussed in more detail later when consideration is given to the preferred style and content of youth services.[52]

The young women appeared just as likely as young men to attend a youth group, but there was an important gender difference that may have

---

[52] 'Mainstream' is used here to refer to Community Education Service or voluntary sector provision which is 'open to all' young people aged 12 years and above.

influenced the motive for participation. Young women spent most of their spare time in the company of family members so that attending an organised youth activity was a means of extending their social lives.

> The worst problem for girls is getting out, having a place to meet up with their friends. They are stuck in the house all the time. [Male, aged 19]

> We weren't interested in the activities, we just did it to get out. [Female, aged 23]

Young men, on the other hand, experienced few restrictions on their social activities.

> If I am not working I am usually out with my friends. [Male, aged 19]

> In the evenings my son goes out with his friends or he works out in the gym. At the weekends he does the same. You know, you can't put any restrictions on a boy. [Female, aged 50]

A number of respondents suggested that this disparity related to the customary arrangement through which the eldest son supported his parents in later life.

> They are afraid to put restrictions on a son because he might go against them and not support them financially when they get older. [Female, aged 23]

This relative freedom as an adolescent was confirmed by observations during the interviewing process as many young men appeared to pop in and out of the house at will. Thus it was unlikely that they felt the need to participate in organised youth work activities in order to expand their social lives in the same way as their sisters. In fact, participation in organised youth work might be seen as imposing restrictions. Some respondents expressed concern that the freedom some young men experienced could place them at risk:

> I feel sorry for young men. There is nowhere for them to go to. There's no support for them in any of the aspects they want help. They are roaming about the streets. Then they have the attitude 'Nobody cares about us'. It's a shame. [Female, aged 19]

> I know of twelve-year-old boys who get to stay out until eleven o'clock at night and things like that. I'm not saying that within the European community you don't get this, but I just feel that a lot of males within a Muslim household get too much freedom and the girls are very restricted. [Female, aged 30]

While there was broad agreement that young people could participate in youth service activities, they were under-represented as service users in Govanhill. This suggests that existing provision was inappropriate, unattractive or was insufficiently promoted to minority ethnic groups. To consider this in more detail the opinions of respondents were sought concerning style and content of 'appropriate' youth service provision.

Separate Muslim Provision

The majority of respondents indicated that it was not important for organisations working with young people to cater for Muslims only, and expressed a preference for 'all religions and cultures' to be included. It is interesting to note that Table 8.8 appears to indicate that younger respondents were less committed to 'all religions and cultures' than their parents generation, but this was not born out by those who were working in the field, or by the comments of younger respondents. While the younger age-bands preferred to socialise more widely, particularly young women, they suggested that their parents would not allow this.

> Right now the club I go to has only got Muslim girls in it and I think that it is quite important. If it's for girls our parents would expect that. [Female, aged 15]

> I belonged to a group in the Muslim House at Charing Cross. Mum found out about the group from her friend. She was trying to find a place where we could go to spend some time but she didn't want us to get corrupted. [Female, aged 23]

Younger women were quite specific about the composition of a group that would be acceptable to their parents, although they felt this would change with time.

> The group I went to was for Asian girls but it was really Muslim girls ... A couple of Hindu and Sikh girls came to the group for a while and then left. My mum didn't mind. I think she would have minded if it was White girls but I don't know. We've always had White friends coming into the house, that hasn't been a problem,

but I think if it was a group she would be hesitant. [Female, aged 23]

> I feel it is important that groups are open to all religions and cultures but society is not ready for it just now and I feel if we rushed that we could knock back ten years of work rather than let it take it's natural course. [Female, aged 30]

Table 8.8 Govanhill Sample: Separate Muslim Provision (Youth)

Which of the following points are 'very important' for organisations working with young men/women?

	14-24		25-50		50+		Total
	f	m	f	m	f	m	
Total respondents:	10	10	11	11	10	10	62
Young women:							
All religions & cultures	6	3	9	8	9	6	41
Young Muslim women only	0	3	5	1	7	5	21
Young men:							
All religions & cultures	5	5	9	6	8	8	41
Young Muslim men only	1	1	2	0	2	3	9

The situation was not clear cut and some older respondents felt it was important for young people to mix as long as specific religious and cultural requirements were acknowledged.

> It is not very important that the group is only for young Muslim women. To me there must be freedom. I am broad minded. But they need to discuss their problems in a similar manner in which they are brought up. If they complain about their mother and father it is better if they have the same background and the same manners of speaking as the others involved in the group. Maybe they could discuss some things openly all together and have some separate discussions with people from the same background. That would probably be better. [Male, aged 59]

While young men had greater freedom to mix socially with non-Muslim peers there were other issues relating to Pakistani and Indian identity:

> Oh dear, with that age range you'd get the exceptions but the exceptions are few and far between and the majority shows that teenage Pakistani boys and teenage Indian boys very rarely mix ... It is not important that it is Muslims only, but what is important is

that things are taken into consideration that won't cause friction within the club. [Female, aged 30]

Religiously Specific Provision

The religious factors included in this part of the interview were the importance of Muslim staff, *halal* food, and Islamic studies as an activity in the curriculum.

Table 8.9 Govanhill Sample: Religiously Specific Provision (Youth)

Which of the following points are 'very important' for organisations working with young men/women?

	14-24		25-50		50+		Total
	f	m	f	m	f	m	
Total respondents:	10	10	11	11	10	10	62
For young men:							
Islamic studies	6	7	7	9	10	10	49
Halal food	4	6	7	8	10	9	44
Muslim staff	2	0	3	2	7	7	21
For young women:							
Islamic studies	7	7	8	8	10	10	50
Halal food	6	6	7	8	9	9	45
Muslim staff	2	5	5	3	8	6	29

The importance attributed to these factors appeared to increase with age, with no clear differences in relation to gender. The importance of *halal* food was acknowledged but where food or snacks were provided this could be catered for through the availability of vegetarian choices. Meanwhile the presence of Muslim staff was regarded as the least important of the three factors, and even those who felt it was important to have Muslim staff were inclined to suggest that some, rather than all, the staff should be Muslim.

> It is important that there are Muslim staff but I wouldn't say that all of the staff should be Muslim. I think it's very important that at least one member of staff is Muslim and can relate to things that may come up that a non-Muslim person may not know about. [Female, aged 30]

However, the majority of respondents thought Islamic studies should be included as an activity in a youth work setting and it appeared that young people were taking an interest in Islam even if they questioned some of the cultural mores of their elders.

> I think they are kind of getting back into it. When I look at young people now they know a lot about their religion. [Male, aged 28]

> Every young person that we know praises their religion like anybody's business. They are proud to be Muslim, they are proud to be following the faith of Islam, but they're a new generation of Muslims. These are Muslims that live their culture within another culture and they have got to make adaptations to be able to survive this way. [Female youth worker, aged 30]

Culturally Specific Provision

The culturally specific factors examined related to language and gender.

Table 8.10 Govanhill Sample: Culturally Specific Provision (Youth)

Which of the following points are 'very important' for organisations working with young men/women?

	14-24		25-50		50+		Total
	f	m	f	m	f	m	
Total respondents:	10	10	11	11	10	10	62
For young men:							
Urdu lessons as an activity	7	7	7	9	10	7	47
Written information/Urdu	3	1	5	4	9	4	26
Some staff speak Urdu	2	1	4	3	9	5	24
Written information/Punjabi	2	1	4	4	8	3	22
Some staff speak Punjabi	2	1	3	2	8	3	19
For young women:							
Urdu lessons as an activity	8	8	8	9	10	8	51
Written information/Urdu	4	3	8	3	8	5	31
Some staff speak Urdu	1	1	4	5	9	8	28
Written information/Punjabi	3	3	6	3	7	3	25
Some staff speak Punjabi	1	1	4	4	8	4	22

It should be remembered that Urdu is the national language of Pakistan and is regarded as a 'book' language. Thus a leaflet or poster translated into Urdu alone could be considered to be aimed solely at the population of Pakistani Muslim origin, while to suggest that written Punjabi is 'very important' may indicate a willingness to extend membership to Sikhs who are more likely to read and write Punjabi. More women than men regarded both spoken and written Punjabi as important. Bearing in mind the majority of respondents, irrespective of gender, spoke Punjabi, this suggests women took a more pragmatic approach to language and were possibly more willing than men to encourage or permit mixed Muslim/Sikh activities.

The importance attributed to most of the language factors tended to increase with age, with older women in particular regarding bilingual staff and translated literature as 'very important'. But the majority of young people, irrespective of gender, shared the view of the older respondents that Urdu lessons should be included as a youth work activity. This indicated a commitment to retain, and in many cases acquire, the language.

Table 8.11 Govanhill Sample: Gender Separation (Youth)

Which of the following points are 'very important' for organisations working with young men/women?

	14-24		25-50		50+		Total
	f	m	f	m	f	m	
Total respondents:	10	10	11	11	10	10	62
For young men:							
All staff are male	1	0	3	0	5	7	16
No young women allowed	1	1	4	4	5	9	24
For young women:							
All staff are female	2	5	7	7	9	9	39
No young men allowed	3	5	6	5	9	8	36

Ensuring that staff were of the same gender as the young people in the group was considered to be much more important for young women than young men, and age influenced opinion. It appeared that younger women felt it was preferable in order to gain parental consent to attend a group, rather than essential in its own right, although some did have specific concerns about the appropriateness of men working with young women.

> We can't have a male because our parents wouldn't approve of it, plus we'll be dancing about and all that. It's not really good to have a male there. Not being sexist or anything, but they would prefer it if it was a woman. [Female, aged 15]

> Muslim girls would not be allowed to go to the group if a man was organising it. They would think he was weird anyway wanting to set up a girls group! [laughs]. He would have to go and see the parents,

> the mums, talk to them individually, and I don't think they would agree. [Female, aged 24]

Single sex groups were also seen as more important for young women than for young men. Only one respondent used the sort of argument more commonly expressed in 'mainstream' youth work debates.

> I find when the girls are on their own and the guys are on their own they can get on with it. When they get mixed, the guys seem to take over. [Male, aged 37]

The majority of respondents were more concerned with separation of the sexes to preserve modesty.

> Definitely no young men in the group at all. Men and women don't mix. [Male, aged 67]

Equal Opportunities

A number of factors were included in the interview to assess the relative importance placed on multiculturalism, anti-racism, and equal opportunities between men and women. Racism was identified earlier as one of the main problems affecting young people and, in line with this view, the majority of respondents felt it was very important that youth groups and organisations should have an anti-racist policy. Racism was also considered to be an important topic for discussion.

It has already been noted that most respondents declared a commitment to the inclusion of 'all religions and cultures', but some had specific views about the degree of mixing that would be acceptable in practice. Similarly, the majority of respondents indicated that an organisation working with young people should believe in equal opportunities for men and women but the interview transcripts revealed a complex picture. Older men felt that men and women should be treated with equal respect, but that they had different roles.

> In a youth club there should be equal opportunities but there are certain things that girls can't do and there are certain things that boys can't do. [Male, aged 67]

Younger men were less likely to hold this opinion, but it was the younger women who were most outspoken about the lack of equality they experienced.

I just feel that in our culture it's more of like a man's world. If you've got females and males in the same household, from a young age the girls are taught not to do certain things and the boys are taught that it's fine ... The male has that dominant role and I feel that they take advantage of it. I suppose in a way they can't help themselves because they've been brought up that way and it's a behaviour pattern that carries on, but I feel parents should give more equality to males and females from day one. [Female, aged 26]

Table 8.12a Govanhill Sample: Equal Opportunities (Youth)

	14-24		25-50		50+		Total
	f	m	f	m	f	m	
Total respondents	10	10	11	11	10	10	62

Which of the following are 'very important' for a group working with young men/women?

For young men:

	f	m	f	m	f	m	
Anti-racist policy	9	9	10	11	10	8	57
Equal opps. for men & women	9	7	9	11	10	6	52
All religions & cultures	5	5	9	6	8	8	41

For young women:

	f	m	f	m	f	m	
Anti-racist policy	10	9	10	9	9	8	55
Equal opps. for men & women	8	6	8	6	9	4	41
All religions & cultures	6	3	9	8	9	6	41

Table 8.12b Equal Opportunities Discussion (Youth)

Should the following be discussed in a group for young men/women?

For young men:

	f	m	f	m	f	m	
Racism	9	10	11	11	10	8	59
Equal opps. for men & women	10	9	10	10	10	7	56

For young women:

	f	m	f	m	f	m	
Racism	9	10	11	10	10	8	58
Equal opps. for men & women	10	9	10	10	10	7	56

It appeared that the situation would change with time. Some young women intended to use their influence within the home to allow more freedom for their daughters, while others were keen to study Islam in order to promote equality. The majority of younger women interviewed were confident that things were changing.

Parents are a lot stricter on girls, that's why I'm not going to be [laughs]. I'm going to go easy on them. [Female, aged 25]

> Equality would have to be brought in. That is why I am saying it's important for children to go to mosque to learn Islam from the *Qur'an*, not man-made Islam. Because the *Qur'an* doesn't say that there shouldn't be equality in a Muslim household. [Female, aged 30]

In the meantime, single sex provision, with sensitivity towards the cultural and religious mix of the group, were required if a youth group was to be viable. Care was also required in planning a suitable programme of activities.

Issue-based Youth Work

In common with many projects serving young people, the youth project in Govanhill encouraged participation in issue-based group work concerning topics thought to be particularly relevant to adolescence. While respondents expressed general approval for topics such as careers advice, racism and drugs awareness, difficulties became apparent over the inclusion of contraception and sexual health.

> If you had a Muslim group and you started teaching them about contraceptives then the parents would whip them out of the group and you wouldn't have a group left. There is no way you could do that type of issue-based work. Issue-based work in an Asian group or a Muslim group is very, very hard to do, particularly with young females. [Female, aged 30]

Questions were included in the interview to determine whether sexual activity was thought to be a problem for young people and the responses confirmed that sexual activity was a very sensitive issue. Just over half of the respondents indicated that it was a problem for young men, but were less inclined to say that it was a problem for young women. Those who elaborated on this point felt that the extent of sexual activity was unlikely to be admitted.

> Most of my friends have had sex before marriage but they can't really talk about it. They don't believe if they go to the clinic or the doctor that it won't go back to their parents, so they try to get someone else to get contraception or they just don't bother. [Female, aged 23]

> There is sexual activity, but they hide it very well. They seem to either disappear or they stay in the house or something. You just don't see them. But I know through the shop, one or two people.

> You hear that something has happened and then you don't see them for ages, and then you see them again later on. Nothing gets said but I think it does happen. [Male, aged 37]

If sexual activity was taking place, then issues of sexual health were relevant and the list of possible discussion topics included contraception and HIV/AIDS awareness. Although the majority of respondents had not seen HIV/AIDS as a major problem affecting young people, it was regarded as a more acceptable topic for discussion than contraception.

> You see it is very delicate because you can only discuss so much. I mean if you are going to tell parents that you are talking about contraception then they won't let you go. I mean HIV/AIDS, yes, because there are other ways of contracting that. [Female, aged 24]

Table 8.13a Govanhill Sample: Sexual Health Problems (Youth)

	14-24 f m	25-50 f m	50+ f m	Total
Total respondents	10 10	11 11	10 10	62
Which of the following problems affect young men/women?				
Sexual activity				
Young men	5 3	6 8	7 6	35
Young women	4 3	4 6	2 3	22
HIV/AIDS				
Young men	3 4	3 4	3 3	20
Young women	1 1	2 3	3 2	12

Table 8.13b Sexual Health Discussion (Youth)

	14-24	25-50	50+	Total
Should the following be discussed in a group for young men/women?				
Contraception				
Young men	8 8	10 11	5 8	50
Young women	7 9	10 10	6 8	50
HIV/AIDS awareness				
Young men	10 10	11 11	9 8	59
Young women	9 9	11 10	8 8	55

It was also suggested that discussing sexual health issues in a group would not be easy, particularly for young women.

> See when it comes to group discussion, girls are afraid to speak their opinions. Every get together with Muslim girls is a farce. They are

one thing inside and they are another thing to your face. There is a lack of trust between groups of Asian girls. They are scared about their sexuality, they are just not honest. I've done it. I do it all the time. I can't be myself because I'm scared that they'll think 'She's wild' [laughs]. [Female, aged 26]

Schools were felt to be a more acceptable place to impart such information. Thus some of the older respondents stated that young people should not know about contraception, whilst at the same time accepting that it was part of the school curriculum. In fact, the Education Act 1993 allows parents to withdraw their children from sex education, but this was rarely done. This confirmed the more pragmatic approach taken towards sensitive issues within a school context.

> I think everybody knows about this by the time they leave school. [Male, aged 50]

> Girls should be taught that having sex before marriage is a grave sin. They should not know about contraception. They get taught in school anyway. [Female, aged 64]

Guidance and Counselling

The Scottish Office had identified 'guidance and counselling' as an important aspect of youth work [SOED 1992b] and Govanhill Youth Survey had shown that 36% of the Asian boys and 62% of the Asian girls interviewed had expressed interest in an advice service. But responses during the fieldwork interviews suggested that this was another sensitive area. Older respondents felt that problems should be discussed and solved within the family, and there was mistrust of outside agencies.

> Problems should not be discussed outside the house. All problems should stay in the house. [Female, aged 50]

Younger people felt there were times when the family could not offer appropriate support.

> Really with our culture they just say that things should be kept at home, you know, if you've got a problem or anything, but really you need to talk to someone else. [Female, aged 25]

But it was generally agreed that anyone offering support should share similar cultural or religious values with the young person concerned, even where problems were thought to stem from those values.

> I wouldn't go to any special organisation. I still don't think that's right unless they are Muslim because only a Muslim can truly understand a Muslim. [Female, aged 26]

> Having an outside agency to do it is basically like taking someone right out from where they exist and landing them somewhere totally different, and it's like they've got to start from zero. And they don't have any of that culture left, or the lifestyle they lived, and they end up living a totally different lifestyle, a totally westernised lifestyle. OK we don't agree, most young Asian people don't totally agree, with like the arranged marriages and the strict religion. But they definitely do not agree with being pulled right out of it. There's a lot of that about, all or nothing. They want somewhere in-between. Somewhere they can still hold on to part of the culture, you know. [Male, aged 29]

Recreational Activities

Data from the interviews suggests that parents and grandparents favoured youth work activities that focused on 'the imparting of knowledge and information' and 'teaching of skills'. Thus, first aid classes, self defence and sports were generally acceptable but activities such as discos, trips to the cinema and young people's holidays were much more controversial.

Table 8.14 Govanhill Sample: Recreational Activities (Youth)

Which of the following activities should young people take part in at youth groups/organisations?

	14-24		25-50		50+		Total
	f	m	f	m	f	m	
Total respondents:	10	10	11	11	10	10	62
Discos							
Young men	7	4	4	5	1	1	22
Young women	6	5	3	5	0	1	20
Trips to the cinema							
Young men	9	7	8	10	6	6	46
Young women	10	9	7	9	5	6	46
Holidays							
Young men	10	10	9	10	5	9	53
Young women	9	7	6	9	3	6	40

Older people strongly disapproved of discos for both young men and women, although some acknowledged that their sons might attend without their permission.

> If my son goes I don't want to know about it. I don't want him to come home and tell me about it, that's all. [Female, aged 50]

Although younger people were more inclined to think discos were acceptable, this was the least favoured activity on the list and there was no strong evidence of resentment towards elders over this issue.

> We were born and brought up here and we have different views from what our parents had and in their time it was different. They had never been to those kind of places or allowed to do these things, and half of them are illiterate and things like that. It would be the same for anyone if they went abroad and they couldn't speak the language. They would be scared to let their children go somewhere unless they knew exactly what it was like. [Male, aged 27]

Trips to the cinema were less controversial although older respondents might have concerns about the content of films.

> I did an Asian girls group in Shawlands and one of the mothers was totally against them going to the cinema even though it would have been within the certificate. If the group was all twelve year olds it wouldn't have been any higher than a twelve, but the parent was against it because she couldn't get to see what her daughter was watching beforehand. [Female, aged 30]

> Girls should not really go but maybe boys could go to the cinema. [Male, aged 63]

Both young men and young women indicated that they would like to take part in holidays and residential activities, but older parents showed reluctance to allow young people, especially their daughters, to stay away from home unless they were visiting relatives.

> There is no need for girls to go on holidays. A holiday can only be to visit relatives. It must be a blood relative. [Female, aged 50]

> Holidays would be all right if they are with elders, but not without elders. [Male, aged 50]

Sports

When younger respondents were asked about their hobbies and interests it became clear that sports and physical recreation were popular with both young men and women.

> My hobbies are football, tennis and swimming. [Male, aged 19]

> I play badminton and at the weekend I go swimming with my sisters. [Female, aged 21]

> I used to love netball, rounders, football and cricket. I was a bit of a tomboy. [Female, aged 25]

Both genders and all ages thought sports and games were an important and acceptable aspect of youth work.

Table 8.15 Govanhill Sample: Sports (Youth)

Which of the following activities should young people take part in at youth groups/organisations?

	14-24		25-50		50+		Total
	f	m	f	m	f	m	
Total respondents	10	10	11	11	10	10	62
Sports & games							
Young men	10	10	10	11	10	10	61
Young women	10	10	11	9	10	7	57

Meanwhile, the popular perception of football as a male obsession in Glasgow, was supported by a number of respondents.

> I used to go to the Asian Boys Club, but it was closed down. It was good. You could play football there, meet your friends there and have a good laugh. Football was the main thing. That's what everybody used to play there. It would be good if they could have extended it by another couple of hours! [Male, aged 19]

> My son enjoys football. In the evenings he plays football. He spends his weekends playing football [laughs]. He belongs to a football club and they play in the Sunday league in different areas. He brought the group together himself and they have won a lot of medals. He is football mad. [Female, aged 50]

> My son doesn't belong to any groups or organisations. All the boys get together and play football. [Male, aged 54]

It is also tempting to speculate that a new role model was emerging through the successful boxing career of 'Prince Naseem'.

> I am thinking of joining boxing. The training at the boxing club is good. One of my friends goes there. He was fat [laughs]. He has been going for nine months and he is dead fit. [Male, aged 14]

> I belong to the boxing club in Govanhill. My cousins went to the boxing club. I went to karate for a while but I found it was always messing about, different age groups and all that and you never learned nothing. Then I went there, to the boxing club, and everybody who was in there was over fourteen and mature and there was good heavy training. In boxing it's proper training. The boxing club itself isn't in a very good state but they've got a grant and should be doing it up soon. [Male, aged 17]

Thus young men appeared willing to commit time and energy to sport (even in 'unglamorous' situations such as a school youth wing or a run down boxing club) with potentially positive implications for health and self esteem. And young women also expressed an interest in sport, with the approval of their parents. However, this type of activity was regarded as the 'old school' of youth work practice.

> There used to be more of a crossover between youth work and sports. In fact I took a sports option in my second year when I was training. It was seen as a low priority option then and now it's really polarised. Youth workers concentrate on empowerment and group work theory. [Youth project leader]

Overall it appeared that the style and content of youth work provision in Govanhill, focusing on a 'socialisation model' and emphasising issue-based group work interspersed with recreational activities such as discos and cinema trips, tended to inhibit the participation of many young people from Pakistani households.

Interaction Between Service Providers and Service Users

In focusing on a socialisation model of youth work the Scottish Office made no specific references to work with young people from minority ethnic groups. At best there appeared to be an assumption that the guidelines on good practice were broad enough to encompass a wide range of approaches. A similar 'culture of inexplicitness' existed in Glasgow where youth service providers were encouraged to develop flexible responses to include young people from minority ethnic groups, but there were no specific directives as to how this could or should be achieved.

At local level, it was difficult to ascertain a clear approach taken by the youth project as a service provider to the Pakistani population of Govanhill. It appeared that the project began with an 'open door' approach but soon acknowledged that 'working practices would have to be altered'. However, there was very little evidence that significant changes were implemented. Lack of competition from other service providers may have contributed to this apparent lack of urgency. As the main provider of youth services in the area, the project had little difficulty in recruiting young people or demonstrating that it was meeting a need. Thus, although the Community Education Service noted that there should be 'a far clearer input into working with the ethnic minority communities within Govanhill', this issue was deflected towards applications for additional funding rather than a radical change of working practices.

There appeared to be greater commitment to working with young women from minority ethnic groups than young men, and a number of factors may have contributed to this. Within mainstream youth work, emphasis was placed on counteracting sexism and promoting equal opportunities for girls and this, combined with popular conceptions of the oppression of South Asian women, particularly within Islam, stimulated a commitment to provide services for them. Moreover, because of the restricted opportunities for social activity outside of the home and family, young women were often keen to attend such groups. These factors fostered the development of the Asian Girls Group in Govanhill and similar groups in other parts of the city.

The establishment of this group was not matched by any involvement of their male peers at the project although the closure of the youth wing at a local school, and the consequent demise of a successful Asian Boys Group, suggested that an opportunity did exist to work with some of these young men. Their apparent freedom gave them greater access to commercial activities and was regarded as an advantage they had over their female peers. A number of these young men were 'at risk' in terms that mainstream youth projects would recognise, such as involvement with gangs and drugs. But youth workers appeared less concerned to develop services for them. There was evidence that these young men, in common with many other young men of their age, and with the sons of previous immigrants, were keen to play football and other sports. But they were unable to assert this as a priority in a paradigm that regarded sport as the 'old school' of youth work.

The project did assert an anti-racist stance, and issue-based group work with young (White) people included challenging racism, but it appeared that the strategy of anti-racism was not sufficiently informed by 'appropriate ethnic histories'.[53] This was illustrated when the possibility of including Islamic studies in the Asian Girls Group was raised in a team meeting. The response of a number of White workers (which included comparing Islam with the Orange Order) suggested that their views were shaped by the particular history of Catholic/Protestant antagonism in the West of Scotland, mixed with fears of colluding with Islamic fundamentalism. There appeared to be little understanding that Islamic studies might include debates about equality, feminism or anti-racism. The incident revealed the need for specialised staff training in multicultural and multi-faith issues, but the matter was resolved away from the full staff team as a separate issue relating specifically to the Asian Girls Group.

The lack of a coherent policy in relation to work with young people from minority ethnic groups in Govanhill arose, at least in part, from the initial recruitment of staff. White local activists employed White senior staff members despite recourse to anti-racist and multicultural terminology in the original funding application. Thereafter, several applications for additional funding made reference to the fact that the staff team lacked the skills and experience to undertake multicultural youth work. Both the Community Education Service and the youth project showed some commitment to the recruitment of sessional staff from minority ethnic groups, but these workers were not in a strong position to influence the overall development of policy. Furthermore, they were more inclined to leave if permanent employment was offered elsewhere, as was evident when the Asian Girls Group was unable to meet for two-and-a-half months after a key sessional worker found full-time employment.

The initial statement that the youth project would work with young people from minority ethnic groups was later replaced by recognition of the need to 'reprioritise' in order to undertake such work and then by an assertion that additional funds were required before such work could be developed. It appeared that, having established a successful pattern of recruitment and group work with young (White) people, this continued as the dominant paradigm even though it was recognised as ineffective in recruiting and working with young people from minority ethnic groups.

Meanwhile, as was the case with previous immigrant populations, Pakistani elders in Scotland expressed fears that the cultural and religious values of their children would be undermined by inappropriate social contact. Broad agreement about the acceptability of public, co-educational

---

[53] See introductory references to Modood 1997c.

schools may have resulted from a belief that the school day was sufficiently structured and supervised to minimise inappropriate social contact. But in the case of youth services there was very little evidence of this pragmatic approach. The majority of respondents indicated that they were not against youth work participation *per se* but had concerns about the style and content of provision.

Single sex provision appeared to be essential if young women were to participate in youth groups and, while separate Muslim provision was not stipulated by the majority of those interviewed, 'all religions and cultures' was likely to have a restricted definition. These specific priorities were asserted when the youth project attempted to establish an Asian Girls Group, resulting in a group with all-Muslim membership that met at an earlier time and had a different programme of activities from the other groups at the Project.

It was not just parents who had concerns, and a degree of religious and cultural sensitivity in youth service provision was expected by the majority of respondents. Although it was acknowledged that young people needed guidance and support during adolescence, older respondents mistrusted outside agencies and felt that problems should be discussed and solved within the family. Younger respondents, who indicated that it was not always possible to resolve problems in this way, nevertheless felt that outside support should be offered by someone who shared, or at least understood, their cultural or religious background.

Issue-based group work, a key element in the curriculum of many mainstream youth projects, was thought to be more suitable in a school environment and recreational activities involving a risk of 'inappropriate' social contact (such as discos) were generally thought to be unacceptable. Thus a good deal of mainstream youth service activities posed problems for young people from Pakistani family backgrounds. Meanwhile, respondents of both genders and all ages thought sports were an important and acceptable aspect of youth work. The doctrine that sports were no longer an important element of youth service provision appeared to result in a lost opportunity to recruit these young people with the approval of their parents.

While interaction between White youth service providers and service users of Pakistani background was limited, a more dynamic interaction was evident between the young people and their parents. It appeared that young people were not completely rejecting the values of their parents but were negotiating a new identity in relation to them. Some were emphasising a religious perspective in order to do so. A number of younger respondents suggested that with increased knowledge of Islam they would be able to negotiate concessions from their parents regarding 'acceptable' behaviour. Others were willing to comply with the wishes of their elders, acknowledging that they had grown up in a very different environment and were genuinely worried about the welfare of their children, but indicated that they would apply different standards to their own children. This suggests that although Islamic studies were perceived by some White workers as placing restrictions on young people, such studies offered an opportunity for both young men and women to negotiate a Scottish Muslim identity. However, it appeared that young people in Govanhill were engaging in this process despite, rather than because of, existing youth service provision.

If integration is conceptualised as an interactive process then it can be argued that this process was inhibited in relation to youth service provision in Govanhill. The voluntary nature of youth services made non-participation much more feasible than was the case with school-age education. This was the favoured option where existing services were considered inappropriate, and the benefits of participation were less tangible than acquiring recognised academic qualifications. In the next chapter consideration is given to a service where participation was also voluntary, but the perceived benefits were more tangible than those of the youth project - care of the elderly.

9 Elderly Care: a Case of Benevolent Trial and Error

Both Catholic and Jewish immigrants in Scotland established welfare organisations to care for the frail and needy, including homes for the elderly in which they could observe dietary requirements and religious obligations. In this chapter the provision and use of elderly care services are examined through consideration of the current policy framework within which care is offered to elderly people from minority ethnic groups; the interpretation of these policies by the main service provider in Govanhill; and, the priorities of Pakistani immigrants and their descendants as actual or potential service users. Finally, some conclusions are drawn concerning the interaction between the providers of elderly care services and the Pakistani population.

Care in the Community

In recent years policies relating to care of the elderly have been shaped by the more general move towards 'Care in the Community'. In 1989 the government published the White Paper, *Caring for People: Community Care in the Next Decade and Beyond*, setting out its policy for the management and delivery of services for a range of client groups. This was followed by the National Health Service and Community Care Act 1990 which aimed to 'shift the provision of care away from institutions and towards facilities based in the community provided not only by local authorities but also by the private and voluntary sectors and by the primary health care services' [Scottish Office 1993]. Section 52 of the Act required local authorities to prepare and publish relevant plans every three years with effect from 1992 and to review them annually.

In 1992 Strathclyde Regional Council produced its first Community Care Plan in which it was asserted that community involvement was already an essential dimension of service delivery. It was stated that the council's general commitment to community development included supporting and promoting community groups, involving local people in the development of policies and services, and providing opportunities for individuals and community groups to take greater responsibility and control of their own resources. Reference to 'black and ethnic minority groups' was under specific sections entitled 'Corporate Council Policies' and 'Social Work Policies'. It was stated that the council 'will seek to ensure that its mainstream provision and that of other agencies is sufficiently sensitive to meet different cultural expectations and requirements, and to ensure equality of access to all forms of provision' whilst at the same time recognising that 'there is a need for separate provision in particular cases where services to black and ethnic minority groups are more effectively provided in a particular environment and by persons of the same background' [SRC 1992].

Strathclyde Community Relations Council expressed concerns about the approach taken in the Plan and made a number of key recommendations.[54] It was argued that the local authority should recognise ethnic minorities as members of different care groups rather than as a separate policy issue. Furthermore, a strategic framework should be developed and should include: procedures for monitoring and assessment with identifiable statistics; involving ethnic minority groups in the planning and designing of care packages; buying services from ethnic minority service providers; employing specialist workers; and providing 'cultural awareness' training for all staff.[55] The Deputy Director of Social Work responded by confirming that Strathclyde Community Relation Council's comments would be taken into consideration in regional planning and in the preparation of the next Community Care Plan [Iqbal 1995].

In November 1994 a Consultation Draft of the next Joint Community Care Plan was produced and circulated. A short sub-section entitled Black and Ethnic Minority Communities contained the assertion that:

> ... access to general services across all agencies is available to people from black and ethnic minorities [SRC et al 1994: 39].

Despite this confident statement about access, it was suggested that the challenges for service providers were: understanding the needs of 'black and ethnic minority' service users and carers; provision of information; recruitment policies and procedures; interpreting services; housing adaptations; and involvement in joint planning. A number of actions were proposed in response to these challenges including: the establishment of a

---

[54] Strathclyde Community Relations Council became West of Scotland Community Relations Council following local government reorganisation.

[55] The full range of care groups were: elderly, people with dementia, people with mental health problems, children and young people with special needs, people with mental handicap, people with physical disabilities, people with sensory impairment, people with head injuries, alcohol, drugs, and HIV/AIDS.

working group to monitor and promote 'racial equality' in the provision of community care services; promoting self help and advocacy groups; encouraging 'black and ethnic minority groups' to become involved in the list of authorised providers; monitoring service relevance and sensitivity; and establishing research projects into the medium and long term need for community care services within 'the black and ethnic minority community'. Despite these lists of challenges and proposals, the phrase concerning access revealed a somewhat complacent 'open door' approach to service provision. This was pounced on by those who had taken time to make recommendations concerning the previous Plan. A special issue of *Interchange*, a monthly newsletter published by Glasgow Council for Voluntary Services, was dedicated to the Joint Community Care Plan and was widely circulated in the voluntary sector. It was argued:

> The section of the plan which refers to Black and Ethnic Minority Communities (pages 39-40) is grossly unacceptable when it states that "access to general services across all agencies is available to people from black and ethnic minorities". This incredible statement masks the fact that most mainstream services pay scant attention to the needs of black and ethnic minority communities, and, as a consequence, uptake may be low. [GCVS 1995a]

A meeting was jointly organised by Strathclyde Community Relations Council and Glasgow Council for Voluntary Services to consider the implications of the Plan. The minutes indicated unanimous agreement that 'the portion of the Plan dealing with services to black and ethnic minority communities was grossly inadequate in all aspects, as well as dangerously misleading in its assertion that services are accessible to all' [GCVS 1995b]. Concern was expressed that there was no clear corporate strategy about the development, monitoring and evaluation of community care services for 'black and ethnic minority groups' who were 'lumped together' as a homogeneous group rather than being recognised as having a wide range of needs. Criticism was levelled at the nature of training for local authority employees because it focused on anti-racism while 'cultural awareness' was slow to develop. In addition the 'black voluntary sector' needed resources and training in order to develop their role in community care, particularly in the field of contracting where investment was required to enable them to compete.[56] It was argued that the patchwork of funding through relatively

---

[56] Through the system of contracting, organisations made bids to provide services previously provided by the local authority. While this was supposed to encourage competition, large established organisations had a distinct advantage over those that were smaller and less experienced.

short-term grants should be replaced by a commitment to funding from mainstream budgets.

When the *1995-1998 Greater Glasgow Joint Community Care Plan* was finally published, cursory reference was made to the 'lack of proper reference' to 'black and ethnic minorities' [SRC et al 1995: 17-21]. It was stated:

> As a result of recent discussion it is recognised that individual choice and access to general services will be available to people from black and ethnic minorities. [Ibid: 60].

This statement replaced the controversial assertion that 'access to general services across all agencies is available to people from black and ethnic minorities', although the replacement of '*is*' with '*will be*' and the addition of 'individual choice' was barely less controversial and invited such questions as 'When?' and 'How?' Nevertheless some of the comments made during the consultation process were incorporated in the Plan. A number of issues were identified for priority action including: recruitment of bilingual staff; funding services from mainline service budgets rather than short term developmental budgets; improved communication through interpreters, translated text, audio and video tapes; anti-racist and cultural awareness training; consultation and service monitoring; and the provision of assistance to enable 'black voluntary organisations' to become approved providers [Ibid: 61].

Overall, the history of the Plan suggested reluctance on the part of the existing statutory service providers to acknowledge that mainstream services had not made adequate provision for minority ethnic groups. To some extent this reflected wider concerns amongst social workers that the basic tenets of the welfare state were being undermined:

> To treat ethnic minority groups as different strikes at the heart of the philosophy of the Welfare State. Ideas of different or separate provision for these groups contradict the universalistic principles that lie at the heart of contemporary liberalism, that all should be equal before the law and have equal rights to public facilities. [McCluskey 1991: 114]

Nevertheless, by the mid-1990s a policy framework existed that offered some encouragement to the development of 'culturally sensitive' and even 'culturally specific' services. It was within this climate that services were provided to the elderly population of Govanhill.

Elderly Care in Govanhill

In 1972 a voluntary sector lunch club was established in Govanhill with the initial aim of 'providing a nutritious meal for the elderly'. The need for elderly day care services in Govanhill was so great that within four years the small lunch club had become a thriving day care centre with 500 members. But it was not until the 1990 Annual Report that Govanhill's 'Asian' population was mentioned:

> A very important new feature of our care began with an Asian Friendship Evening in the Centre. This was a very colourful and lively occasion where Asian families with our Members and Staff sang and danced and ate together. From that hospitable opening an Elderly Ethnic Group has been formed and will meet every week in the Centre. Five Asian volunteers have offered their services to the Good Neighbour Scheme. Through these two beginnings we hope to improve communications and relationships with our ethnic minority neighbours so that we can offer their elderly our services and support.

While it could be argued that the Centre had been slow to recognise the presence of elders from minority ethnic groups, it should also be noted that Census data indicated there were 31 Pakistani and 10 Other (i.e. non-White) residents of pensionable age in Govanhill in 1991. These figures were likely to have been even lower during the previous twenty years when the project was developing its services. When the Centre took positive action to contact Asian elders, the new members were soon included in the somewhat possessive terminology. The 1991 Chairman's Report[57] at the Annual General Meeting stated:

> Our ethnic group have adopted the title *Ittifaq*, meaning union and friendship. The group consists of 14 elderly and a mixed age group of about 30. *Ittifaq* meet once a week to have lunch followed by an afternoon of activities in the Centre. Other social events, which include bus runs and parties, have been valuable in providing opportunities for the staff to learn more about the customs and culture of the group.

The group held weekly meetings which alternated between unstructured social gatherings and more structured meetings with visiting speakers. None of the staff supporting the group could speak Urdu or Punjabi - the first

---

[57] This was the terminology used although the 'Chairman' was consistently a woman.

languages of the members - and this difficulty was overcome by expanding membership to include younger bilingual women who acted as interpreters:

> The presence of the younger women, most of whom are able to speak English, facilitates communication between the group and workers who do not have language skills in Urdu or Punjabi. However, language barriers do not pose a great problem, as the group members and workers have become more familiar with each other and are now very relaxed in each other's company. [*Race & Housing* February 1993: 3]

The women were Muslim and the fact that since efforts were made to obtain *halal* meals suggests that they were able to assert some of their religious priorities. Food was provided through Catering Direct, who operated the school meals service but it soon became clear that the choice of two menus was somewhat limited:

Menu 1
soup
halal meat, mashed potato, vegetables
vegetarian cake and custard

Menu 2
soup
korma mince, mashed potato, vegetables
vegetarian apple pie and custard

Members voted with their feet and numbers at the lunch club temporarily declined. Following unsuccessful attempts to obtain a more varied menu, the group eventually settled for 'fish and chips and sweet'. Although this was served every week, *Ittifaq* thrived and it was asserted that 'the 30 members attending the Tuesday lunch are regular attendees and enjoy this menu as it is different from their usual daily diet'.

The successful establishment of *Ittifaq* encouraged the Centre to apply for Urban Programme funding for a 'Black Elderly Initiative' to develop and promote 'ethnically sensitive services to Asian/Black elderly'. The new project would provide day care services including a lunch club, group activities, arts and crafts, welfare rights advice, health promotion and advice, housing advice, a library, films and a separate prayer facility. Transport would be provided and outreach work would identify frail and vulnerable 'ethnic elders'. It was asserted that the project 'would wish to employ properly skilled and experienced bilingual workers' but the tentative language reflected a lack of confidence that skilled and experienced bilingual workers would be forthcoming. The vocabulary used in the application was not religiously specific although reference to a separate prayer facility was clearly an acknowledgement that religious practice would be important to some of the elderly clients.

The 1992 Chairman's Report indicated that Urban Programme funding had been secured and that the project had advertised for staff, although there had been a 'disappointing response from suitably experienced or qualified candidates'. The posts were not filled until the following year which was described as a year of consolidation when the project successfully recruited bilingual staff as well as 10 volunteers and 70 members [Chairman's Report 1993]. At this point the 'Black Elderly Initiative' became the 'Friendship and Support Centre for Ethnic Minority Elderly', reflecting the fact that members did not regard themselves as 'Black'. The project was open four days per week with a programme that included a lunch club, keep fit, English language classes, arts and crafts activities and *daras* (prayers). However, all the members were female and it was acknowledged that 'elderly men from the Asian community still find it difficult to join in the social activities provided by this project' [Ibid]. The solution, implemented the following year, was to provide separate men's sessions.

There was an expressed commitment to 'integration'. The term was not defined but it appeared to refer to positive interaction and mutual understanding. It was asserted that the project 'has provided the focus for integration between the ethnic and indigenous populations which have strengthened the links between them and produced empathy and understanding in both cultures' [Ibid]. The following year a progress report stated:

> Despite the language problems friendships have developed. Members in all parts of the [Centre] are able to say hello, smile and say a few words to each other, both in and outside of the Centre. At least once a month we try to have an event where the two communities can integrate.

Concerns about integration did not only focus on relationships between 'the ethnic and indigenous populations'. In practice the project was catering for Pakistani Muslims and in the 1995 Annual Report it was stated:

> In an effort to reach other minority groups, we had a very successful Multi-Cultural Event. Successful in the sense of being a great night's entertainment; not successful in attracting elderly people of other communities.

At the same time the Centre was anxious to retain its existing clients and to ward off perceived competition. In 1991, the *Jamiat Ittihad-ul-Muslimin* at Glasgow's Central Mosque began work on an Urban Programme application to develop services for Muslim elders in disused school buildings close to Govanhill. Between 1992 and 1994 the Area Liaison Committee in Govanhill undertook a series of meetings to discuss this and other Urban Programme applications. This Committee was made up of voluntary sector representatives, community education staff and a local councillor, and had considerable influence over the final outcome of applications which could not progress without its support [Urban Programme Guidelines for Glasgow DCDC 10/3/93]. Concerns were expressed that the project proposed by the Central Mosque would involve duplication of services and would have a detrimental effect on the existing project in Govanhill. The discussion also revealed a degree of cultural racism. It was suggested that the management structure would be 'undemocratic' and that the project would 'target Pakistani and particularly Muslim men to the exclusion of other ethnic minority and black groups of both genders'. The local councillor, who chaired the meeting, intervened:

> I have to say something about the legitimacy of the Mosque doing social work like this. I must admit to reservations but as a Regional Council we have to be even-handed. The Catholic Church and the Church of Scotland are an integral part of Social Services in the Region. I'd be happy if that was not the case, but we have to be even-handed.

This quotation, while arguing for equal treatment, suggests that concerns about the potential for denominational schools to perpetuate religious antagonism were also evident in relation to welfare facilities. The Area Liaison Committee, the local authority and the Scottish Office all appeared more comfortable with terminology such as 'black', 'ethnic minority', 'multicultural' and 'integrated', where religious identity was not specified. In the event the proposal did not gain Urban Programme funding, but the Social Work Department and a group of Muslim elders did work together to develop an elderly care centre based in Glasgow's Central Mosque.[58] While there had been worries about competition it will be shown later that a number of elderly respondents enjoyed attending both groups.

In practice, while a proposal for a Muslim-founded project had struggled to gain political and financial support, the Centre in Govanhill was running a group for Muslims. This had come about because the earliest 'ethnic

---

[58] Greater Glasgow Joint Community Care Plan 1995-1998: 100.

minority' members had negotiated provision for their specific religious obligations (such as facilities for *daras* and the provision of *halal* food) which then signalled to others that the services were geared towards the needs of Muslim elders. The extent to which membership could be broadened appeared to be limited, but to consider this in more detail the next section focuses on the views of actual or potential service users from a Pakistani Muslim background.

Priorities of Pakistani Immigrants and Their Descendants

To gauge the significance placed on cultural and religious factors by service users five key areas were considered during the interviews. How did Pakistani elders spend their time and what were their interests? What were the main problems they faced? Who should care for them? What services were considered important? And, how much importance was placed on religiously or culturally specific provision, and on multicultural, anti-racist and equal opportunities policies?

Interests of the Elderly

As was the case with young people, the interviews revealed different social spheres for men and women. The social lives of the elderly women tended to revolve around their families and a good deal of time was spent visiting or entertaining relatives.

> My mother spends her days looking after her grandchildren because my elder brother stays with them. And she visits friends and relatives. [Female, aged 32]

> My mother comes over to my house, and she's got lots of nephews and nieces. She visits all of us. [Female, aged 33]

While visiting and childcare were important activities for elderly women, there was often a reduction in household chores. These became the responsibility of younger females and a number of respondents raised the concept of a 'retired housewife'.

> My aunt hasn't got a job but she used to be a housewife. Now she mainly sits and reads the *Qur'an*. [Female, aged 21]

> My mother is retired. She used to be a housewife. She doesn't have hobbies. She stays in the house. She is very sociable and has her friends and relatives to visit. [Female, aged 42]

While the social lives of the elderly women were centred around the home and family, the men were more likely to be involved in social and political activities in the wider community.

> My father started up the Pakistani Welfare Trust with two other people ... They meet in different houses roughly every month. [Female, aged 21]

> I am involved with various housing associations. Positive Action in Housing is a forum to look after all the housing associations. They have paid staff, and I am on the committee, unpaid, voluntary. I go whenever there's a meeting. [Male, aged 67]

Irrespective of gender it was generally accepted that in the later stages of their lives the thoughts of the elderly turned towards religion. Men were more likely to centre their religious activities around the mosque while women prayed and read the *Qur'an* at home or with small groups of other women.[59]

> My mother goes to *Qur'an* readings with friends. They have a wee Asian committee going. They give wee parties, and read the *Qur'an*. She'll go if she can. My mother likes listening to stories from the *Qur'an*. It is about the holy events that have been passed down. My mum loves the stories. She's daft on prayers. She has problems bending but she puts a chair in front of her to help her bend down. [Female, aged 38]

> Mosque is a very good place for the elderly people because when the men come senior in age, in every religion they tend to go back to God and religion. So when older people go to the mosque they feel something very close, they feel happy. [Male, aged 68]

Problems Affecting the Elderly

In order to assess the relevance of specific services the interviews included questions about problems facing the elderly. There was broad agreement that family problems, language and poor health were all significant issues for the elderly, although the emphasis placed on each of these issues showed

---

[59] Even 'illiterate' women were able to read the *Qur'an* in Arabic

some variation with age and gender. Comments made during the interviews revealed why problems such as racism and poverty were seen as less important, as well as revealing the interplay between various factors (for example, family problems were seen as contributing to loneliness). In a number of cases, problems arose from historically and culturally specific circumstances and so it appeared unlikely that the younger respondents would face the same issues, or interpret them in the same way, as their elderly relatives.

Table 9.1a Govanhill Sample: Which of the Following Problems Affect the Elderly?

	14-24		25-50		50+		Total
	f	m	f	m	f	m	
Total respondents	10	10	11	11	10	10	62
Family problems	10	8	10	8	10	9	55
Problems with language	9	9	11	10	10	6	55
Poor health	8	8	10	10	9	9	54
Not enough organisations for Asian elderly	8	7	9	9	6	8	47
Not enough organisations for all elderly	9	5	8	10	5	8	45
Loneliness	6	4	9	8	9	8	44
Racism	8	6	8	6	5	9	42
Poverty	6	2	5	3	6	7	29

Table 9.1b Which are the Two Worst Problems Affecting the Elderly?

Family problems	5	4	3	5	9	6	32
Problems with language	2	6	7	3	4	1	23
Poor health	3	4	5	5	1	3	21
Loneliness	2	1	4	3	4	3	17
Not enough organisations for Asian elderly	6	0	2	4	0	3	15
Racism	1	4	0	0	0	2	7
Poverty	0	1	1	1	2	2	7
Not enough organisations for all elderly	1	0	0	0	0	0	1
Other:							
Not aware of facilities available	-	-	-	1	-	-	1

The majority of respondents took pride in the extended family system.[60] This was the case irrespective of age or gender, and even where individuals

---

[60] This involved maintaining close relationships with grandparents, aunts, uncles and cousins. In addition it was usual for the parents to live with their eldest son and his wife.

were critical of some aspects of family relationships. It is important to acknowledge this because it became clear that the family was also a source of considerable worry. The 'generation gap' was a common source of tension and was likely to be more pronounced where elders had been brought up in a different country from their offspring. However, the resulting difference of perspective was often well understood and negotiated.

> My grandparents have been great. Some grandparents say 'You shouldn't go out wearing trousers' but my grandparents are cool about that, so long as you are covering your body up, obviously, that's the main factor. They're not absolutely liberal but they are trying to understand western society. My parents are trying to teach them. [Female, aged 19]

> It might be a wise point that they are actually making. The reason I said that is because my mum's aunt came and I never listened to her point of view and I was always arguing with her. This is a few years back. Then recently I found out her history and what she has actually been through. I thought 'Oh God, she has been through hell'. So it makes you think twice about the things you actually say to a person. She has been really nice to me, genuinely really nice to me. [Male, aged 21]

> They feel rejected by the young ones. Maybe to some extent they are because they come from a different culture. Their children don't listen. The elders are more sentimental. When they were young they respected their parents in a different way and now their children have grown up they feel neglected. Maybe their children do respect them but the culture is different and they feel hurt. [Male, aged 50]

Some serious concerns were expressed over the introduction through marriage of new family members. The majority of respondents described the expected arrangement as one in which the daughters and younger sons left the family home when they married while the eldest son and his wife remained to take care of his parents. For this reason the eldest son's choice of marriage partner was particularly important. There was very little confidence that a White daughter-in-law would take on these duties.

> If sons have gone off with a Scot's girl for them it is a major crisis. I'm not being racist but it's a crisis because they want their son to marry a Muslim girl ... They have wed their daughters off and the son is meant to stay at home to take care of them, you see. [Female, aged 24]

> A lot of older people have family problems about their children. Maybe boys have married White girls. [Female, aged 50]

It was not only a White daughter-in-law who could be a problem. A wife born or brought up in Scotland may have very different views from those of her mother-in-law from Pakistan.

> My mother-in-law, she hasn't been educated or anything, so it's very hard to explain things like me working. You have to say 'Everyone does it. Life's like this'. They don't really understand. [Female, aged 25]

Not all family problems related to tensions between different generations. The sensitive issue of husbands having more than one wife was raised by one elderly woman who did not wish to elaborate, and two younger women who discussed the matter in more detail.

> My friend is a doctor. Recently her dad went to Pakistan and got married again. He got married to someone who is twenty-three, twenty four. Just like that. He came back and told his wife he got married while he was in Pakistan. It happens quite a lot. I don't know if I'm the only person who has told you that. It is all quite hush, hush. Especially older men going for a younger wife. It happens a lot but it's not discussed. [Female, aged 23]

> There have been quite a few men who have gone through a mid-life crisis and found a new wife in Pakistan and taken the house from under their first wife. The house is maybe tied up in the business and the wives don't know how to make themselves partners so they can't get access to it. Or they end up selling the house and they don't realise that they could actually have half of it by law even if it was not in their name. There have been a lot of sad things like that and cases of depression. I know about two cases like that in Govanhill. [Female, aged 24]

The frankness with which this issue was described by the younger women, and their reluctance to see this as anything other than male irresponsibility, make it unlikely that they would be as vulnerable in later life. However, the consequences could clearly be very serious for an elderly woman who was reluctant or ashamed to seek support from others. Difficult family issues were linked to social exclusion and loneliness by a number of respondents.

> My mother needs someone of her own age to say 'Come on, let's go out'. Because of the problems my family have had, a lot of the elderly won't come to the house.[61] Loneliness is a problem lately, because I've started college. I say 'Go out mum, go see someone'. She says 'How can I show my face when you have put me down?' It's like I'm starting to feel guilty for trying to make my own life. It's messing up my mum's life because she cannot go and see her friends and family because of me. [Female, aged 25]

Even where there were less specific issues, loneliness could still be a significant problem. In contrast to the notion of a close-knit family structure, a number of the younger respondents were not really aware of the interests of their elderly relatives even when they lived in the same house. This suggests that physical presence did not always equate with social interaction. Younger respondents were not always sensitive to this issue and were less likely to regard loneliness as a problem affecting the elderly.

> No, loneliness isn't a problem because what tends to happen is they seem to live with the family. My gran lives with my uncle and most of his family. I mean all my cousins and that, everyone just meets up at the house. My gran lives there, my uncle, and seven kids he's got. So everyone gathers there nearly every day. [Male, aged 17]

> Loneliness isn't a problem. They have a good social life, really they do. I wouldn't say any of my grandparents or their friends are lonely. Obviously they have children and their kids to look after or they go back to Pakistan for a wee holiday. [Female, aged 19]

Members of the middle age-band were more likely to recognise that loneliness can result from a lack of company of others of the same age or with the same interests.

> It could be loneliness in the way that there is maybe not someone from their generation you know. [Female, aged 30]

> Loneliness and family problems sort of ties in. 'I'm too busy to take you there. Why don't you ask what's-his-name?' They're all like that you know. 'Oh no, I'm lumbered with the old person for the day'. [Male, aged 29]

A tendency to rely on younger family members resulted from language difficulties. This was seen as particularly significant for older women, many

---

[61] This young woman was divorced.

of whom were thought to be dependent on others for even routine activities outside of the home.

> See if my mother ever got lost she would never know her way back. I mean she couldn't explain to a taxi driver. You would have to write it on a card and put it in her purse. You'd think all the years she has been here she would know. I'm not making a joke out of it, a lot of people are like that. [Female, aged 24]

> There is a problem with the language because they have not put enough effort into learning it. They've been too busy bringing up the kids and supporting the husband to think about themselves, but now they are being left on their own and it is a big problem. My mother can't read. She used to go out shopping in town and get by making signs instead of speaking English, but now she says 'You go, you do it'. [Female, aged 38]

Younger respondents explained how they were often called upon to escort elderly relatives to the doctor. This led to difficulties in understanding a diagnosis and, in addition, undermined privacy and confidentiality in the doctor-patient relationship.[62]

> The worst problem for them is getting to the doctors and explaining what is wrong with them. [Male, aged 20]

> My mother is diabetic. The worst problem I think is trying to understand for what reasons she isnae well, or what is exactly wrong with her. I mean I know I could go along with her and the doctor will discuss her problem with me and explain to me and then I'll explain to my mother, but that is like second hand material really. It's not coming first hand from an expert to her. She takes insulin and basically my mum knows she's taking it because the sugar isnae staying at the right level. All she knows is to take it in the morning and at night and she avoids eating sugar all day, so she doesn't understand why there's still a problem with sugar. I reckon speaking to a doctor in her language would be better for explaining things. [Male, aged 27]

The immediacy of family and personal problems took precedence over broader issues such as racism and poverty. Thus there was a tendency

---

[62] Consultations can be especially difficult if, for example, a woman has gynaecological problems and is required to discuss this through her son. See Pharaoh 1995.

amongst elderly respondents not to regard racism as a problem for themselves unless it took the form of physical harassment.

> Racism is a problem but they probably don't realise that people are being racist towards them. To them it is a problem if it is physical. [Female, aged 23]

> For older people I don't think racism is a problem. It's only the young people when they are trying to get jobs, but I don't think so for the elderly. [Male, aged 50]

However, respondents did give examples of racism including physical harassment.

> My gran has had problems with quite young kids actually. She was taking my little cousin to school and this guy with these wee kids went and splashed water all over them for some reason. It was terrible. The lollipop lady went chasing after them and she said 'I know where you live, and I'm going to get you' and all that.[63] [Female, aged 15]

> Yes, they suffer racism. My dad was attacked twice, once in his shop and the other time was an attempted mugging. [Female, aged 42]

> Sometimes they are robbed. They know that our people have some money with them all the time so they are the targets. It can happen when you are afraid and you are not strong enough to defend yourself. [Male, aged 72]

And yet, as had been the case throughout the interviews, there was a belief amongst the elderly that racism was less of a problem in Scotland than it was in England.

> I like Scottish people you know, they are very friendly. I mean the English people, they are a wee bit biased. They think they are a superior race or something. I was working in Coventry on the buses and I had a dispute, an argument, with my inspector there on the buses and I told him, I said, 'Do you think you belong to a superior race or something?' I said 'Hitler thought the same way as well and you know how he ended up.' He was surprised to hear that [laughs]. [Male, aged 72]

---

[63] It is worth noting that the lollipop lady was White. Thus, this incident revealed how individuals may regard the White population as manifesting both racism and support.

The tendency to regard the situation in Scotland as more favourable than elsewhere was also evident in comments relating to poverty, although in this case comparison was made with Pakistan.

> When we say someone is poor in Pakistan we mean they don't have enough money to clothe themselves, they maybe are not wearing shoes, they don't have shelter, they can't afford food. So they would maybe say poverty is not a problem here. [Female, aged 23]

> Define poverty. Here they've got welfare, nobody will starve. If you've spent all your life here you would call it poverty going on welfare, but I'm going by my mum's point. My dad was the same. They wouldn't call it poverty. [Female, aged 38]

Some respondents suggested that the elderly were protected from poverty because they were cared for by their children, but one young woman suggested that there were disadvantages to financial dependence on younger members of the family.

> Some of the elderly people who are living at home, when their pension comes through, their son or their daughter-in-law handles their money. I'm not saying that people are being cruel to them but it's because they have language problems and they don't get out and about as much. It means that they always think that they are having to penny pinch. They don't realise that that money is theirs. They feel they are relying on the family. The family thinks 'We'll just take care of it' but not having the money as their own means that they don't have their own independence. So a lot of them are too reliant on the family. It would be better if they had the pension book in their own hand like a lot of the Scottish elderly who go in and cash their pension. It's not that they have a great time, a pension is only so much, but it's in their hand. [Female, aged 24]

This perceived difference was mentioned by other respondents who suggested that Pakistani elders were not as independent as their White peers. If they were dependent on others, then questions arose about who should provide care when it was required.

Who Should Care for Pakistani Elders?

This question prompted considerable discussion that reflected the impact of migration and settlement on relationships within the family and on 'traditional' arrangements for elderly care. The overwhelming majority of respondents, irrespective of age or gender, felt that the elderly should be cared for by their children. Some respondents indicated that this was a religious obligation.

> In Islam it says you should look after the elders because if it wasn't for them you wouldn't be in this world. You wouldn't have got anything if it wasn't for them. [Male, aged 33]

> That is the proper Islamic way, that children look after their parents. [Male, aged 67]

Table 9.2a Govanhill Sample: Who Should Care for the Elderly?

	14-24 f m	25-50 f m	50+ f m	Total
Total respondents	10 10	11 11	10 10	62
Their children	9 10	11 10	10 9	59
Local voluntary organisations	8 9	9 11	3 9	49
Social Services	6 7	10 10	2 10	45
Other family members	5 10	8 5	7 6	41
Religious organisations e.g. mosque	6 6	9 9	2 8	40
They should look after themselves	5 2	5 4	1 4	21

Table 9.2b Who Should have the Most Responsibility for Care of the Elderly?

Their children	7 8	9 8	10 7	49
Social Services	1 0	2 1	0 2	6
Other family members	1 2	0 0	0 0	3
Religious organisations e.g. mosque	1 0	0 0	0 1	2
Local voluntary organisations	0 0	0 2	0 0	2
They should look after themselves	0 0	0 0	0 0	0

Younger respondents felt they should repay their parents for the substantial sacrifices made on their behalf.

> Their children should look after them. Our parents have done so much for us. They have done so much. When I was younger I used to be angry with my dad because I didn't see him but now I realise how hard he worked. [Female, aged 23]

> Asian families sacrifice a lot for their children. They work long hours and they do not have holidays. They buy them houses and they

give them everything. So yes, the children should give something back to their parents. [Male, aged 26]

Although the eldest son was considered responsible for his parents, in practice the daughter-in-law undertook the day-to-day care while her husband's responsibility was largely financial. It has already been shown that the relationship between mother and daughter-in-law can be strained, particularly where they have different countries of origin. Other problems can occur where there is no son, or where he is unwilling or unable to fulfil his responsibilities.

> Obviously if they've got no sons the daughters should help, but the daughters have their husband's parents to consider so there is a big fight about who should come first. [Female, aged 19]

> Having only one child is a problem. If it is a girl then she will get married and leave you, and if it's a boy and he doesn't do well then who will look after the parents? [Female, aged 64]

Some younger women suggested that, with their own changing financial status, parents need not always be the responsibility of their sons.

> The reason why they don't live with the daughter is because the husband is the breadwinner so the mother feels 'If I live with my son-in-law, he's the breadwinner and I'm eating off him'. Now things have changed, because I don't think my mum would mind coming to live with me because I work. I earn money as well, so there is no reason why she cannot come. [Female, aged 23]

However, individuals of both genders and all ages indicated that there were practical issues threatening the extended family system.

> Most of Asian children are still doing it, but what can they do if they find a job outside of the house? [Female, aged 33]

> Hinduism, Islam and Sikhism all respect their elders. They never throw them out. Now we have a different environment. It's very hard if you have a man and wife and children and elderly people in a small house. Not everyone has four bedrooms. I don't know. It used to be that way, but it's very hard. [Male, aged 59]

There were mixed views about whether other family members should help with the care of the elderly but the majority of respondents felt that this should only be considered if children were not available. There was not a great deal of confidence that other relatives would want to take on this responsibility.

> Other family members or a sincere person should help if children are not available. [Female, aged 64]

> Other family members would not bother. [Male, aged 54]

Whatever the potential problems, when asked to choose who had the greatest responsibility, no-one felt the elderly should have to fend for themselves.

> Can I tell you honestly, they need someone else. I know people who are living alone. Honestly, they cry and they need help. [Female, aged 33]

> There is a limit if you are frail. How can you look after yourself if you are suffering from some disease? It would be difficult. [Male, aged 72]

Although there was a tendency to emphasise the potential frailty of the elderly, there was also evidence that both young and old felt the elderly would benefit from being more independent.

> I think they should look after themselves in the sense that some of them just get themselves down too much, d'you know what I mean? I'm not being cruel when I say that. [Female, aged 24]

> Not if that means disowning your parents, no, but if it means encouraging them to keep on the go then that would be all right. [Male, aged 27]

It appeared that the ideal would be for children to care for their elderly parents while additional support and social activities were offered through voluntary sector groups.

> My grandmother goes. She loves it. She goes on outings and they're teaching her to speak English and write English. It's changed her whole life. I've never seen her so happy to be honest with you. She's socialising. She's not stuck with her daughters or her sons or her grandchildren. She's got friends of her own and they're knitting and gossiping. [Female, aged 19]

> I can have a chit chat with other women my age. They understand how I feel much more than my children or my husband. [Female, aged 50+]

In addition it was felt that staff were supportive in dealing with a number of tasks which might otherwise fall on other family members.

> They fix up appointments for them or they change appointments. They find things out and they phone around. It's good because they don't feel they have to rely on the family as much. They feel they can go to the [Centre] and they will help them out. [Female, aged 24]

The benefits of sympathetic assistance appeared to outweigh concerns about the denomination of staff.

> These girls, they look after us well, the Sikh girl. If I've got a doctor's appointment they will go with me and explain in English to the doctor what is wrong with me, or to the optician. I feel very, very comfortable here. [Female, aged 50+]

Given the importance of religion to the elderly, it might be thought that they would look to the mosque as the most appropriate outside agency to offer them support. However, the mosque was regarded primarily as a quiet place where men prayed and studied Islam. Furthermore, there were concerns about the practicalities of mosques undertaking care in the community.

> The mosque should if they could manage it, but they haven't got many people to do activities for them. The majority of people at the mosque are working class. They are working and it is very hard to get the time to spare. [Male, aged 19]

> I think they should help the elderly in a supporting capacity, but they shouldn't have to go and raise funds to build sheltered housing or something. That's the government. [Female, aged 32]

There was also some concern that groups based in one mosque may not be attractive to Muslims of another sect, or to non-Muslims.

> Some people believe one thing and some people believe something else. They are all Muslims but these people are fighting amongst themselves and somebody who is maybe a little bit not towards religion won't be encouraged to go in. [Male, aged 28]

> I think the mosque should help, yes, but I don't believe it should be for just Asian people. I know it's difficult to mix communities together but with a new generation coming on that will be a lot easier. For the older generation now that would be difficult because they feel there is a barrier. [Male, aged 27]

Some elderly people attended groups at the Centre in Govanhill and at Glasgow's Central Mosque. The following quotation illustrates the importance to service users of the social, rather than specifically religious, aspects of provision.

> At the [Centre] it tends to be ladies looking after the place so it tends to be better. You get more attention from the ladies. But at the mosque you have all the advantages of being a club in the mosque. We have all the mosque facilities as well as the club facilities. It means we have the use of their library and recreational hall, and for prayers the use of showers and toilets. We make use of all that but we are trying for a separate unit outwith the mosque. It means that when we have our club, it is our club. [Male, aged 67]

Irrespective of venue, concern was expressed about the funding of projects.

> Voluntary organisations are good, but to what extent? It depends on what their funds are. [Female, aged 33]

> We have been struggling hard for the last four years and the Social Work Department has no finance to get us a big building.[64] Our Director, he contacted the Social Work Department and we get a figure, we do get a grant, but it is not enough. [Male, aged 68]

Concerns about the financial viability of voluntary sector organisations may have contributed to the fact that, when asked to choose who had greatest responsibility for care of the elderly, respondents were more likely to choose social services than voluntary organisations. It was, perhaps not surprisingly, the middle age-band who were most accepting of the idea of social services involvement. The majority of them had been brought up in Scotland and were more likely to be aware of the facilities available. Furthermore, these were the people who were most likely to have the responsibility of caring for both ageing relatives and growing children.

---

[64] This respondent was involved in organising the group at the Central Mosque.

> This is a hard one because in terms of their children taking care of them I think that would be preferable for the elderly person, but it is whether it would be realistic. I wouldn't want to put pressure on people dealing with their own lives. Social services should really have most responsibility. [Female, aged 26]

> You see our lot are changing to the same way as here. We are changing completely. Before it was just family but now you feel sorry for the husband and wife who have got children to look after as well. [Long pause]. I think it will have to be outside help, I think the Social Work Department. [Male, aged 28]

One woman suggested that social work involvement could be seen as beneficial for the elderly people themselves rather than as simply offering relief to carers. This was in keeping with the comment of another respondent who had suggested that it would help if the elderly received their own pensions and were able to spend their own money. Although in interviews of this kind it is unlikely that difficult personal problems will be shared to any great degree, this does suggest that some elderly people were not well cared for by their immediate family.

> Social services should have greatest responsibility because sometimes elderly people find that they are very much at the mercy of their children and family. The bottom line should be social services. [Female, aged 32]

However, it was suggested that the elderly often did not understand which services were available to them.

> Social work departments should make the elderly more aware of what is available. I think racism comes into that. I think some of the people employed by the Social Work Department are not doing their job properly. Language comes into it as well. Nobody has explained. [Male, aged 28]

This supports the assertions of Strathclyde Community Relations Council and Glasgow Council for Voluntary Services that greater efforts were required by social work departments to make their services accessible and attractive to minority ethnic groups.[65] To examine this in more detail the fieldwork interviews included questions about which services were

---

[65] Such arguments are also supported by research in Scotland which has shown that much greater sensitivity to religious and cultural requirements is required [Bowes & Dar 1997].

considered important, and the significance of religious and cultural factors in care services for the elderly.

Services for the Elderly

Residential care was considered the least important service for elderly people when respondents were asked to tick as many services as they wished from a list of eighteen. Additional comments alluded to notions of abandonment and humiliation.

> No way would I dump my parents in a home. Why would I put my mother in a home because I can't cope with her. Why shouldn't I cope with her? She coped with me. When I was ill my mum didn't dump me. They still care for me when I am ill. They comfort me and they deserve me to do it for them. [Female, aged 19]

> In our country there are not homes like you have got here for older people, because they don't allow their parents to suffer in those homes. They keep them with them as a family member. [Male, aged 72]

But when asked to choose the two most important services, residential care moved up the list slightly. There appeared to be reluctant recognition that not all elderly people would be cared for by their families and in such cases it would be important that there was appropriate care available.

> It is important that there should be residential care for people that don't have family, but I wouldn't want my grandparents to be in residential care. It's degrading. [Female, aged 19]

> Residential care is important even though I hope my son won't throw me out. [Male, aged 56]

While the majority of respondents continued to reject the notion of permanent residential care for elders, it was acknowledged that a range of services for the elderly and their carers was desirable. In line with the assertion that poor health was a significant problem for the elderly, medical services were thought to be the most important. Priority was also given to religious celebrations and Islamic studies, confirming the importance of religious obligations to the elderly.

Table 9.3a Govanhill Sample: Which Services are Important for the Elderly?

	14-24 f	14-24 m	25-50 f	25-50 m	50+ f	50+ m	Total
Total respondents	10	10	11	11	10	10	62
Dental check-ups & eye tests	8	6	8	10	10	9	51
Medical treatment	7	6	8	9	10	10	50
Religious celebrations	8	5	9	9	10	9	50
Cultural celebrations	7	5	8	10	10	9	46
Day trips	7	4	7	10	9	9	46
Health education & advice	6	2	7	11	10	9	45
Welfare rights advice	6	3	9	8	9	9	44
Friendship groups	7	3	7	9	10	8	44
Islamic studies	6	4	6	5	10	9	40
Housing advice	6	1	9	8	7	8	39
Library	4	4	4	8	9	9	38
Keep fit	5	1	5	7	10	7	35
Lunch club	3	2	5	8	10	7	35
English language classes	5	1	4	6	10	6	32
Urdu classes	4	3	3	6	10	5	31
Learning about other cultures	5	1	4	5	10	4	29
Films	4	1	3	5	4	4	21
Permanent residential care	0	2	4	5	3	3	17

Table 9.3b Which are the Two Most Important Services for the Elderly?

	14-24 f	14-24 m	25-50 f	25-50 m	50+ f	50+ m	Total
Medical treatment	6	5	3	4	7	1	26
Islamic studies	3	3	4	1	7	3	21
Friendship groups	1	2	1	5	0	4	13
Day trips	2	2	1	2	1	2	10
Health education & advice	2	2	2	2	0	1	9
Keep fit	3	0	1	1	3	1	9
Welfare rights advice	0	1	2	2	0	1	6
English language classes	1	1	2	0	1	0	5
Religious celebrations	0	0	1	1	0	2	4
Lunch club	0	0	1	0	0	3	4
Permanent residential care	0	1	1	0	0	1	3
Learning about other cultures	0	0	2	1	0	0	3
Cultural celebrations	1	1	0	0	0	1	3
Films	0	1	0	1	0	0	2
Library	1	1	0	0	0	0	2
Dental check-ups & eye tests	0	0	1	1	0	0	2
Housing advice	0	0	0	1	0	0	1
Urdu classes	0	0	0	0	0	0	0
Other:							
Transport	0	0	0	0	1	0	1

If health and religious requirements were catered for, there appeared to be general agreement that part-time voluntary groups, offering a range of social activities and practical support, could give the elderly some independence and relieve pressure on other family members. However, the elderly were not a homogeneous group who inevitably enjoyed socialising with each other, and there was some evidence of perceived differences that could preclude social mixing.

> You find that sometimes someone will be reading an Urdu newspaper and they'll say 'Oh, look at this in the newspaper'. My mum said that someone did it to her and she can't read. Even if someone is the same age as them they might come from an educated background and they can't read so they feel awkward. [Female, aged 24]

For some, attending such groups was regarded as accepting charity.

> She doesn't want hand outs. She won't go for lunch. She says she's got her own house and her own food. She says 'I'll live on my own money'. [Female, aged 38]

For others, it could be seen as neglecting family duties or breaking social mores.

> My mum is not interested. She would not go to a thing like that because she organises her time between me and my sister, and her daughter-in-law, my brother's wife. Sometimes if they go out she looks after the children. And she wouldn't want to go just now because my sister is single and not married and people talk, you know. [Female, aged 33]

> My mother spends all day on her own. If you are aware of the customs for Asian women, after her husband dies she doesn't go out as much. My mother is very old fashioned in her way of thinking. [Female, aged 38]

Nevertheless, the majority of respondents, irrespective of age or gender, recognised that groups for the elderly had many benefits. To make such groups accessible to Pakistani elders it was clear that a number of religious and cultural factors would have to be taken into account. The existing groups were based around the idea of a lunch club and this may be the reason why, given a choice, a relatively high priority was placed on the availability of 'Asian' food. However, it has been shown through the story of the development of *Ittifaq* that where this was not provided a lunch club could still survive as long as food was *halal*. This suggests that the social aspects of a lunch club could override at least some concerns about the menu.

> It doesn't have to be Asian food. We like fish and chips as well! [Male, aged 63]

> Food is food. Rice is neither Asian nor British. As long as it's *halal*, it's all right. [Male, aged 67]

Table 9.4 Govanhill Sample: Which of the Following Points are Important for Organisations Working with the Elderly?

	14-24		25-50		50+		Total
	f	m	f	m	f	m	
Total respondents	10	10	11	11	10	10	62
Anti-racist policy	9	10	10	11	10	9	59
Prayer facilities available	8	7	10	8	10	9	52
Transport is available	7	8	11	10	10	9	52
Asian food is available	9	7	9	10	10	6	51
Trained medical staff	6	7	9	9	10	10	51
Close to home	7	7	11	9	9	7	50
All food is halal	6	7	8	9	10	9	49
Services are free of charge	7	6	8	9	9	9	48
Equal opps for men & women	8	5	8	9	7	8	45
Some staff speak Urdu	5	4	10	8	10	7	44
Written information/Urdu	5	5	10	6	10	7	43
Some staff speak Punjabi	7	4	8	8	10	6	43
All religions and cultures	5	5	7	10	6	8	41
Written information/Punjabi	7	5	8	6	10	4	40
Staff keep family informed	5	5	7	7	8	7	39
The group is 'single sex'	5	4	8	2	8	8	35
There are Muslim staff	6	4	7	2	8	7	34
Elderly plan own activities	3	1	4	4	9	8	29
Social events for family	1	3	7	6	9	2	28
The group is for Muslims only	4	0	5	0	2	7	18

While the importance attributed to prayer facilities and *halal* food indicate the importance placed upon meeting religious obligations, the denomination of staff was given a relatively low priority. This may have been because many of the respondents were aware that the co-ordinator of the Centre in Govanhill was not Muslim. However, it appeared unlikely that elderly respondents would feel confident attending a group where there were no Muslim workers at all.

> It depends on your members if you need Muslim staff. Our Senior Careworker is Indian so when she started she didn't know about our people's needs, so I think it is important. If we are multicultural, one of each staff must be there because we might make a mistake. [Female Careworker, aged 33]

> It doesn't really matter if the staff are Muslim. If they are paid staff they have got a duty to do and it's according to social services needs. I don't think it is important for paid staff to be Muslim. Unpaid staff is a different story. Unpaid staff would look after religious matters, like *halal* food.[66] [Male, aged 67]

It was generally not thought to be important that the group was for Muslims only and this point was bottom of the list of twenty. Some respondents, including the majority of older men, indicated that both 'Muslim only' and 'all religions and cultures' were important. This suggests that the existence of the group, rather than the denomination, was the important factor.

> It can be for all religions and cultures or for Muslims only. Both are OK. [Male, aged 50]

However, additional comments revealed practical reasons why the majority of older respondents were inclined to restrict social interaction to other South Asian cultures.

> I think when they say other cultures the elderly would mean Sikhs and Hindus, maybe Pakistani Christian as well, but not really others because they feel they don't have a lot in common with them. It's the language and then there is a lot of difference between a White woman that's sixty and an Asian woman at sixty, you know. A lot of difference in their way of thinking and everything. You couldn't really have them up line dancing together![67] [Female, aged 23]

> Muslim only is not important, but it is the language. If Chinese women came to the group we wouldn't understand what they were

---

[66] This reflects the fact that, following the difficulties experienced in obtaining an appropriate menu, part-time workers and volunteers prepared food on the premises.

[67] This conjures up a wonderful image, and is further evidence of the belief that White elderly have more fun than their Pakistani peers.

> saying and they won't understand us. It could be all right for Hindu and Sikh women to come but not really Arabic women or anything like that because of the language barrier. [Female, aged 64]

Difficulties arose when balancing the need for specific religious observances with the desire to make people of other religions and cultures feel welcome. On the whole, this resulted in single faith groups despite 'multicultural' intentions.

> It's meant to be an ethnic minority project but all the people are Muslim and they end up doing the things that Muslim women do like the prayers, and they go to the mosque. You can end up doing that and forgetting what you started off as. It should meet the needs of everyone. It makes it more difficult then for people from the Sikh community to come in. D'you know what I mean? [Female, aged 24]

The potential for antagonism between faiths was evident in comments relating to the importance of an anti-racist policy. Within the context of a group for the elderly, the definition of racism appeared to be influenced by political concerns in the country of origin.

> We don't allow them even to discuss politics. We put up a notice. Like if Muslim people start saying 'Hindus are doing this and that', and some people start saying 'Muslims are doing this in Israel'. We don't allow them to do that. [Female Careworker, aged 33]

> There is a wee bit of racism, a wee bit. Most of the members here are Pakistanis but nobody is there to represent us, either in the staff or anywhere. I mean they have got the girls who cook for us, they are Muslim you know, they are Pakistanis, but at a higher level there is nobody to represent the majority of the people here. I am not against Indians or anybody but we should be represented there as well. They have got the Project Coordinator. I mean she is Indian you know. I am not against her but we should have a Pakistani person at policy level, either man or woman, to represent us because we are the majority. [Male, aged 72]

There were some signs that older women placed less emphasis on religious differences. Only two of the elderly women thought it was very important for the group to be Muslim only. Some had memories of mixing with Sikh friends when they were children. Furthermore, in Scotland, it was sometimes easier for Muslim women to attend a Sikh venue than a mosque.

> My grandmother remembers when she was in India. She was seven years old when there was independence but she remembers having Sikh friends. The state where we come from in India was mainly Sikhs and Muslims. That was mixed religions then, but it's not like that now in Britain. Muslims stick to their own community and Sikhs stick to their own community. So I think they find it hard because when they were young they were mixed and they used to get involved in celebrating other festivals. [Female, aged 19]

> We put on some English classes in the *gurdwara*[68] and people said it would end up all Indian women so we did taster courses for two weeks. In the end we decided to use it because actually four Muslim women did come. You see, men and women can go to the *gurdwara*, whereas mosques are restricted to men. [Female, aged 24]

Although there was some limited mixing of faiths, strict separation by gender remained important to the elderly.

> The organisations should be single sex. You would get bad ideas if it was mixed. [Male, aged 54]

> Yes definitely single sex. That's the way it is and that's the way it should be. [Male, aged 67]

However, gender separation was not thought to be as important by younger people.

> You see by that age Islamically you are allowed to mix freely. You are allowed to mix because you are usually free of any sexual desire. [Female, aged 23]

> We have started a men's group as well, and now we are going to try to mix them but that is hard, really hard. I think it is a better way than men sitting alone or women sitting alone, if they can sit together. They can discuss each other's problems, they listen. But it is hard. [Female Careworker, aged 33]

It appeared that such a departure from established cultural mores was likely to occur between rather than within generations. Overall, it appeared that the Pakistani elderly had been able to maintain and assert those aspects of their religious and cultural identity to which they attached greatest

---

[68] Sikh temple.

importance, while in other areas they had shown considerable pragmatism. This process is reconsidered in the concluding section.

Interaction Between Service Providers and Service Users

By the early 1980s, agencies working with the elderly expressed concerns about the lack of recognition of cultural and religious requirements that were effectively excluding minority ethnic elders from available services.[69]

> The argument for total integration seems ludicrous for this age group ... The provision of housing and welfare facilities to bring about integration has the effect of limiting choice and imposing, for example, certain types of food, leisure and other facilities totally unsuited to the needs of ethnic elders, while also limiting their opportunities to relate to others of their own culture. [Age Concern/Help the Aged 1984: 26]

The discourse surrounding the development of the *Greater Glasgow Joint Community Care Plan* revealed reluctance amongst mainstream service providers to acknowledge that their services were not accessible to minority ethnic groups. This appeared to be influenced, at least in part, by a prevailing social work ideology that emphasised equality and universality and was unwilling to focus on difference. In the draft of the second Plan this approach emerged as a somewhat complacent 'open door' attitude to service provision and was challenged by Strathclyde Community Relations Council and Glasgow Council for Voluntary Services who stressed the importance of combining anti-racist training and practice with cultural awareness. The difference of opinion was publicised and debated within the voluntary sector and did have some influence over the final content of the second Plan.

Early moves towards Care in the Community coincided with the availability of Urban Programme funding in Areas of Priority Treatment such as Govanhill and enabled the voluntary sector to develop a number of new initiatives.[70] Within this framework the development of services for minority ethnic elders in Govanhill illustrated some of the ways in which services were negotiated at local level. The early years of *Ittifaq*, from a

---

[69] See also Bowes & Dar 1997, Anderson & Brownlie 1997, Chakrabarti & Cadman 1997.

[70] The policy of Care in the Community has been criticised as a cost cutting exercise and as an attempt to undermine state welfare provision. These are important arguments but for the purposes of this dissertation the move towards Care in the Community is accepted as the framework within which services were operating.

'multicultural friendship evening' to a group supported by staff who relied on unpaid volunteers as interpreters, could be criticised on a number of counts by the academic theorist or anti-racist strategist. How can 'colourful' evenings of singing and dancing address the structural causes and effects of racism? Why should interpreters command a high salary if they speak French or German, but be unpaid volunteers if they speak Punjabi? And even the most naive optimist might question how a lunch club for elderly Pakistani women could survive for several years with no bilingual staff and a consistent menu of fish and chips. But it did.

Positive action had been taken to contact elders from minority ethnic groups, the friendship evening was regarded as a success and the resulting group and lunch club were popular. Lessons were learned and, by the time Urban Programme funding was secured to expand the service, it was accepted that properly skilled and experienced bilingual workers were a priority. Posts were held open when recruitment proved difficult rather than being filled by non-bilingual workers. Meanwhile arrangements were made to prepare appropriate food on the premises. And, in the Project's name, 'Black' was changed to 'ethnic minority', to reflect the fact that members did not regard themselves a Black. Thus the project appeared to evolve through a process of trial and error.

To attract and retain its initial client base the Centre had acknowledged the cultural and religious obligations of the largest minority ethnic group in the area i.e. Muslims of Pakistani origin. From this point there was a tendency to attract other Muslim elders who felt comfortable with the services. This process was not confined to services for elderly Muslims and in other parts of the city 'multicultural' groups were also serving elders of predominantly one faith, culture or national origin. As it was increasingly recognised that an 'open door', or even 'multicultural', approach was inappropriate for the current generation of elderly, a degree of pragmatism emerged amongst policy makers and service providers who appeared not to delve too deeply into composition of group membership. There was also some recognition that if Christian denominations received financial support from the local authority to provide services it was difficult to justify refusing such support to other faiths.

However, the reluctance to specify religious denomination remained. While it could be argued that this was to avoid perpetuating religious antagonism, other factors appeared to be involved. When the Central Mosque submitted its Urban Programme application the discussions at the Area Liaison Committee revealed a degree of anti-Muslim stereotyping. Competition for clients resulted in some rivalry between the Centre in Govanhill and the Central Mosque over who should provide care to Muslim elders. In practice, potential clients were not particularly concerned about who provided the services but were able to benefit from both projects.

Religion played an important part in the lives of the elderly respondents. Many of them had retired from full-time employment and household responsibilities and had more time to focus on religious obligations which were considered to be a source of comfort. Despite this, separate Muslim provision was not seen as essential for addressing many of the problems they faced in daily life. Health, family problems and loneliness were identified as significant issues for the elderly and it was felt that voluntary groups providing opportunities to socialise, as well as practical assistance when required, were well-suited to meeting many of their needs.

As service users the elderly valued the opportunity to gather together in a sympathetic environment more than other factors, even including the language skills and denomination of staff. But there was no compromise over specific obligations such as *halal* food and gender separation, and while older women were prepared to communicate with staff through younger bilingual women, it was clear that they would not be comfortable socialising in groups where they were unable to communicate with other members in their first language.

Meanwhile, anti-racist and equal opportunities policies that were not informed by cultural sensitivity appeared largely irrelevant to the current generation of elderly service users. Most of the respondents felt it was inconceivable that a 'multicultural' group for elderly clients of Pakistani origin would include, for example, Chinese or White members, since the cultural differences were thought to be too pronounced. The fact that there were groups for Chinese, Jewish and Polish elderly in other parts of the city suggests that this was a common feeling and not limited to immigrants from Pakistan.[71]

As with previous immigrant populations, ties with the country of origin continued to influence relationships in Scotland so that there was some evidence of animosity between Muslims and Sikhs. Diasporic ties also influenced definitions of poverty (which was not regarded as a serious problem in comparison with conditions in Pakistan) and of gender equality, (which was interpreted in relation to culturally defined social spheres). Nevertheless, it was recognised that attempts to reproduce 'traditional' relationships in Scotland could be a source of difficulty for the elderly and their carers. Women could be particularly vulnerable when relationships broke down since they were most likely to have language difficulties and were often dependent on younger family members for routine assistance with

---

[71] Such projects are listed in Greater Glasgow Community Care Plan 1995-1998, Appendix 6.

medical and financial matters. The middle age-band were thought to be under pressure where they were working and had responsibility for elderly relatives and children, and where their accommodation was inappropriate for an extended family system.

Yet, despite the fears of some elderly people that they might be abandoned by their children, the vast majority of younger respondents were committed to the idea of living with, and caring for, elderly parents. Respondents showed some pride in this aspect of their family life particularly when compared with 'western culture' which was thought to 'dump' and 'neglect' the elderly. At the same time it was acknowledged that too much dependence on younger family members could have a detrimental effect on the health and well-being of elders. Younger people expressed the view that the White elderly were generally fitter and more independent than their Pakistani peers, and there appeared to be some admiration for those pensioners who were out and about 'doing their own thing'. Culturally and religiously sensitive voluntary groups were thought to be an excellent way of providing Pakistani elders with a more varied social life, maintaining a degree of independence and relieving younger family members of the more routine tasks. Furthermore, it appeared that some members of the current generation of Pakistani elders were gaining confidence in accessing, and shaping, local voluntary sector projects. Services at the Centre in Govanhill developed through an initial attempt to take positive action followed by a process of 'benevolent trial and error' in which both parties participated. During this process staff gained knowledge and experience, and clients gained confidence in asserting their priorities.

Younger respondents were committed to the idea that current services should be relevant and accessible to their elders, but they anticipated that their own needs and preferences would be quite different. Younger women were particularly aware of the vulnerability of their elderly female relatives and were taking steps to ensure that they themselves were less vulnerable. Most younger respondents did not regard it as essential to separate the elderly by gender and most had a much broader definition of 'multicultural' than their parents. In the future they would negotiate services appropriate to their needs and to historical circumstances. Thus multiculturalism in relation to elderly care appeared to be a gradual process with definitions changing between, rather than within, generations.

10 Conclusion: the Process of Multiculturalism

In discussing issues of methodology it was asserted that theoretical reflection alone was insufficient to understand processes such as integration and multiculturalism, or to contribute to effective anti-racist strategies. In the preceding chapters an attempt has been made to contribute to a broader understanding of such issues through qualitative fieldwork contextualised by historical investigation and analysis of quantitative Census data. In this final chapter some conclusions are drawn in relation to the assertion and negotiation of identity by Pakistani immigrants and their descendants in Scotland; the historical continuity of multiculturalism; and the importance of multiculturalism as an integrative process.

The Preferred Identity of the Pakistani Population

During the fieldwork, respondents were interviewed primarily as residents and service users in Govanhill, rather than as Pakistanis, Asians, Muslims etc. It became clear that different aspects of identity were asserted in different contexts, and that identity was not simply based on country of origin. The majority of elderly respondents were born in India before partition, about half of the middle age-band were born in Pakistan and half in Britain, and the majority of younger respondents were born in Scotland. This pattern broadly reflects the history of the partition of India and migration to Scotland.

Respondents were comfortable selecting multiple identities, including reference to national allegiance, but none of those born in India identified themselves as Indian. This suggests that the foundation of Pakistan had a significant impact on those who lived through partition, and it has been shown that this has continued to shape the identity of Pakistanis in Scotland.[72] The majority of respondents indicated four or five aspects of a

---

[72] Thus at the project for the elderly it was acknowledged that an important aspect of the anti-racist policy was to reduce animosity between Pakistanis and Indians, and when considering youth services there was evidence that some young men were projecting a Pakistani versus Indian identity.

multiple identity without hesitation but most found it difficult to choose only one from the list. In fact, five respondents insisted that they were unable to do so and gave 'hybrid' identities instead. Comments made during this process confirm that identity is dependent on relationships with others and a sense of location [Bhabha 1994: 185].

Table 10.1 Govanhill Sample: Country of Birth

	14-24 f m	25-49 f m	50+ f m	Total
Scotland	8 7	3 2	0 1	21
Pakistan	1 1	5 6	2 3	18
India	0 0	0 0	7 5	12
Other:				
England	1 2	3 1	0 0	7
Kashmir	0 0	0 1	0 1	2
Bangladesh	0 0	0 1	0 0	1
Kenya	0 0	0 0	1 0	1
Total	10 10	11 11	10 10	62

Notes:
Where Pakistan is given as country of birth by those aged 50+, this must have been India before partition because the interviews were conducted before India and Pakistan celebrated fifty years of independence.
Kashmir is a region of India, rather than a separate country, although there is an independence movement.

Pakistani

Pakistani ancestry was readily acknowledged in the list of multiple identities but this was usually omitted when respondents were asked to select only one. Older women were the exception and Table 10.2b shows that their preference for Pakistani tended to skew the results. A possible reason for this choice of identity by the elderly women, all of whom were born before the partition of India, related to the fact that they had migrated from Pakistan to join husbands and children rather than through personal choice.

> I think the women they feel more strongly towards Pakistan, maybe because the men came here and they got more of an education and they didn't really think about going back home. Maybe it was their choice to come here, to live here and to work here and it wasn't

really the wife's choice. She's kind of hung on to Pakistan, but I'm not really sure. [Multi-lingual interviewer discussing older women's responses]

It should also be noted that Pakistan was created as a Muslim state and so, for some older respondents who experienced the upheaval of partition, Pakistani and Muslim identity are closely connected.

Table 10.2a Govanhill Sample: How Would You Describe Your Identity? (Tick as many as you wish)

	14-24		25-49		50+		Total
	f	m	f	m	f	m	
Total respondents	10	10	11	11	10	10	62
Muslim	10	9	9	10	5	10	53
Pakistani	5	8	8	9	9	9	48
Asian	5	7	11	9	0	8	40
Scottish	7	8	4	9	0	6	34
British	6	7	7	6	1	7	34
Black	3	3	4	2	0	1	13
Indian	0	0	0	0	0	0	0
Other:							
English	1	0	0	0	0	0	1
Kashmiri	0	0	0	1	0	0	1
Bangladeshi	0	0	0	1	0	0	1

Table 10.2b Which Single Identitiy Would You Choose?

Muslim	7	6	5	3	1	5	27
British	0	2	1	3	1	2	9
Pakistani	0	0	1	0	8	0	9
Scottish	2	2	0	1	0	0	5
Asian	1	0	1	1	0	1	4
Black	0	0	1	2	0	0	3
Indian	0	0	0	0	0	0	0
Other:							
Pakistani Muslim	-	-	-	-	-	1	1
Asian Muslim	-	-	1	-	-	-	1
Scottish Muslim	-	-	-	1	-	-	1
Scottish Pakistani	-	-	-	-	-	1	1
British Asian	-	-	1	-	-	-	1

Black

Only 13 of the 62 respondents chose Black as part of a multiple identity and only 3 as a preferred identity. The majority of those who chose Black indicated that it was used by others but had no real significance to them as individuals.

> I don't mind people calling me Black. I don't mind anything actually, but I don't think of myself as Black. [Male, aged 28]

> Even though we are not Black, we get called Black you know [ticks Black]. Personally I don't think I'm Black, but you know. [Female, aged 39]

Thus, although the vast majority of respondents asserted the importance of anti-racist policies throughout the interviews, it appeared that few regarded Black identity as an important aspect of an anti-racist strategy. Some strongly resented the term.

> I know they use it for politics but I don't think that's right ... we are seen as Black workers, and Chinese people are seen as Black workers. Someone at [work] says we have two Black workers. Now those two workers could be Pakistani and Chinese. I don't like that. I think people are individuals. You have been brought up in one culture, I have been brought up in another culture, but our two cultures interact with each other. [Female, aged 19]

> I hate the word Black. I don't think anybody is Black and I don't think people should be classed as Black or White. I think it's insulting and I know it's the PC word but I think who ever makes up the PC word should start looking at finding something else. [Female, aged 30]

Asian

The term Asian tends to be used in Britain to refer to immigrants from the Indian sub-continent, partly in recognition of their South Asian origins, but also in acknowledgement of the fact that few regard themselves as Black. But while this term appeared to be much more acceptable than Black as part of a multiple identity (40 of the 62 respondents included it), when respondents were asked to select a single identity it was chosen by only 4 respondents. Again, it appeared to be selected primarily because it was used by others.

> I would maybe just go for Asian ... I'm just thinking of the reasons why I would choose that [pause]. Why would I choose that? It's maybe mild brainwashing [laughs]. Whenever you fill in forms they always ask you what's your ethnic origin and you just tick Asian or Pakistani. But if they asked me my nationality I would say British. [Female, aged 32]

Muslim

Religious identity was important to the vast majority of respondents and its relative strength was even more pronounced when respondents were asked to choose only one from the list. However, it was often linked to national origins and there clear signs of an emerging Scottish-Muslim identity.

> I don't classify myself as being Asian because I'm a Scottish Muslim. [Female, aged 19]

> I am a Scottish Muslim. I could not separate them. I could not choose one. [Male, aged 26]

> I am a Muslim first, then a Scot, and of Pakistani origin. This is my home though. I'm proud to be Scots. [Male, aged 28]

> I have always said I am a Scottish Muslim. If I had to choose one of the two it has got to be Muslim. It's like saying you're Scottish but are you a Catholic or a Protestant. It's hard to choose but your religion has to come first. [Male, aged 67, born in Scotland]

Scottish

A number of respondents emphasised that they were Scottish rather than English.

> I was born in England but I would still say I'm more Scottish [Female, aged 26]

> I think because I have been brought up here I would say Scottish. On the passport you have to say British or Pakistani but I would like to say Scottish. [Male, aged 37]

> I am not English. I will tell you a story. I worked one year in London transport. After two months on the top deck as a conductor a passenger said 'You are Scottish!' He was a Scottish man and he heard my voice. He said 'You are Scottish, you are my brother' and

he hugged me! [laughs]. An English person would not do that. The Scots say 'Hello Jimmy'. They are friendly people. [Male, aged 63]

Of the seven respondents born in England, only one chose English as an aspect of multiple identity and no-one chose it as their single preferred identity. The sense of 'not being English' is a factor that shapes the identity of many people who are born or brought up in Scotland, irrespective of religious denomination or ancestral origins. This does inject a strand, albeit tentative, of shared loyalty between people who may appear to have very little else in common. This, combined with the fact that Black is regarded as an inappropriate term imposed by others rather than as a genuine aspect of identity, suggests that an anti-racist strategy based on the conceptualisation of Black immigrants subjected to White racism is inappropriate in Scotland.

Changing Aspects of Identity

The fieldwork confirmed that cultural and religious differences were significant, but it was also clear that some aspects of identity were negotiable. A comparison of the priorities of respondents in relation to school-age education, youth services and care of the elderly indicated that the benefits and disadvantages of asserting identity as service users were evaluated. If there was a degree of compulsion and the benefits of participation were highly valued (such as academic achievement), then a pragmatic approach was adopted and some compromises were made. Where a service was optional but participation was perceived as beneficial (as with groups for the elderly), a degree of pragmatism was again evident while specific religious and cultural concessions were negotiated. But where a service was optional, the benefits of participation were less tangible (as in youth work provision), and there were perceived disadvantages (such as inappropriate social mixing for young women, or an unattractive programme for young men), then the service was likely to be rejected. The greater the perceived benefits, the greater the potential for negotiation and compromise.

Some religious and cultural obligations appeared non-negotiable in the short-term but there were differences between the views of respondents born in India or Pakistan and their descendants born in Scotland. These differences were particularly evident in relation to gender. Equality of opportunity for men and women was interpreted by older respondents in terms of 'separate but equal' gender roles, while their children were more likely to define it in terms of parity within the same fields. The younger women had received considerably more formal education than their mothers and some were pursuing career ambitions. At the same time the majority of these young women regarded family life and the role of mother as a priority.

Some suggested that they would use this crucial role in the family to influence the views of the next generation particularly in relation to gender equality and broader definitions of 'multicultural'.

Modood asserted that for many migrants becoming part of British society had to be justified in terms compatible with a Muslim faith [1997b: 157]. This was confirmed by the fieldwork in Govanhill, but it was also evident that what was considered to be compatible with the Muslim faith was subject to change. A number of young people suggested that their elders confused the obligations of Islam with those of Pakistani culture and, while they did not wish to reject the values of their parents altogether, there was evidence that they were attempting to negotiate a Scottish-Muslim identity. Furthermore, while Muslim remained an essentially religious identity for the majority of young people, the interviews did not support the notion that Islam is impervious to secularisation. Some respondents asserted that they were Muslim but were 'not religious'. This suggested a sense of ownership of a religious heritage even where it was not practised by the individual and hence the potential for a 'secular Muslim' identity to develop.

The Historical Continuity of Multiculturalism

Biological and Cultural Racism

It might be argued that a crucial difference between Pakistani immigrants and Irish, Italian and Jewish immigrants is that the Pakistani population in Britain are victims of biological racism as a result of perceived phenotypical differences, notably skin colour. It is, therefore, important to point out that phenotypical differences, whether real or imagined, were cited in racist discourse concerning Irish, Italian and Jewish immigrants. In racist discourse these perceived differences were linked to a supposed threat that the cultural, religious, or national identity of the newcomers posed to the Scottish 'way of life'. Furthermore, these differences were thought to be passed on to their children so that the Scottish-born descendants of immigrants were also perceived as undermining social cohesion by their habits, religious affiliation and overseas allegiances.

In Scotland religious affiliation has been particularly significant. Some attempts were made to convert Catholics and Jews to the Protestant faith but more widespread was their deliberate exclusion from employment, the housing market and membership of clubs and associations. The extent to which Islamophobia takes hold in Scotland remains to be seen. It does appear that there is increased recognition of Muslim identity, and there is some evidence of a perceived association between Islam and fundamentalism, but the particular history of religious antagonism in the West of Scotland has also engendered an atmosphere in which religious intolerance is denounced in many quarters.

The Assertion of Identity

Each of the nineteenth and early twentieth century migrant populations studied could not be described as a united, homogeneous community. Each manifested internal differences based on religious practice, class difference and geographical origins. But there was also considerable evidence that the majority played an active part in maintaining and reproducing aspects of a shared cultural and religious identity. Attempts were made to create a suitable atmosphere at home, while parents and religious leaders did their best to encourage endogamy in the hope that specific cultural and religious traditions would be maintained by future generations.

What goes on in people's homes and personal relationships may be relatively unnoticed by the wider public but, in spite of the potential to trigger hostility, many of the shared beliefs and patterns of behaviour were not simply relegated to the private sphere. Appropriate shops and places of worship were clearly visible, and negotiations took place with existing institutions such as schools and hospital authorities over specific cultural and religious obligations. This process played a part in shaping local conditions, from changes in the physical environment and eating habits to influencing housing and education policies.

For Catholics and Jews, religious affiliation was a key aspect of identity and a source of practical, social, spiritual and emotional support. Many showed considerable tenacity in asserting the right to practice their faith and celebrate rites of passage, but this did not mean that they all exercised unquestioning religious commitment or were dominated by authoritarian leaders. Some Jews played and watched football on their Sabbath, and the Catholic hierarchy accepted some 'socialist' values as a form of radical Christianity when it became clear that working class parishioners were increasingly drawn to the Labour Party. Thus, as with other aspects of identity, religious identity was shaped by a sense of location. Nevertheless, diasporic ties ensured that identity was not solely defined by events at one end of the migratory chain. Perceptions amongst the wider population that the relative newcomers had loyalties elsewhere were not entirely misplaced as was evident in campaigns for Irish Home Rule, Jewish support for Zionist causes, and Italian membership of the *fascio*.

It has been shown that members of the current Pakistani population are also attempting to create a suitable atmosphere in their homes, promoting endogamy, establishing separate institutions to meet cultural and religious obligations, negotiating with wider public institutions over specific requirements, and maintaining national, cultural and religious diasporic ties.

Acknowledgement of Identity

While Irish, Jewish and Italian immigrants and their descendants were subjected to biological and cultural racism, there were also signs of sympathetic attitudes, tolerance of diversity and a commitment to fair and equal treatment. For example, the case for Catholic schools was presented in terms of equal citizenship; the House of Commons forced a change in company policy after a Jewish applicant had been refused a house in a Glasgow suburb; and during the Second World War Italian women were supported by sympathetic neighbours. While religion was a particular source of social conflict, it might be overlooked in some circumstances. A Jew could be a hero if he played well for the local football team, and Italian cafes could be popular with customers who 'hated Catholics'.

The identity of immigrants, and especially their descendants, was undoubtedly influenced by local conditions. The English language was given priority and there was evidence of secularisation, social mixing and out-marriage. These factors altered the identity of the relative newcomers, but cultural influences were reciprocal and the physical and social environments were changed by the arrival and settlement of each immigrant population.

While the prominence of recent debates about the place of Islam in a western liberal democracy prompted the assertion that religious migrants are in the vanguard of a 'new European multiculturalism', this study has illustrated some of the ways in which migrants who asserted a religious identity have negotiated forms of multiculturalism in Glasgow for more than a hundred years. And, while it has been suggested that 'new multiculturalism' does not relegate cultural diversity to the private sphere, this study has shown that cultural diversity has been asserted and accommodated in the public sphere in Glasgow for at least a hundred years. Multiculturalism developed through the inevitable interaction between an existing population (who exhibited hostility and exclusionary practices mixed with sympathy and notions of fair treatment) and relative newcomers (who asserted and modified aspects of their cultural and religious identity). The fieldwork case studies illustrate some of the ways in which this process was operating at the end of the twentieth century.

Multiculturalism in the 1990s

During the 1970s and 1980s the key issue identified by the Scottish Office and the local authority in relation to the educational needs of immigrants and their children was that of language. By the 1990s, greater emphasis on the legal obligation to avoid indirect discrimination, combined with the practices developed through the day-to-day realities of teaching children from minority ethnic groups, resulted in a broad ethos in which concessions to religious and cultural requirements were the norm in local authority schools. However, different schools adopted different approaches. Some complied with directives from the Scottish Office but made no additional concessions; others accommodated additional needs as they were identified; and some took positive action and developed initiatives that preceded and sometimes informed broader policy guidelines.

The tendency to omit references to religious identity in local authority welfare services was less apparent in the field of school-age education because religious education and observance have always been part of the education system. However, current attitudes towards religious identity in Scottish schools have been influenced by the perceived repercussions of the 1918 Education (Scotland) Act which incorporated Catholic schools into the local authority education system. The persistence of antagonism between Catholics and Protestants prompted political concerns about the desirability of separating children on religious grounds for educational purposes. At the same time it was acknowledged that to challenge the existence of Catholic schools would be politically unpopular. Faced with this dilemma, local councillors appeared anxious not to increase the number of denominational schools and manifested a strategic pragmatism towards the educational requirements of religious groups. This resulted in a commitment to meeting the needs of Muslims within existing local authority schools, and even some financial assistance for *Qur'an* schools through the 'language and culture' budget.

The legal obligations on local authorities to ensure the 'efficient education' of children, combined with 'race relations' legislation that outlawed direct and indirect discrimination, ensured that local schools accommodated some of the specific needs of children from Pakistani families. This was not the case with youth service provision. In focusing on a socialisation model of youth work, there were no clear Scottish Office directives concerning multicultural or anti-racist provision or curriculum content. This lack of specificity permeated to local level so that in Glasgow youth service providers were encouraged to develop flexible responses to the needs of young people from 'black and ethnic minority groups' with no clear directives as to how this could or should be achieved. Within this framework it was difficult to ascertain a clear approach taken by youth service providers in Govanhill. An imprecise anti-racist stance was asserted, but this was not sufficient to develop work with young people from minority ethnic groups. Meanwhile the Youth Project, as the main provider of youth services in the area, had no difficulty recruiting young White members.

However, when positive action was taken to meet cultural and religious requirements it proved possible to establish an Asian Girls Group. The group was in practice catering for Muslim girls, but the reluctance to openly acknowledge religious identity was clear when a request to include Islamic studies in the programme of activities was refused. The establishment of the Asian Girls Group may have been prompted by a broader youth work emphasis on counteracting sexism and promoting equal opportunities for girls, combined with popular perceptions of the oppression of Muslim women, since there was no evidence of similar positive action being taken to accommodate the priorities of their male peers. The absence of competition, combined with a lack of compulsion from monitoring bodies, appeared to have influenced this lack of urgency.

As with youth service provision, the voluntary nature of participation in services for the elderly meant that inappropriate or unattractive services could be avoided. Thus, interaction between mainstream service providers and service users from minority ethnic groups was not inevitable. The likelihood that services would be considered inappropriate was increased by the prevailing Social Work ideology that emphasised equality and universality. However, moves towards Care in the Community in the 1990s coincided with the availability of Urban Programme funding in Areas of Priority Treatment and enabled the voluntary sector to develop a number of new initiatives.

In Govanhill positive action was taken to contact the local 'ethnic minority' population and to work with them in developing appropriate services. While there was some reluctance to specify religious denomination, the resulting services catered for the needs of the largest minority ethnic group in the area i.e. of Pakistani Muslim origin. Worries about competition for clients, when the Central Mosque applied for funding to establish similar services, reinforced a commitment to meet the needs of Muslim clients. A similar process was evident in other parts of the city as separate projects developed serving Sikh, Jewish, Polish and Chinese elders. From an initial reluctance to encourage separate provision the local authority and voluntary agencies showed a degree of pragmatism over group membership and eventually acknowledged that culturally and religiously specific projects were an important part of provision for the elderly. Within this shifting framework, benevolent trial and error, informed by close interaction between service providers and service users, was shown to be more effective in developing appropriate services than the rhetoric of equality and universality.

Multiculturalism as an Integrative Process

In this book the terms multiculturalism and integration refer to a process through which newcomers arrive and settle and, in negotiating aspects of their identity, shape local conditions into which subsequent newcomers arrive and repeat the process. However, it is important to note that the process is non-linear and that immigrants and their descendants do not follow a steady path from initial hostility to subsequent acceptance. In practice, hostility and exclusionary practices intermingle with notions of fair and equal treatment. Meanwhile, events abroad, and local and international responses to them, have the potential to reinforce or reshape the identity of immigrants and their descendants, and to influence the attitudes of others towards them.

To undermine racism and disadvantage, it is important to challenge those who allege that immigrants and their descendants, in asserting specific values and customs and maintaining diasporic ties, threaten the social cohesion of the country to which they have migrated. This study has shown that historical comparison and empirical fieldwork can play a part in challenging such allegations.

Historical comparison confirms that the arrival and settlement of immigrants with cultural and religious identities distinct from those of an existing 'Scottish' population is not new. Such evidence can strengthen anti-racist discourse at local level by illustrating how an apparently established way of life is the product of a continual process of migration and settlement. Meanwhile, empirical investigation indicates that acknowledging difference can be more 'integrating' in the long term than the premature application of universal principals. The participation of both service providers and service users in a practical process incorporating goodwill and pragmatism, can be more effective in the development of services than dogged adherence to a precise theoretical perspective.

The Scottish Context

It has been argued that, while racism exists, the political process has not been racialised in Scotland. Explanations for this lack of racialisation have included the persistence of antagonism between Catholics and Protestants, and the existence of a political nationalism focusing on the perceived economic and political disadvantages of the Union. While these factors have clearly shaped local conditions, they do not constitute a complete explanation. With regard to the first, history does not support a 'zero-sum' notion of intolerance: being Catholic constituted one basis for exclusionary practices, being Irish or Italian constituted another, while there was concurrent hostility towards Jews. Furthermore, by the 1970s, when Pakistani settlement in Scotland increased, antagonism between Catholics and Protestants in Scotland appeared to be declining in significance, at least in the political and economic spheres.

The second factor, the perceived economic and political disadvantages of the Union, may currently have greater significance. Firstly, it undermines racist discourse that might seek to blame the arrival of immigrants from Pakistan for the increase in unemployment resulting from post-industrial decline. In addition, resentment of the Union has reinforced a sense of identity that is 'not English'. Part of this identity has involved the assertion that 'the Scots' are not as racist as 'the English' and this may have had an impact on behaviour.[73] Certainly, the notion of the 'friendly' Scot was articulated by a number of the fieldwork respondents. Furthermore, immigrants and their descendants who speak with a Scottish accent, and display loyalty to Scotland, also manifest an identity that is 'not English' and may be perceived, at least in part, as sharing a sense of belonging with others who were born north of the border. It is probably true that no English person would hear a bus conductor of Pakistani ancestry speak with an English accent and feel moved to hug him and exclaim 'You are English, you are my brother!'

Anti-racism and Multiculturalism

Racialisation is shaped by both racism *and* anti-racism [Solomos & Back 1996: 104], and so it is important to consider the consequences of anti-racist strategies:

> Antiracism seems very comfortable with this idea of blacks as victims. I remember one simplistic piece of Greater London Council propaganda which said 'We are all either the victims or the perpetrators of racism'. Why should this be so? Suffering confers no virtue on the victim; yesterday's victims are tomorrow's executioners. [Gilroy 1992: 60-61]

The fieldwork interviews in Govanhill indicated that while respondents were aware of racism they did not define themselves primarily as victims of racism. Of greater importance was commitment to Islam, to family relationships, to property ownership, and to academic achievement and

---

[73] A similar assertion of a 'non-English' identity is evident amongst Scottish football supporters abroad. Whilst Old Firm rivalry can engender bigotry and aggression, Catholic and Protestant fans of the Scottish national team take considerable pride in displaying exemplary behaviour abroad in contrast to that of some English 'supporters'.

professional status. This picture may seem stereotypical, and even naive, but it does appear to have yielded some positive results. Analysis of the 1991 Census data offered an opportunity to outline some characteristics of the current Pakistani population in Scotland. There was evidence of low cost property ownership, poor housing conditions, overcrowding, higher rates of unemployment, and self employment involving working long hours in small businesses. But there was also evidence of movement into wealthier suburbs, the expansion of businesses, 'over-representation' in higher educational qualification categories, and entry into the professions. Furthermore, evidence from the fieldwork suggested that Pakistanis in Scotland have played an active part in undermining the racialisation of the political process. Rather than engage with the political process as a racialised, and victimised, group there is evidence of attempts to fashion a Scottish-Muslim identity.

An emphasis on multiculturalism was evident in initial responses to the arrival of Pakistani immigrants in Scotland in the 1970s. However, since the 1980s attempts have been made by researchers and political activists to shift the perspective by highlighting incidents of racism and the disadvantage experienced by victims. Serious consideration needs to be given to whether this is the most effective strategy in challenging exclusionary practices. While racism must not be ignored, the evidence of this thesis suggests that it would be counter-productive to insist that service users and service providers focus on anti-racism at the expense of promoting multiculturalism. It has been shown that multicultural policies, which recognise and accommodate the cultural and religious priorities of minority ethnic groups within a wider collectivity, have an important contribution to make in meeting the needs of relative newcomers, stimulating positive interaction between them and the wider population, and challenging exclusionary practices.

Researchers and political activists are increasingly acknowledging that Black/White terminology and related anti-racist strategies imported from the USA have not been entirely appropriate in a British context. Similarly, it can be argued that there are dangers in developing policies in Scotland based on 'British' research that frequently contains no Scottish data. Much more work needs to be done to advance and link empirical and theoretical research relating to the Scottish experience. This book is a contribution to such a body of work.

Bibliography

Age Concern and Help the Aged [1984] *Housing for Ethnic Elders*, Mitcham, Age Concern England
Ahmed A and Hastings D [1994] 'Islam in the Age of Modernity' in Ahmed A and Hastings D (eds) *Islam, Globalization and Postmodernity*, London, Routledge
Alderman G [1992] *Modern British Jewry*, Oxford, Clarendon Press
Anderson I and Brownlie J [1997] 'A Neglected Problem: Minority Ethnic Elders with Dementia' in Bowes A and Sim D (eds) *Perspectives on Welfare: the Experience of Minority Ethnic Groups in Scotland*, Aldershot, Ashgate
Anthias F [1992] 'Connecting "Race" and Ethnic Phenomena', *Sociology*, 26, 3, 421-38
Appiah K [1994] 'Identity, Authenticity, Survival: Multicultural Societies and Cultural Reproduction' in Gutmann A (ed) *Multiculturalism*, Princeton, Princeton University Press
Armstrong B [1989] *A People Without Prejudice?* London, Runnymede Trust
Askham J, Henshaw L and Tarpey M [1995] *Social Communities and Health Authority Services for Elderly People from Black and Minority Ethnic Groups*, London, HMSO
Aspinwall B [1982] 'The Formation of the Catholic Community in the West of Scotland: Some Preliminary Outlines' *Inness Review*, Vol XXIII
Aspinwall B [1991] 'The Catholic Irish and Wealth in Glasgow' in Devine T (ed) *Irish Immigrants and Scottish Society in the Nineteenth and Twentieth Centuries*, Edinburgh, John Donald
Ball W & Solomos J (eds) [1990] *Race and Local Politics*, London, Macmillan
Ballard R [1997] 'The Construction of a Conceptual Vision: 'Ethnic Groups' and the 1991 UK Census' in *Ethnic and Racial Studies*, 20, 1
Banton M [1977] *The Idea of Race*, London, Tavistock Publications
Banton M [1983] *Racial and Ethnic Competition*, Cambridge, Cambridge University Press
Banton M [1987] *Racial Theories*, Cambridge, Cambridge University Press
Banton M [1996] 'The Racism Problematic' in Barot R (ed) *The Racism Problematic: Contemporary Sociological Debates on Race and Ethnicity*, Lampeter, Edwin Mullin Press
Barkan E [1992] *The Retreat of Scientific Racism: Changing Concepts of Race in Britain and the United States Between the World Wars*, Cambridge, Cambridge University Press
Barker J [1984] *Black and Asian Old People in Britain, Research Perspectives on Ageing*, Age Concern England, Mitcham, Surrey
Barker M [1981] *The New Racism*, London, Junction Books
Barot R (ed) [1996] *The Racism Problematic: Contemporary Sociological Debates on Race and Ethnicity*, Lampeter, Edwin Mullin Press

Barth F [1993] *Balinese Worlds*, Chicago, University of Chicago Press
Beharrell L V [1965] 'Our New Immigrants' in *Glasgow Herald* 24 November 1965 and 25 November 1965
Belson W [1986] *Validity in Social Research*, Aldershot, Gower
Benski T [1981] 'Identification, Group Survival and Inter-group Relations; the Case of a Middle Class Jewish Community in Scotland', *Ethnic and Racial Studies*, 4, 3, 307-319
Berger P L [1969] *The Social Reality of Religion*, London, Faber and Faber
Berthoud R [1997] 'Four National Surveys of Ethnic Minorities' in *Measurement and Indicators of Integration*, Strasbourg, Council of Europe
Bevan V [1986] *The Development of British Immigration Laws*, London, Croom Helm
Bhabha H [1994] *The Location of Culture*, London, Routledge
Bhalla A and Blakemore K [1981] *Elders of the Minority Ethnic Groups*, Birmingham, All Faiths For One Race (AFFOR)
Bishop I M [1987] *The Education of Ulster Students in Glasgow University in the Eighteenth Century*, MA Thesis, Queens University Belfast
Bowes A and Dar N [1997] 'The Social Work Service and Elderly Pakistani People' in Bowes A and Sim D (eds) *Perspectives on Welfare: the Experience of Minority Ethnic Groups in Scotland*, Aldershot, Ashgate
Bowes A, Dar N and Sim D [1997] 'Pakistanis and Social Rented Housing: a Study in Glasgow' in Bowes A and Sim D (eds) *Perspectives on Welfare: the Experience of Minority Ethnic Groups in Scotland*, Aldershot, Ashgate
Bowes A, McCluskey J and Sim D [1989] *Ethnic Minorities and Housing Problems in Glasgow*, Glasgow City Council
Bowes A, McCluskey J and Sim D [1990] 'The Changing Nature of Glasgow's Ethnic Minority Community', *Scottish Geographical Magazine*, 106, 2, 99-107
Bowes A and Sim D [1991] *Demands and Constraints: Ethnic Minorities and Social Services in Scotland*, Edinburgh, SCVO
Bowes A and Sim D (eds) [1997] *Perspectives on Welfare: the Experience of Minority Ethnic Groups in Scotland*, Aldershot, Ashgate
Brah A [1992] 'Difference, Diversity and Differentiation' in Donald J and Rattansi A (eds) *'Race', Culture and Difference*, London, Sage
Bryant B and Bryant R [1982] *Change and Conflict: a Study of Community Work in Glasgow*, Aberdeen, Aberdeen University Press
Bryant G [1985] 'Scots in India in the Eighteenth Century', *Scottish Historical Review*, LXIV, pp 22-41
Bulpitt J [1986] 'Continuity, Autonomy and Peripheralisation: the Anatomy of the Centre's Race Statecraft in England' in Layton-Henry Z and Rich P (eds) *Race, Government and Politics in Britain*, London, Macmillan
Bunt S [1975] *Jewish Youth Work in Britain*, London, Bedford Square Press
Butler D and Stokes D [1969] *Political Change in Britain*, London, Macmillan
Cable V [1969] *Whither Kenyan Immigrants?* London, Fabian Society
Caglar A [1997] 'Hyphenated Identities and the Limits of 'Culture' ' in Modood T and Werbner P (eds) *The Politics of Multiculturalism in the New Europe*, London, Zed Books

Cain A [1986] *The Corn Chest for Scotland: Scots in India*, Edinburgh, National Library of Scotland
Cambridge A and Feuchtwang S [1992] *Where You Belong*, Aldershot, Avebury
Campbell A [1979] *The Lanarkshire Miners: a Social History of their Trade Unions 1775-1874*, Edinburgh, John Donald
Campbell T and Woods P [1987] *The Glory and the Dream: the History of Celtic FC 1887-1987*, London
Cant B and Kelly E with Wing Sau Sit K [1995] *The Roads to Racial Equality*, Edinburgh, SCVO
CES [1994a] *Area 10 Development Plan 1994-1997 Strathclyde Regional Council Department of Education*, Glasgow Division, Community Education Service
CES [1994b] *Project No 324/90 Interim Evaluation*, Glasgow Division, Community Education Service
Chakrabarti M and Cadman M [1997] 'Minority Elders in Scotland: Facing the Challenge' in Bowes A and Sim D (eds) *Perspectives on Welfare: the Experience of Minority Ethnic Groups in Scotland*, Aldershot, Ashgate
CHC [1936] *Jubilee of the Mission 1886-1936*, Church of the Holy Cross Souvenir Booklet, Crosshill, Glasgow
CHC [1961] *Golden Jubilee of the Church of the Holy Cross*, Souvenir brochure 1911-1961, Crosshill, Glasgow
Cohen P [1988] 'The Perversions of Inheritance: Studies in the Making of Multi-Racist Britain' in Cohen P and Bains H (eds) *Multi-Racist Britain*, London, Macmillan
Collins B [1991] 'The Origins of Irish Immigration to Scotland in the Nineteenth and Twentieth Centuries' in Devine T (ed) *Irish Immigrants and Scottish Society in the Nineteenth and Twentieth Centuries*, Edinburgh, John Donald
Collins K [1987] *Aspects of Scottish Jewry*, Glasgow Jewish Representative Council
Collins K [1988] *Go and Learn: the International Story of Jews and Medicine in Scotland*, Aberdeen, Aberdeen University Press
Collins K [1993] *Glasgow Jewry: a Guide to the History and Community of the Jews in Glasgow*, Glasgow, Scottish Jewish Archives Committee
Colpi T [1991] *The Italian Factor*, Edinburgh, Mainstream
Cooper H and Morrison P [1991] *A Sense of Belonging: Dilemmas of British Jewish Identity*, London, Weidenfeld and Nicolson
CRE [1990] *Schools of Faith: Religious Schools in a Multicultural Society*, London, Commission for Racial Equality
CRE [1991] *Code of Practice for the Elimination of Racial Discrimination in Education*, London, Commission for Racial Equality
Crowley J [1996] 'Immigration and 'Race Relations' in Britain and France' in Carmon N *Immigration and Integration in Post-industrial Societies*, London, Macmillan
Curtis E [1990] *A History of Ireland*, London, Routledge
Dahya B [1974] 'The Nature of Pakistani Ethnicity in Industrial Cities in Britain' in Cohen A (ed) *Urban Ethnicity*, London, Tavistock
Dalton M and Daghlian S [1989] *Race and Housing in Glasgow: the Role of Housing Associations*, London, Commission for Racial Equality

Dalton M and Hampton K [1995] *Housing Needs of Ethnic Minorities in Govanhill: a Community Perspective*, Report Prepared for Govanhill Housing Association

Davis G [1991] *The Irish in Britain 1815-1914*, Dublin, Gill and Macmillan

de Azevedo R and Sannino B [1997] 'A European Research Project on Migrants' Integration' in *Measurements and Indicators of Integration*, Strasbourg, Council of Europe.

Devine T (ed) [1991] *Irish Immigrants and Scottish Society in the Nineteenth and Twentieth Centuries*, Edinburgh, John Donald

Docherty C [1997] 'Survey of Clergy Perceptions on the Present and Future of Youth Ministry in Glasgow Parishes', Archdiocese of Glasgow Youth Office

Donald J and Rattansi A (eds) [1992] *'Race', Culture and Difference*, London, Sage

Dummett A [1976] *Citizenship and Nationality*, London, Runnymede Trust

Dummett M and Dummett A [1982] 'The Role of Government in Britain's Racial Crisis' in Husband C (ed) *'Race' in Britain*, London, Hutchinson & Co.

Dunlop A [1988] *Aspects of Scottish Migration History with Particular Emphasis on Contemporary Pakistani and Bangladeshi Migration*, Unpublished M.Litt Thesis, Department of Sociology, University of Glasgow

Dunlop A and Miles R [1990] 'Recovering the History of Asian Migration to Scotland', *Immigrants and Minorities*, 9, 2, July 1990, 145-67, London, Frank Cass

Durie A [1979] *The Scottish Linen Industry in the Eighteenth Century*, Edinburgh, Donald

Durkheim E [1954] *Elementary Forms of Religious Life*, London, Allen and Unwin

Edward M [1993] *Who Belongs to Glasgow? 200 Years of Migration*, Glasgow City Libraries

Elahi K [1967] *Some Aspects of Social Adaptation of Pakistani Immigrants in Glasgow*, Unpublished MA Thesis, University of Edinburgh, Department of Social Anthropology

Engels F [1958] *The Condition of the English Working Class*, Oxford, Blackwell

Esposito J L [1991] *The Islamic Threat: Myth or Reality*, New York, Oxford University Press

Eunson E [1994] *Old Govanhill*, Ayrshire, Richard Stenlake

Fenton S [1996] 'The Subject is Ethnicity' in Barot R (ed) *The Racism Problematic: Contemporary Sociological Debates on Race and Ethnicity*, Lampeter, Edwin Mullin Press

Fife Regional Council [1991] *Racial Equality in Fife*

Fitzgerald M [1997] 'Measurement and Indictors of Integration' in *Measurement and Indicators of Integration*, Strasbourg, Council of Europe

FitzPatrick T [1986a] *The Parish of Holy Cross Glasgow 1886-1986*, Centenary History

FitzPatrick T [1986b] *Catholic Secondary Education in South West Scotland before 1972: its Contribution to the Change in Status of the Catholic Community*, Aberdeen, Aberdeen University Press

Foddy W [1993] *Constructing Questions for Interviews and Questionnaires*, Cambridge, Cambridge University Press

Forbes C [1993] *Alternatives: a Report on Research into the Possibilities for Developing the Work of the Church of Scotland in the Asian Community on the South Side of Glasgow*, submitted to the Asian Bookshop Support Group, 2 February 1993

Gallagher T [1985] 'A Tale of Two Cities: Communal Strife in Glasgow and Liverpool before 1914' in Swift R and Gilley S (eds) *The Irish in the Victorian City*, London, Croom Helm

Gallagher T [1987] *Glasgow: the Uneasy Peace*, Manchester, Manchester University Press

Gallagher T [1991] 'The Catholic Irish in Scotland: in Search of Identity' in Devine T (ed) *Irish Immigrants and Scottish Society in the Nineteenth and Twentieth Centuries*, Edinburgh, John Donald

GCC [1996] *Glasgow City Council Key Objectives 1996-1999*

GCVS [1995a] *Interchange: Special Issue on the Community Care Plan*, Glasgow Council for Voluntary Services, February 1995

GCVS [1995b] Minutes of the Meeting on Consultation about the Greater Glasgow Community Care Plan with Regard to the Services to the Ethnic Minority Communities, Glasgow Council for Voluntary Services, 31 January 1995

GDC [1979] *Govanhill Local Plan Survey Report*, Glasgow District Council Planning Department

GDC [1980] *Govanhill Local Plan*, Glasgow District Council Planning Department

Geertz C [1993] *The Interpretation of Cultures: Selected Essays*, London, Fontana

Gellner E [1994] Foreword to Ahmed A and Donnan H (eds) *Islam, Globalization and Postmodernity*, London, Routledge

Gerholm T [1994] 'Two Muslim Intellectuals in the Postmodern West: Akbar Ahmed and Ziauddin Sardar' in Ahmed A and Donnan H (eds) *Islam, Globalization and Postmodernity*, London, Routledge

GHA [1984] *Annual Report 1983-1984*, Govanhill Housing Association

GHA [1990] *15 Years of Govanhill Housing Association*, Govanhill Housing Association

GHA [1994] Statistics Compiled for Local Report, Govanhill Housing Association, Glasgow

Gilley S [1980] 'Catholics and Socialists in Glasgow 1906-1912' in Lunn K (ed) *Hosts, Immigrants and Minorities: Historical Responses to Newcomers in British Society 1870-1914*, Folkstone, Dawson

Gilroy P [1987] *There Ain't No Black in the Union Jack*, London, Hutchinson

Gilroy P [1992] 'The End of Anti-racism' in Donald J and Rattansi A (eds) *'Race', Culture and Difference*, London, Sage

Glasgow Corporation [1972a] *Areas of Need in Glasgow*

Glasgow Corporation [1972b] *Glasgow Planning District 41*, Govanhill, Environmental Studies Planning Department, October 1972

Glasgow Corporation [1973] *Housing and Social Deprivation*

Govanhill ALC [1995] *An Investigation into the Need for Additional Youth Facilities in Govanhill*, Govanhill Area Liaison Committee Sub-Group on Youth Issues.

Gregory J [1987] *Sex, Race and the Law*, London, Sage

Gutmann A [1992] 'Introduction' in Taylor C et al *Multiculturalism and 'The Politics of Recognition'*, Princeton, Princeton University Press

Hall S [1991] 'Old and New Identities, Old and New Ethnicities' in King A (ed) *Culture, Globalization and the World System*, London, Macmillan

Hamilton W [1977] Internal Memorandum and Draft Report Subject: 'Ground Consolidation Cost - SDD Grant', Glasgow District Council Planning Department

Hampton K and Bain J [1995] *Poverty and Ethnic Minorities in Scotland: a Review of Literature*, Scottish Ethnic Minorities Research Unit, Research Paper No 4, Series 2, Glasgow Caledonian University

Handley J [1943] *The Irish in Scotland 1789-1845*, Cork, Cork University Press

Handley J [1947] *The Irish in Modern Scotland*, Cork, Cork University Press

Hannan J [1988] *The Life of John Wheatley*, Nottingham

Hannerz U [1992] *Cultural Complexity: Studies in the Social Organisation of Meaning*, New York, Columbia University Press

Hickman M [1995] *Religion, Class and Identity*, Aldershot, Avebury

Howell D [1983] *British Workers and the Independent Labour Party 1888-1906*, Manchester, Manchester University Press

Husband C [1982] *'Race' in Britain: Continuity and Change*, London, Hutchinson & Co

Iqbal B [1995] 'Overview on Community Care Services for Ethnic Minority Communities in Glasgow', Strathclyde Community Relations Council, 31 January 1995

Jacobson J [1998] *Islam in Transition: Religion and Identity among British Pakistani Youth*, London, Routledge

Jeffrey J and Seagar R [1993] *Housing Black and Ethnic Elders*, London, FBHO

Jenkins R [1996] ' 'Us' and 'Them': Ethnicity, Racism and Ideology' in Barot R (ed) *The Racism Problematic: Contemporary Sociological Debates on Race and Ethnicity*, Lampeter, Edwin Mullin Press

Joly D [1986] *Making a Place for Islam in British Society: Muslims in Birmingham*, Research Papers in Ethnic Relations, ESRC

Jones C [1977] *Immigration and Social Policy in Britain*, London, Tavistock

Jones T [1993] *Britain's Ethnic Minorities*, London, Policy Studies Institute

Kay B [1982] 'From Gorbals to Gweedore' in Kay B (ed) *Odyssey: Voices from Scotland's Recent Past*, The Second Collection, Edinburgh, Polygon

Kearsley G and Srivastava S [1974] 'The Spatial Evolution of Glasgow's Asian Community', *Scottish Geographical Magazine*, 95, 110-124

Kenneth, Rev Brother [1968] 'The Education (Scotland) Act 1918 in the Making', *Innes Review*, XIX

Khan V [1980] 'Asian Women in Britain: Strategies of Adjustment of Indian and Pakistani Migrants' in de Souza A (ed) *Women in Contemporary India*, Delhi

Kinealy C [1992] 'Irish Immigration into Scotland in the Nineteenth and Twentieth Centuries' in *European Immigration into Scotland*, Proceedings of the 4th Annual Conference of the Scottish Association of Family History Societies, 12 September 1992

Kolmel R [1987] 'German-Jewish Refugees in Scotland' in Collins K (ed) *Aspects of Scottish Jewry*, Glasgow Jewish Representative Council, Glasgow

Kraditor A [1982] *The Radical Persuasion*, Baton Rouge, Louisiana State University Press

Lawrence E [1982] 'In the Abundance of Water the Fool is Thirsty: Sociology and Black 'Pathology'' in CCCS *The Empire Strikes Back*, London, Hutchinson

Lee J [1973] *The Modernisation of Irish Society 1848-1918*, Dublin, Gill and Macmillan

Lees L [1979] *Exiles of Erin: Irish Immigrants in Victorian London*, Manchester, Manchester University Press

Levi-Strauss C [1994] 'Anthropology, Race and Politics: a Conversation with Didier Eribon' in Borofsky R (ed) *Assessing Anthropology*, New York, McGraw Hill

Lewis P [1994] *Islamic Britain*, London, I B Tauris

Lewis P [1997] 'Arenas of Ethnic Negotiation: Cooperation and Conflict in Bradford' in Modood T and Werbner P (eds) *The Politics of Multiculturalism in the New Europe: Racism, Identity and Community*, London, Zed Books

Luckmann T [1967] *The Invisible Religion: The Problem of Religion in Modern Society*, London, Collier-Macmillan

Lyon W [1997] 'Defining Ethnicity: Another Way of Being British' in Modood T and Werbner P (eds) *The Politics of Multiculturalism in the New Europe: Racism, Identity and Community*, London, Zed Books

Lythe C and Majmudar M [1982] *The Renaissance of the Scottish Economy?* London, George Allen & Unwin

Maan B [1992] *The New Scots: the Story of Asians in Scotland*, Edinburgh, John Donald

Maan B [1994] *No Problem Here: an Investigation into Racism in Scotland*, Unpublished M.Sc Thesis, University of Strathclyde

McCaffrey[1] [1991] 'Irish Issues in the Nineteenth and Twentieth Centuries: Radicalism in a Scottish Context' in Devine T (ed) *Irish Immigrants and Scottish Society in the Nineteenth and Twentieth Centuries*, Edinburgh, John Donald

McCluskey J [1991] 'Ethnic Minorities and the Social Work Service in Glasgow' in Bowes A and Sim D (eds) *Demands and Constraints: Ethnic Minorities and Social Services in Scotland*, Edinburgh, SCVO

MacEwen M [1991] 'Housing Allocations and the Law: Ethnic Minorities in Edinburgh' in Bowes A and Sim D (eds) *Demands and Constraints: Ethnic Minorities and Social Services in Scotland*, Edinburgh, SCVO

McFarland E [1986] *The Loyal Orange Institution in Scotland 1799-1990*, Unpublished PhD Thesis, University of Glasgow

McFarland E [1991] 'Clyde Opinion on an Old Controversy: Indian and Chinese Seafarers in Glasgow', *Ethnic and Racial Studies*, 14, 4, October 1991

McFarland E, Dalton M and Watson D [1987] *Personal Welfare Services and Ethnic Minorities: a Study of East Pollokshields*, Scottish Ethnic Minorities Research Unit, Caledonian University

---

[1] Mc and Mac are treated as 'Mac' and listed alphabetically according to the next letter in the name

McLean I [1983] *The Legend of Red Clydeside*, Edinburgh, John Donald

McLellan D [1972] *The Thought of Karl Marx*, London, Macmillan

Manchester Computing Centre [1992] *SASPAC User Manual* Parts I and II, London Research Centre, First Edition

Marx K and Engels F [1962] 'The Eighteenth Brumaire of Louis Bonaparte' in *Marx and Engels Selected Works*, Vol I, Moscow, Foreign Language Publishing House

Mason D [1996] 'Some Reflections on the Sociology of Race and Racism in Barot R (ed) *The Racism Problematic: Contemporary Sociological Debates on Race and Ethnicity*, Lampeter, Edwin Mullin Press

Massie A [1989] *Glasgow*, London, Barrie & Jenkins

Miles R [1982] *Racism and Migrant Labour*, London, Routledge & Kegan Paul

Miles R [1989] *Racism*, London, Routledge

Miles R [1993] *Racism After 'Race Relations'*, London, Routledge

Miles R [1996] 'Racism and Nationalism in the United Kingdom: A View from the Periphery' in Barot R (ed) *The Racism Problematic: Contemporary Sociological Debates on Race and Ethnicity*, Lampeter, Edwin Mullin Press

Miles R and Dunlop A [1986] 'The Racialization of Politics in Britain: Why Scotland is Different', *Patterns of Prejudice*, 20, 1, 23-31

Miles R and Dunlop A [1987] 'Racism in Britain: the Scottish Dimension' in Jackson P (ed) *Race and Racism: Essays in Social Geography*, London, Allen & Unwin

Miles R and Muirhead L [1986] 'Racism in Scotland: a Matter for Further Investigation', *Scottish Government Yearbook*, pp 108-136

Miller S, Schmool M and Lerman A [1996] *Social and Political Attitudes of British Jews: Some Key Findings of the JPR Survey*, Institute for Jewish Policy Research

Modood T [1988a] 'Who is Defining Whom?' *New Society*, 4 March 1988

Modood T [1988b] 'Black, Racial Equality and Asian Identity', *New Community*, XIV, 3, 397-404

Modood T [1992] *Not Easy Being British: Colour, Culture and Citizenship*, London, Runnymede Trust and Trentham Books

Modood T et al [1994] *Ethnic Minorities in Britain: Diversity and Disadvantage*, London, PSI

Modood T [1996] 'If Races Do Not Exist, Then What Does? Racial Categorisation and Ethnic Identities' in Barot R (ed) *The Racism Problematic: Contemporary Sociological Debates on Race and Ethnicity*, Lampeter, Edwin Mullin Press

Modood T [1997a] 'Culture and Identity' in Modood T (ed) *Ethnic Minorities in Britain: Diversity and Disadvantage*, London, PSI

Modood T [1997b] 'Difference, Cultural Racism and Anti-racism' in Werbner P and Modood T (eds) *Debating Cultural Hybridity: Multi-cultural Identities and the Politics of Anti-racism*, London, Zed Books

Modood T [1997c] 'Introduction' in Modood T and Werbner P (eds) *The Politics of Multiculturalism in the New Europe: Racism, Identity and Community*, London, Zed Books

Murray B [1984] *The Old Firm: Sectarianism, Sport and Society in Scotland*, Edinburgh, John Donald

Murray C [1991a] 'Ethnic Minorities and Community Work: the Experience of Crossroads Youth and Community Association' in Bowes A and Sim D (eds) *Demands and Constraints: Ethnic Minorities and Social Services in Scotland*, Edinburgh, SCVO

Murray J [1991b] *Three Tears for Glasgow*

Muus P [1997] 'Concepts of Migrants' Integration: a Comparison of National Policies' in *Measurement and Indicators of Integration*, Strasbourg, Council of Europe

Neustatter H [1955] 'Demographic and Other Statistical Aspects of Anglo-Jewry' in Freedman M [ed] *A minority in Britain*, London, Valentine Mitchell & Co Ltd

Nicholson M and O'Neil M [1987] *Glasgow: Locomotive Builder to the World*

Papastergiadis N [1997] 'Tracing Hybridity in Theory' in Werbner P and Moody T (eds) *Debating Cultural Hybridity: Multi-Cultural Identities and the Politics of Anti-Racism*, London, Zed Books

Parker J [1985] 'Scottish Enterprise in India 1750-1914' in Cage R (ed) *The Scots Abroad*, London, Croom Helm

Parkin D [1993] 'Nemi in the Modern World', *Man*, 28 (I) 79-99

Pieri J [1997] *Isle of the Displaced: an Italian-Scot's Memoirs of Internment During the Second World War*, Glasgow, Neil Wilson Publishing

Porter R [1980] *Govanhill Church of Scotland 1880-1980*, Alloa

PP [1837-38] Reports from Commissioners of Religious Instruction, *Parliamentary Papers*, Scotland 1837-1838 XXXII, App III

PP [1936] Report on the State of the Irish Poor in Great Britain, *Parliamentary Papers*, 1836, 40, XXX, IV

Pugh M [1985] *The Tories and the People 1880-1935*, Oxford, Blackwell

Rees T [1982] 'Immigration Policies in the United Kingdom' in Husband C (ed) *'Race' in Britain: Continuity and Change*, London, Hutchinson & Co

Rex J [1991] *Ethnic Identity and Ethnic Mobilisation in Britain*, Warwick ESRC Centre for Research in Ethnic Relations

Robinson V [1986] *Transients, Settlers and Refugees*, Oxford, Clarendon Press

Rodgers M [1982a] 'Italiani in Scozzia' in Kay B (ed) *Odyssey: Voices from Scotland's Recent Past*, The Second Collection, Edinburgh, Polygon

Rodgers M [1982b] 'Glasgow Jewry' in Kay B (ed) *Odyssey: Voices from Scotland's Recent Past*, The Second Collection, Edinburgh, Polygon

Rossi V Rev Mgr Gaetano [1991] *Memoirs of 1940: Impressions of Life in an Internment Camp*, Glasgow, Glasgow University Department of Italian

Runnymede Trust [1997] *Islamophobia: a Challenge for Us All. Report of the Runnymede Trust Commission on British Muslims and Islamophobia*, London, The Runnymede Trust

Saggar S [1996] 'The Politics of Racial Pluralism in Britain and Problems of Evaluation' in Barot R (ed) *The Racism Problematic: Contemporary Sociological Debates on Race and Ethnicity*, Lampeter, Edwin Mullin Press

Save the Children and Glasgow Caledonian University [1995] *Child and Family Poverty in Scotland: the Facts*

Schimmel A [1992] *Islam: An Introduction*, State University of New York Press
Scott A [1912-14] *Scott Diaries*, Glasgow University Special Collection
Scottish Office [1983] *Ethnic Minorities in Scotland*, Edinburgh, HMSO
Scottish Office [1993] *Caring For People: Information for Voluntary and Private Providers in Scotland*, Edinburgh, HMSO
Scottish Office [1994] *Ethnic Minorities*, Factsheet 15, Edinburgh, HMSO
SCVO [1988] *Irrespective of Race, Colour or Creed: Voluntary Organisations and Minority Ethnic Groups in Scotland*, Edinburgh, SCVO and Commission for Racial Equality
SED [1989] Ethnically-based Statistics on School Pupils, Circular No 8, Edinburgh, Scottish Education Department
Selltiz C, Jahoda M, Deutsch M and Cook S [1965] *Research Methods in Social Relations*, revised edition, London, Methuen
Sereni B [1974] *They Took the Low Road: a Brief History of the Barghigiani to Scotland*, translated by M Moscardini, Barga, Giornale di Barga
Shaw A [1988] *A Pakistani Community in Britain*, Oxford, Blackwell
Sloan W [1991] 'Religious Affiliation and the Immigrant Experience: Catholic Irish and Protestant Highlanders in Glasgow 1830-1850' in Devine T (ed) *Irish Immigrants and Scottish Society in the Nineteenth and Twentieth Centuries*, Edinburgh, John Donald
Smith P [1991] *Ethnic Minorities in Scotland*, Edinburgh, Scottish Office
Smout T [1986] *A Century of Scottish People 1830-1950*, London, Collins
SOED [1992a] *Religious and Moral Education 5-14, Curriculum and Assessment in Scotland*, National Guidelines, Scottish Office Education Department
SOED [1992b] *Youth Work in Scotland: a Report by HM Inspectors of Schools*, Edinburgh, HMSO
SOED [1993] *Devolved School Management: Guidelines for Schemes*, OM(DPPS)GE 1653, Scottish Office Education Department
SOED [1994a] *Education 5-14 A Guide for Parents*, Edinburgh, HMSO
SOED[1995a] *Scottish Education*, Factsheet 3, Edinburgh, HMSO
SOED [1995b] *St Albert's Primary School*, HM Inspectors Report, Edinburgh, Scottish Office Education Department
Solomos J and Back L [1995] *Race, Politics and Social Change*, London, Routledge
Solomos J and Back L [1996] *Racism and Society*, London Macmillan
Spivak G [1987] *In Other Worlds*, London, Methuen
SRC [1990] *Tackling Racist Incidents Within the Education System*, Strathclyde Regional Council Department of Education
SRC [1992] *Community Care Plan 1992/93-1994/5*, Strathclyde Regional Council
SRC [1993] *Social Strategy for the Nineties*, Chief Executives Department, Strathclyde Regional Council
SRC [1994] *Priority Area Profile: Govanhill*, Strathclyde Regional Council
SRC [1995] *Review of Priority Areas in Strathclyde*, Social Strategy Communications, Strathclyde Regional Council
SRC et al [1994] *Greater Glasgow Joint Community Care Plan 1994/5-1997/8* Consultation Draft, Strathclyde Regional Council

SRC et al [1995] *Greater Glasgow Joint Community Care Plan 1994/5-1997/8*, Strathclyde Regional Council
Srivastava S [1975] *The Asian Community in Glasgow*, Unpublished PhD Thesis, University of Glasgow, Faculty of Arts
St Catherine's Conference [1991] *Islam: the British Experience*, Report No 29, St Catherine's Conference 27-29 November 1991
Stepan N [1982] *The Idea of Race in Science: Great Britain 1800-1945*, London, Macmillan
Strathclyde Poverty Alliance [1994] *Race and Poverty: Issues and Opportunities for Action in Strathclyde*, Preliminary Draft Report
Strathclyde Regional Archives [1858] *Poor Law Applications*, Irish Series, Glasgow
STUC [1992] *Unemployment: the Race Bias in Scotland*, Report of the Scottish Trades Union Council
Swann [1985] *Education for All: the Report of a Committee of Enquiry into the Education of Children from Ethnic Minority Groups*, London, HMSO
TCRC [1987] *Racial Tension in Tayside*, Tayside Community Relations Council
Third H and MacEwen M [1997] 'The Housing Experience of Minority Ethnic Groups in Scotland' in Bowes A and Sim D (eds) *Perspectives on Welfare: the Experience of Minority Ethnic Groups in Scotland*, Aldershot, Ashgate
Thomas S [1982] *The Qualifying Round: a Study of Second Generation South Asian Women approaching the Labour Market*, Unpublished MSc Thesis, University of Bristol
Treble J [1973] Irish Navvies in the North of England 1830-50, *Transport History*, vi
Turner B [1985] 'Knowledge, Skill and Occupational Strategy: the Professionalism of Paramedical Groups', *Community Health Studies*, 9, 1, 38-47
University of Aberdeen [1991] *Measuring the Benefits of Youth Work*, Report to the Scottish Office Education Department, University of Aberdeen Department of Education and Grampian Regional Council
van de Veer P [1997] 'The Enigma of Arrival: Hybridity and Authenticity in the Global Space' in Werbner P and Modood T (eds) *Debating Cultural Hybridity: Multi-cultural Identities and the Politics of Anti-racism*, London, Zed Books
Visram R [1986] *Ayahs, Lascars and Princes: Indians in Britain 1700-1947*, London, Pluto
Walker G [1991] 'The Protestant Irish in Scotland' in Devine T (ed) *Irish Immigrants and Scottish Society in the Nineteenth and Twentieth Centuries*, Edinburgh, John Donald
Walsh D [1987] *Racial Harassment in Glasgow*, Scottish Ethnic Minorities Research Unit, Caledonian University, Glasgow
Watson M [1984] *A Report of the Findings of a Survey of the South Asian community residing in the Crosshill Area of Glasgow between 19 July and 29 August 1984*, Report to Church of Scotland, Glasgow
Watt C [1993] *Ethnic Minority Business and Employment in Glasgow's Inner City*, Unpublished M Phil Thesis, Glasgow Caledonian University

Weber M [1948] 'The Social Psychology of the World's Religions' in Gerth H and C Wright Mills (eds) *From Max Weber: Essays in Sociology*, London, Routledge

Werbner P [1997] 'Introduction: the Dialectics of Cultural Hybridity' in Werbner P and Modood T (eds) *Debating Cultural Hybridity: Multi-cultural Identities and the Politics of Anti-racism*, London, Zed Books

Werbner P and Modood T (eds) [1997] *Debating Cultural Hybridity: Multi-cultural Identities and the Politics of Anti-racism*, London, Zed Books

West of Scotland CRC [1997] *Annual Report*, Glasgow, West Of Scotland Community Relations Council

Wicker H [1997] 'From Complex Culture to Cultural Complexity' in Werbner P and Modood T (eds) *Debating Cultural Hybridity: Multi-cultural Identities and the Politics of Anti-racism*, London, Zed Books

Wieviorka M [1997] 'Is it so Difficult to be Anti-Racist?' in Werbner P and Modood T (eds) *Debating Cultural Hybridity: Multi-cultural Identities and the Politics of Anti-racism*, London, Zed Books

Wood I [1990] *John Wheatley*, Manchester, Manchester University Press

Worsdall F [1979] *The Tenement: a Way of Life: a Social, Historical and Architectural Study of Housing in Glasgow*, Edinburgh, West & R Chambers

Yuval-Davis N [1997] 'Ethnicity, Gender Relations and Multiculturalism' in Werbner P and Modood T (eds) *Debating Cultural Hybridity: Multi-cultural Identities and the Politics of Anti-racism*, London, Zed Books

Index

academic achievement 27, 29, 54, 78, 79, 107, 109, 128, 130, 133, 143, 146, 151-3, 190, 230, 237
access to services 4, 73, 121, 145, 158, 187, 192-4, 213, 216, 221, 224
Act of Union (1707) 10, 13, 14, 61, 236, 237
advice services 157, 158, 180, 182, 196, 215
Aliens Order (1920) 36
anti-Catholicism 18, 21, 104
anti-Muslim (see Islamophobia)
anti-racism 1-7, 9, 110, 121-3, 126, 132, 140-2, 151, 153, 161, 165, 178-9, 188, 193-4, 199, 217, 219, 221-3, 225, 228, 230, 234, 236-8
anti-Semitism 3, 48, 49, 55, 107
Arabic 112, 124, 147, 148, 219
Arandora Star 38, 39
arranged marriage 168-170, 183
Asian
   food 216, 217
   identity 5, 67-9, 83, 95, 105, 106, 111, 156, 225, 227-9, 235
Asian Boys Group 156-7, 162, 185, 187
Asian Girls Group 157, 161-4, 171, 173, 182, 184, 187, 189, 235
assimilation 8, 31, 108, 123

Barga 33, 34, 36
Battle of the Boyne 19
Belfast 18, 20, 31
bilingual staff 136, 144, 177, 194, 197
Black
   Elderly Initiative 196, 197
   identity 3, 5, 6, 67-9, 95, 197, 198, 222, 227, 228, 230
blasphemy law 6
British
   identity 5, 8-10, 227, 229
   immigration legislation 64, 81
   Nationality Act (1948) 63, 81
   Raj 61, 62

Care in the Community 191-4
Casa d'Italia 39-42, 221
Catholic
   identity 22, 23, 28-32, 44, 107
   Irish 11, 13, 21, 23-4, 27-8, 81, 86, 93, 107, 154
   Italian 40, 41, 107
   schools 25, 26, 29-31, 37, 87, 89, 90, 105, 107-8, 121-2, 124, 126, 127, 129, 132-3, 152, 233-4
   Socialist Society 27
   voting patterns 23, 27
   youth work 23, 30, 31
Celtic Football Club 20, 23, 31, 41, 59
Census
   'ethnic question' 67-8, 109
   undercount 67
Central Mosque
   Glasgow 66, 130, 198, 212, 222, 235
   Govanhill 93
chain migration
   Italian 34, 43
   Pakistani 62, 67, 93
chedar schools 54, 57, 107
Chinese 5, 66-9, 80, 95, 218, 223, 228, 235
Church of Scotland 19, 20, 50, 198
'colour' 2, 80-83, 104, 108, 123, 231
Commission for Racial Equality 84
Community Education Service 156, 160, 187, 188, 198
Community Relations Council 11, 192, 193, 213, 221
competition for clients 187, 198, 222, 235
Conservative Party 20, 82, 115
Crosshill 52, 64, 86, 87, 89, 93
cultural
   awareness training 192-4, 221
   racism 3-5, 82, 104, 120, 123, 198, 231, 233

daras 197, 199

denominational schools
  Catholic 25-31, 37, 87, 89, 90, 105, 107-8, 121-2, 124, 126-7, 129, 132-3, 152, 233-4
  concerns about 27, 123, 152, 198, 234
  Jewish 54, 57, 107
  Muslim 129-133, 136, 152
diasporic ties 7, 109, 111, 223, 232, 233, 236
dispersal
  East African Asians 67, 93
drugs 31, 165, 167, 180, 187

East African Asians 67, 93
East India Company 61, 62, 85
Edinburgh 13, 33, 52, 62
education, school-age 118-153
  anti-racist 121-3
  in Govanhill 123-9
  in Scotland 118-121
  multicultural 121-3
Education (Scotland) Acts
  (1872) 26
  (1918) 26-7, 54, 121, 234
  (1980) 118, 120, 124
Eid 112, 125, 134, 151
elderly
  care 191-224
  Jewish 53, 108
  Pakistani
    care of 207-214
    definition 70
    identity 225, 226
    interests 199-200
    problems 200-207
    services for 214-221, 230, 235
  White 207, 218, 224
employment
  Irish 15, 17
  Irish Catholic 104, 108, 231
  Irish Protestant 19
  Italian 34, 36, 43, 104
  Jewish 47, 104, 231
  lascar seamen 62, 80, 81
  Pakistani 63, 74-9, 98-9, 108, 137, 145-6, 165-6, 238
endogamy 30, 44, 58, 168, 232
Engels, Friedrich 17

England 10, 13, 18, 21, 33, 36, 40, 61, 64, 67, 69, 81, 82, 84, 93, 94, 96, 97, 206, 226, 229, 230
English
  identity 10, 14, 206, 227, 229-30, 237
  language 50, 57, 109, 121-2, 127, 130, 135-8, 142, 152, 163, 196, 197, 205, 210-11, 215, 220, 233
Episcopalians 19
equal opportunities 6, 125-6, 132, 140-147, 178-180, 187, 217-220, 223, 235
essentialism 4, 5, 7, 113
'ethnic group' 5, 6, 67-9, 93-6
ethnocentricity 9
extended family 71, 168, 201, 209, 224

Fair Employment (Northern Ireland) Acts (1976, 1989) 6
famine, Irish 15-16, 105
Fascism 36, 38, 40-42, 105
fatwa 83-4, 105, 113
Fenian movement 24
food
  Asian 217
  halal 108, 113, 127-8, 132-5, 175, 196, 199, 217-18, 223
  Italian 39, 41-2, 44, 107-8
  kosher 51, 53, 55, 57, 108
football 20, 23, 31, 41, 58, 59, 108-9, 158, 185-7, 232-3, 237n
'foreigners' 39, 44, 50, 104

Gaelic Football 23, 31
gang fighting 37, 160, 165-7, 187
gender
  expectations 147, 166, 178-9, 230, 231
  inequality 168, 178-180, 188, 223, 230, 231, 235
  separation 131-2, 136, 140, 156, 177-8, 180, 189, 217, 220, 223
generation gap 202
Glasgow
  early history 13, 14
  levels of deprivation 88-9
  Second City of Empire 13, 85
Govanhill
  Area Liaison Committee 156, 198, 222

Area of Priority Treatment 221, 235
 history 85-8
 local plan 88-91
 youth survey 156-8, 182
Greater Glasgow Joint Community
 Care Plan 192-4, 221
gurdwara 220

hadith 112, 113
hafiz 112, 147
halal food 108, 113, 127-8, 132-5, 175,
 196, 199, 217-18, 223
harassment 3, 10, 92, 141, 153, 159,
 206
health problems 70, 200, 201, 214-15,
 223-4
Hebrew
 Benevolent Society 47
 Burial Society 53, 57, 89, 93
 lessons 53, 54, 57
 Philanthropic Society 47
hijab 139, 163
Hindus 63, 66, 125, 133, 150, 173, 209,
 218, 219
HIV/AIDS 181
holocaust 55, 58, 60, 105
home ownership 72-4, 90-2, 101-3, 109,
 237, 238
Home Rule
 India 61
 Ireland 20, 23-5, 27, 105, 106
hospital catering 53, 108, 232
housing
 conditions 88, 92, 100, 101, 109,
 238
 tenure 73, 91, 100, 101

identity
 Asian 5, 67-9, 83, 95, 105-6, 111,
 156, 225, 227-9, 235
 Black 3, 5, 6, 67-9, 95, 197-8, 222,
 227-8, 230
 British 5, 8-10, 227, 229
 Catholic 21-23, 28-32, 44, 107
 English 10, 14, 206, 227, 229-30,
 237
 'hybrid' 5, 226
 Indian 5, 63, 6-9, 83, 94-6, 174,
 218-19, 225, 227
 Irish 18, 24, 25, 28-32
 Italian 39-45

Jewish 51-60
 multiple 8, 9, 225, 226, 228, 230
 Muslim 6, 111, 129-136, 147-153,
 173-6, 188-190, 216-220, 223-4,
 227, 229, 231, 238
 of 'Pakistani' population 225-231
 Protestant 18-21
 Scottish 10, 14, 19-21, 28, 109,
 152, 190, 206, 229, 231, 237-8
imam 66, 113, 149
immigration
 Irish 14-18
 Italian 33-37
 Jewish 46-48
 Pakistani 61-67
India 61-4, 70, 220, 225, 226
indirect discrimination 113, 120, 127,
 151, 234
integration 8, 9, 44, 58, 82, 108, 109,
 190, 197, 221, 225, 236
Irish
 attitudes towards 16-18
 Catholics 21-32
 education 25-28
 employment 15, 17
 famine 15, 16, 105
 Home Rule 23-25
 identity 18, 24, 25, 28-32
 migration 14-16
 Protestants 18-21
Islam 6, 7, 84, 110, 111, 113, 130, 147,
 149, 176, 179, 180, 188, 189, 208,
 209, 231, 233
Islamic studies 130, 133, 135-6, 141,
 147, 149, 152, 163, 175, 188, 190,
 214, 235
Islamophobia 3, 9, 83, 231
Israel 48, 56, 57, 59, 60, 106, 219
Italian(s)
 attitudes towards 37-39
 clergy 40, 44
 'community' 39-42
 employment 33-37
 Fascism 36, 38, 40-42, 105
 identity 39-45
 language 40
 migration 33-37
 prisoners of war 41-42, 44

Jenkins, Lord 8

Jews
    attitudes towards 48-51
    Austrian 47, 55, 56
    East European 46, 55, 56
    employment 46, 49
    German 38, 46, 47, 55, 56, 105
Jewish
    'community' 51-56
    education 53-5, 107
    football team 58, 59
    homeland 48, 56, 59-60
    identity 51-60
    migration to Scotland 46-48
    welfare services 47, 53, 55, 57
    youth services 58-60
jute trade 61

Kashmir 7, 226, 227
Keir Hardie 23, 24
King William, statue in Glasgow 19
Kings Park Estate 49
kosher food 51, 53, 55, 57, 108

Labour Party 23, 24, 27, 28, 82, 232
Larkfield bus depot 89, 90
lascar seamen 62, 80-83, 104, 105
lessons outside of school
    Asian 66
    Italian 40
    Jewish 54, 57, 107
    Qur'an school 123, 147-150, 152, 234
Liberal Party 23, 24
linen industry 15, 18
London 47, 48, 54, 229, 237
loneliness, elderly 201, 203-4, 223
lunch clubs 114, 195-7, 215-7, 222

'mainstream' services
    definition 116
    education 55, 118, 121, 122
    elderly care 192-4, 221, 235
    youth 171, 178, 187, 189
marriage
    arranged 168-170, 183
    endogamy 30, 44, 168, 202, 232
    love 169, 170
    mixed 30, 58, 106
    out-marriage 58, 59, 233
mass
    attendance 27, 29-31

in school 133
Melville, Viscount 61
migration to Scotland
    chain 34, 43, 62, 67, 93
    'internal' from England 64, 67, 70
    Irish 14-16
    Italian 33-37
    Jewish 46-48
    Pakistani 61-65
mining
    in Govanhill 85, 90
    and Labour movement 24, 27
mosques
    establishment of 66, 107-8
    Glasgow Central 66, 130, 198, 212, 222, 235
    Govanhill Central 93
    role of 113, 147, 200, 211, 219-20
    welfare services 200, 208, 211-12
multiculturalism 1, 7, 8, 11, 12, 110, 119, 126, 133, 140, 159, 178, 224, 225, 231, 233, 236-238
    definition xiii, 1, 116
    and integration 8, 9, 236
    'new' 7, 233
multiple identity 8, 9, 225-6, 228, 230
Muslim
    identity 6, 111, 129-136, 147-153, 173-6, 188-190, 216-220, 223, 224, 227, 229, 231, 238
    schools 121-2, 129-132, 136, 152
    staff 132-4, 136, 175, 217, 218
    youth 164, 170, 174
Muslims
    not 'ethnic group' 6
    and *Satanic Verses* 6, 83-4, 105
Mussolini 38, 41, 105

nation state 8
national curriculum 30, 119, 151
navvies 16, 17
nazi Germany 38, 47, 50, 56
New Commonwealth 8, 63-4, 67, 81-2
'new' multiculturalism 7, 233
'new' racism 2, 3, 12
newspapers
    Catholic 23
    Irish 32
    Italian 42
    Jewish 57, 59
    Protestant 21

Urdu 216

'open door' 114, 187, 193, 221, 222
Orange Order 18-20, 109, 163, 188

Pakistan 61, 63, 64, 70, 93, 126, 138, 167, 169, 176, 203, 204, 207, 225-227, 230
Pakistani(s)
   chain migration 62, 67, 93
   'culture', not Islam 136, 170, 231
   elderly care 199-224
   identity xii, 68-9, 106, 226-7, 238
   migration 61-65
   school-age education 129-153
   youth 78, 164-190, 230
Parish of Holy Cross 28-9
partition of India 70, 95, 106, 225-7
pedlars 33, 47, 62-4, 81
Poor Law 17, 21, 25
positive action 114, 127, 142, 144, 159, 195, 200, 222, 224, 234, 235
Powell, Enoch 3, 8, 82
prayer facilities 132-3, 136, 217
Presbyterianism 15, 21, 104
proselytism 23, 50, 104, 231
Protestant
   education 25
   identity 18-21
   Irish in Scotland 18-21
   Orange Order 18-20, 109, 163, 188
Punjabi 124, 132, 136-7, 163, 176-7, 195-6, 217

qualifications 76, 78-9, 129, 133, 142-7, 151, 153, 190, 238
qualitative research, importance 109-10
Qur'an 112, 170, 180, 199, 200
Qur'an school 107, 123, 129, 131, 147-150, 152, 234

'race' 2, 4, 21, 50, 67, 80, 104, 125
Race Relations legislation 2, 6, 11, 67, 81, 82, 84, 120, 121, 125, 234
racial harassment 92, 141, 153, 159
racial typology 2
racialisation 10, 236-8
racism 1-6, 10, 12, 73, 74, 82, 83, 92, 104, 109, 120, 123, 126, 129, 130, 139, 141-2, 152, 156, 159, 161, 156-6, 178-80, 188, 198,
201, 205-6, 213, 219, 231, 233, 236-8
   biological 2, 82, 104, 231, 233
   cultural 2-5, 82, 104, 120, 123, 198, 231, 233
   and elderly 198, 201, 205-6, 213, 219
   at school 123, 126, 129, 130, 139, 141-2, 152
   and youth 156, 159, 161, 165-6, 178-80, 188
Ramadan 112-3, 134
Rangers Football Club 20, 59, 141
religious
   discrimination 84
   education 30, 66, 107, 118-120, 124, 151-2, 234
   identity 3, 6, 13, 20, 22, 23, 83, 98, 106-8, 110, 111, 114-5, 119, 148, 152, 198, 229, 231-5
   intolerance 9
   leaders 6, 52, 107, 232
   migrants 7, 233
   tolerance 9
Religious and Moral Education 119-20
religious requirements (Muslim)
   and elderly care 217-221
   and schools 133-6
   and youth services 173-6
residential care 214-5
'Rome on the Rates' 27
Rushdie, Salman 3, 6, 83, 105

Satanic Verses 3, 6, 83, 105
school
   boards 119, 124, 127
   chaplain 120, 125
   equal opportunities 125
   handbooks 30, 31, 108, 123-9
   meals 121, 134, 151
   uniform 120, 127, 132, 151
Scottish
   context 5, 9-10, 117, 236-7
   friendly attitude 10, 206, 210, 237
   identity 5, 9, 10, 14, 19-21, 23, 28, 109, 152, 190, 206, 229, 231, 237-8
Second World War 8, 36, 38, 39, 41, 42, 44, 47, 53, 56, 60, 87, 88, 105, 115, 233
sectarianism 152, 164, 188

255

secularisation 6, 48, 51, 58-9, 109, 111, 231, 233
self employment 47, 74-5, 77, 105, 145
sexual activity 180-182
shalwar kamiz 127, 132, 136, 138-9
Sikhs 6, 63, 65, 66, 84, 93, 125, 133, 150, 173, 177, 209, 211, 218-20, 223, 235
Sinn Fein 24
small businesses 77, 109, 238
social services 192, 194, 198, 208, 212, 213, 218, 221, 235
sports 23, 59, 89, 158, 183, 185-7, 189
stereotypes 17, 21, 42, 54, 74, 105, 122, 142-3
synagogue(s) 51-5, 57-8, 60, 87, 89, 93, 107-8

Talmund Torah 54
Tebbitt, Norman 10
trade unions 17, 19, 24, 40, 49, 80
training
    anti-racist 156, 221
    cultural awareness 188, 193-4, 221
    youth work 186
translation 132, 136-7, 148, 163
transport
    for Asian Girls Group 163
    and elderly 72, 196, 215, 217
    employment 63-4, 72, 76, 229

UK Islamic Mission 123
ulama 112
Ulster 14, 15, 18-20
unemployment 31, 36, 47, 64, 74-5, 87-8, 96, 98-9, 109, 155, 159, 237-8
Union, Act of (1707) 10, 13-14, 61, 236-7
Unionism 20, 27, 89
Unique Restaurant 31, 45
United Free Church 37
United Irish League 24
United Synagogue of Glasgow 52, 55
universal suffrage 23
universality 113, 194, 221, 235-6
university
    education 26, 35-6, 138, 145-6, 166, 169
    Glasgow 14-15, 21, 35, 42, 48, 56
    Strathclyde 14

Urban Programme 93, 159-60, 196-8, 221-2, 235
Urdu
    language of Pakistan 137, 176
    lessons 157, 176-7, 215
    school subject 128, 130, 135-7
    speaking staff 132, 176, 195, 217
    translation 124, 132, 135-7, 163, 176, 217

'victim', status of 1, 3, 9, 10, 106, 109, 113, 231, 237-8
voluntary sector 4, 11, 26-7, 115, 123, 143-4, 191, 193-5, 198, 200, 208, 210, 212-13, 216, 221, 223-4, 235
voting patterns, Irish 23, 27

wage rates 17, 24, 49, 62, 80, 104
Walfrid, Brother 23
welfare state 113, 115, 194, 207
Wheatley, John 27-8
White, 'ethnicity' 67
working hours 16, 40, 49, 78-80, 109, 167, 208, 238

Yiddish 46, 55-7
Yiddishe Shtimme 57
young people 37, 109, 115, 138-40, 142-7, 153-6, 234-5
    Catholic 23, 29-31
    Italian 34, 40, 43-4
    Jewish 53-4, 57-9
    Muslim 111, 129-36, 147-9, 152, 173-6, 189-90, 229-31
    Pakistani 78, 156-90, 230
youth survey, Govanhill 156-8, 182
youth work 154-190
    benefits of 155
    Catholic 23, 30, 31
    in Govanhill 156-90
    in Scotland 154-6
    issue-based 164, 180-82, 186, 188, 189
    Jewish 58-60

Zangwall, Israel 56
Zionism 58-60, 105, 106, 232

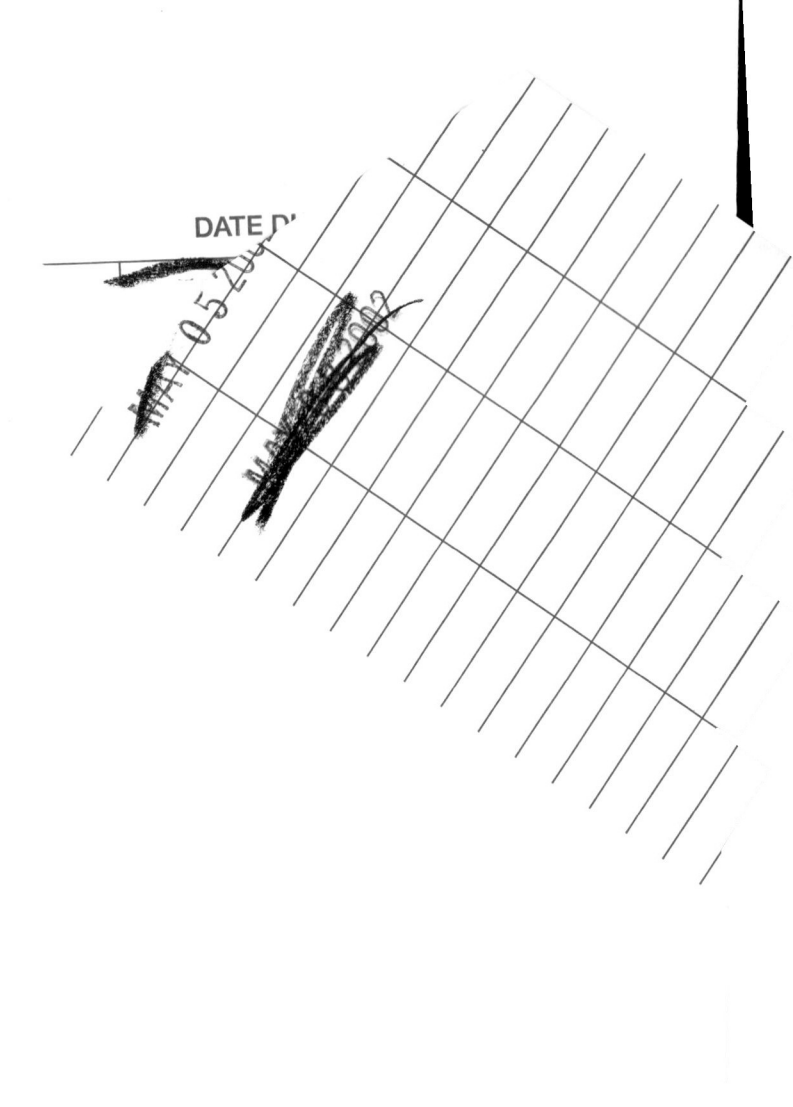